Retrospective and Prospective Views on Information Systems Engineering

Cinzia Cappiello · Marco Comuzzi ·
Massimo Mecella · Pierluigi Plebani · Monica Vitali
Editors

Retrospective and Prospective Views on Information Systems Engineering

Contributions in Honor of Barbara Pernici on the Occasion of Her Retirement

Springer

Editors
Cinzia Cappiello
Dipartimento di Elettronica, Informazione e Bioingegneria
Politecnico di Milano
Milan, Italy

Massimo Mecella
DIAG
Sapienza Università di Roma
Rome, Italy

Monica Vitali
Dipartimento di Elettronica Informazione e Bioingegneria
Politecnico di Milano
Milan, Italy

Marco Comuzzi
Ulsan National Institute of Science and Technology (UNIST)
Ulsan, Korea (Republic of)

Pierluigi Plebani
Dipartimento di Elettronica Informazione e Bioingegneria
Politecnico di Milano
Milan, Italy

ISBN 978-3-032-19577-7 ISBN 978-3-032-19578-4 (eBook)
https://doi.org/10.1007/978-3-032-19578-4

This Springer imprint is published by the registered company Springer Nature Switzerland AG
The registered company address is: Gewerbestrasse 11, 6330 Cham, Switzerland

Chess is in its essence a game, in its form an art, and in its execution a science.

[Tassilo von Heydebrand und der Lasa]

Foreword

A Barbara

Tu che di scacchi eri una regina
in Istituto giungesti una mattina,
di Elettronica allora si chiamava,
ma dei circuiti non ti interessava.
Neppure ti attraeva il transistore;
solo Batini fu il tuo vero amore!

Anche se i Database non eran male
dell'Informatica scegliesti il Gestionale.
Studiavi e pubblicavi molto bene
e, come sempre, il risultato viene;
la cattedra alla fin ti guadagnasti
e al confine orientale riparasti.

Ad Udine per insegnare andavi,
vicino alla patria dei tuoi avi.
Al Politecnico sei poi ritornata,
dai collaboratori circondata,
per studiare i Sistemi Informativi
che tutto san dei morti e anche dei vivi.

Adesso siamo alla conclusione:
anche a Barbara arriva la pensione,
la ricerca continua con passione
come pure il guidar tante persone.
Assapora però anche il riposo
e goditi la vita col tuo sposo.

Milan, Italy
December 2025

Fabio A. Schreiber

Preface

"Why don't we write a book?"

How many times have we heard this sentence from you, Barbara. Sometimes to provide study materials for students, sometimes at the conclusion of a large research project, sometimes on specific research topics. A book has always been a bit of a target (or maybe an obsession) for you. Obsession that, for those who were working with you, often turned into fear. Hours and hours writing articles that, especially at the beginning of our career, were, with a simple comment, dismantled. Ready to be rewritten and reassembled.

Now we can say it: if many times we were able to evade this question it was only because, in our mind, we wanted to save some energy and our best ideas to write a book dedicated to you at the end of your academic career. Well, that moment finally arrived and, as usual, we looked for a way to escape such an immense task but, at the same time, we felt obliged to complete it. And here we began to take advantage of your teachings: study, read, see what others do. Here's the clue! The others! Why not make our lives easier and let others write? There are so many people who have met you, Barbara, and who will want to dedicate a chapter of this book to you.

Scouting, the first phase of the work. We went to the roots of your research activity, we found names unknown to us from your time in Udine, colleagues from Rome with whom you stayed in touch, as well as—of course—the colleagues at the Politecnico di Milano. Some of them have been your Ph.D. students. People who took off to have a brilliant career both in Italy and abroad as entrepreneurs, or people who stayed in academia, achieving prestigious positions in Italy and worldwide. It cannot be said that you have not raised numerous professionals and researchers who want to thank you with this book. Some of them, as you can imagine, were not able—for various reasons—to provide a direct contribution to this book. However, the fact remains that everyone responded with a thought dedicated to you.

The second phase was the *wait*. After defining the deadlines for the delivery of the contributions, we waited for them to arrive. As you taught us, though, a deadline extension request is not denied to anyone. After all, who requests an extension would not have cooperated if they had not asked for it. And, most importantly and as you have always taught us: if you are not the first believing in the goal, no one else will.

We believed in it so much that, in the end, all the contributions arrived, well laid out, and packaged in this book that you have in your hands.

We believe that all the contributions reflect your experience as a researcher who has contributed to different fields in these 40 years: from time databases, to workflows; from services to sustainability. What unites your contributions is definitely your distinctive feature of being able to foresee the most promising research topics. Sometimes the work you have done has been successful even in the short term, other times it has taken some time to be appreciated. Transversally to these topics, you will find mentioned the numerous national and European projects in which you have participated, or even coordinated. Among these, a particular mention goes to the MAIS project. A national project that has allowed to build not only high-level and innovative research, but also a network of relationships between doctoral students, researchers and professors from various Italian universities who, thanks to this project that you thought, proposed, and coordinated, is still standing today.

Let us move now to the last phase: the *surprise*! We present this book today to you in the conference that is perhaps the dearest to you: CAiSE. We are writing these words close to Christmas and far from the event. Everyone is committed to organizing it in the best possible way, in the hope that you will truly enjoy it. Convinced that many of the people who have left a contribution here, as well as many others with whom you have shared your professional adventure, are present to pay you the right tribute.

Milan, Italy — Cinzia Cappiello
Ulsan, Korea (Republic of) — Marco Comuzzi
Rome, Italy — Massimo Mecella
Milan, Italy — Pierluigi Plebani
Milan, Italy — Monica Vitali
June 2026

Contents

Contributors

Mortada Al-Banna Deloitte, Sydney, Australia

Steven Alter University of San Francisco, San Francisco, CA, USA

Danilo Ardagna Politecnico di Milano, Milan, Italy

Luciano Baresi Politecnico di Milano, Milan, Italy

Moshe Chai Barukh Jellow AI, Sydney, Australia

Carlo Batini Università degli Studi di Milano-Bicocca, Milano, Italy

Boualem Benatallah Dublin City University, Dublin, Ireland

Sonia Bergamaschi University of Modena and Reggio Emilia, Modena, Italy

Devis Bianchini University of Brescia, Brescia, Italy

Carlo Alberto Bono Politecnico di Milano, Milan, Italy

Dominik Bork TU Wien, Business Informatics Group, Vienna, Austria

Cinzia Cappiello Politecnico di Milano, Milan, Italy

Fabio Casati Servicenow, Zurich, Switzerland;
University of Trento, Trento, Italy

Silvana Castano Università degli Studi di Milano, Milano, Italy

Tiziana Catarci Università degli Studi di Roma La Sapienza, Rome, Italy

Sara Comai Politecnico di Milano, Milan, Italy

Carlo Combi Università degli Studi di Verona, Verona, Italy

Gianpaolo Cugola Politecnico di Milano, Milan, Italy

Valeria De Antonellis Università degli Studi di Brescia, Brescia, Italy

Johann Eder University of Klagenfurt, Klagenfurt, Austria

Alexandre Mello Ferreira Recod.ai, State University of Campinas, Campinas, Brazil

Xavier Franch Universitat Politècnica de Catalunya, Barcelona, Spain

Mariagrazia Fugini Politecnico di Milano, Milano, Italy

Carlo Ghezzi Politecnico di Milano, Milan, Italy

Gerti Kappel TU Wien, Vienna, Austria

Kyriakos Kritikos University of the Aegean, Mytilene, Greece

John Krogstie Norwegian University of Science and Technology, NTNU, Trondheim, Norway

Andrea Maurino University of Milano Bicocca, Milan, Italy

Giovanni Meroni Technical University of Denmark, Lyngby, Denmark

Raffaela Mirandola Karlsruhe Institute of Technology, Karlsruhe, Germany

Enrico Mussi Sense Reply, Turin, Italy

Selmin Nurcan Université de Paris 1 Panthéon-Sorbonne, Paris, France

Oscar Pastor Universitat Politècnica de València, Valencia, Spain

Giuseppe Pozzi Politecnico di Milano, Milan, Italy

Giovanni Quattrocchi Politecnico di Milano, Milan, Italy

Jolita Ralyté Université of Genève, Geneva, Switzerland

Edoardo Ramalli European Commission-Joint Research Centre, Ispra, Italy

Carlos Rodríguez Universidad Católica Nuestra Señora de la Asunción, Asunción, Paraguay

Chiara Sandionigi Univesité Grenoble Alpes, Grenoble, France

Gaetano Santucci Politecnico di Milano, Milano, Italy

Monica Scannapieco Politecnico di Milano, Milan, Italy

Monique Snoeck KU Leuven, Leuven, Belgium

Dragana Sunaric TU Wien, Vienna, Austria

Letizia Tanca Politecnico di Milano, Milan, Italy

Charlotte Verbruggen TU Wien, Business Informatics Group, Vienna, Austria

Monica Vitali Politecnico di Milano, Milan, Italy

Mathias Weske Hasso Plattner Institut, University of Potsdam, Potsdam, Germany

An Inspiring Journey in Information Systems Design

Carlo Batini, Valeria De Antonellis, Silvana Castano, Mariagrazia Fugini, and Gaetano Santucci

Abstract This chapter explores the evolution of information systems design, examining the long-standing collaboration between the authors and Barbara, characterised by joint publications, methodological contributions and a shared conceptual approach. Drawing on scientific results from national and international projects, the chapter aims to inspire new developments in line with current needs, and to illustrate the historical evolution of information systems design techniques and methods.

1 Introduction

The field of Information Systems Design has long been a research area where methodological rigour, systemic vision and attention to evolving application contexts have converged. This chapter is born from the desire to honor Barbara, a colleague and research partner with whom we all have shared an intense, inspiring and friendly journey, marked by joint publications, methodological dialogue, and a deep conceptual affinity. Together, we explored information systems design as a layered process,

C. Batini
Università degli Studi di Milano-Bicocca, Milano, Italy
e-mail: carlo.batini@unimib.it

V. De Antonellis
Università degli Studi di Brescia, Brescia, Italy
e-mail: valeria.deantonellis@unibs.it

S. Castano (✉)
Università degli Studi di Milano, Milano, Italy
e-mail: silvana.castano@unimi.it

M. Fugini
Politecnico di Milano, Milano, Italy
e-mail: mariagrazia.fugini@polimi.it

G. Santucci
Individual Researcher, Rome, Italy
e-mail: gaetanosantucci02@gmail.com

C. Cappiello et al. (eds.), *Retrospective and Prospective Views on Information Systems Engineering*, https://doi.org/10.1007/978-3-032-19578-4_1

where the formalization of specifications is interwoven with the ability to capture organizational and semantic needs of real-world systems. Our joint contributions, which range from refinement-level modelling to specifications reuse, reflect our shared vision of design as a collaborative process that can evolve over time and across different domains, rather than just a technical construction process.

This chapter continues along those trajectories, presenting:

- scientific results obtained in national and international research projects with the aim of inspiring new questions, models and connections;
- valuable literacy on the application of methods and related techniques in the design of information systems in various areas of application.

2 Methodologies and Tools in Information Systems Design

The emergence of reusing requirements and conceptual schemas during the 1990s was driven by pressing needs. Information systems were becoming increasingly complex, development cycles were under pressure to deliver faster results, and organisations faced the challenge of migrating or integrating legacy systems. In this context, reuse was seen not simply as a way to save effort, but as a methodological strategy to preserve organisational knowledge, reduce ambiguity, and ensure consistency across diverse projects.

It is important to distinguish this from the reuse of software code. While code reuse focuses on technical artefacts at the implementation level, requirements and schema reuse operates at a higher level of abstraction. It involves reusing validated descriptions of user needs, business processes, and conceptual structures. This form of reuse is more strategic, ensuring that new developments build upon established and reliable models rather than reinventing them. Several research projects played a pivotal role in the area of requirements and schema reuse.

The ITHACA project (FP2-ESPRIT 2, 1989–1992) explored advanced techniques for managing and reusing conceptual models across heterogeneous environments, emphasising interoperability and the preservation of organisational knowledge.

The INFOKIT project (Progetto Finalizzato Sistemi Informatici e Calcolo Parallelo, CNR, 1989–1994) concentrated on repositories and toolkits that enabled analysts to classify, retrieve, and adapt requirements and schema components, thereby reducing duplication and improving design quality.

The F3 project (FP3-ESPRIT3 project, 1992–1994), went further by developing a requirements engineering workbench that guided engineers through the entire process, from gathering user needs to analysis, formalisation, and validation. Central to this workbench was the Reusable Requirements Library, an archive of validated specifications designed to support systematic reuse across projects.

Together, these initiatives illustrate how reuse of requirements and conceptual schemas matured into a methodological cornerstone of information systems development. By moving beyond code and focusing on the reuse of knowledge and models, they helped consolidate requirements engineering and conceptual modelling as distinct disciplines, equipped with tools and frameworks capable of reducing risk and accelerating innovation.

2.1 An Environment for Supporting the Development of Large-Scale Application Software Systems: The ITHACA Project

The ITHACA Project has been a UE FP2-ESPRIT2 funded project, started in 1989 and completed in 1992. Its aim was to address the life cycle of large software projects, and to provide tools to support the whole software development cycle. The project has produced the ITHACA—Integrated Toolkit for Highly Advanced Computer Applications—suite of tools constituting an application development environment, based on the ITHACA Software Information System for enhancing reusability of both software components and artifacts (documents, reports, etc.) named development knowledge. Object-oriented techniques were used in the Environment at all levels of the development: requirement specification, scripting, and implementation through class reuse. The ITHACA tools tracked how the products of the development phases were produced by providing tools for the Application Engineer, who is responsible for abstracting or generalizing application skeletons and development knowledge, and for storing these as Application Frames in the ITHACA Software Information System.

In particular, the Requirement Collection And Specification Tool (RECAST) and the Visual Scripting Tool (Vista) of the ITHACA Development Environment have been focused in research at Politecnico di Milano, based on the assumption that applications share common functionalities which can be factored out into reusable elements [16, 17]. RECAST offered facilities for capturing, classifying, and retrieving validated requirements from previous projects, allowing analysts to adapt existing specifications for new contexts. Its key contribution was demonstrating that reuse could extend beyond code to the requirements level by offering structured repositories and retrieval mechanisms that improved productivity and consistency. By demonstrating that reuse could be extended to the conceptual and requirements level, RECAST anticipated later frameworks such as the ESPRIT F3 (From Fuzzy to Formal) project (see Sect. 2.3). It showed how structured repositories and retrieval mechanisms could facilitate the practical and effective reuse of requirements in the development of large-scale information systems.

2.2 Designing Information Systems Through Reuse: The INFOKIT Project

In Italy, research on the design of information systems was initiated primarily within the framework of two major national programmes: Progetto Finalizzato Informatica (1979–1985) and Progetto Finalizzato Sistemi Informatici e Calcolo Parallelo (1989–1994), both promoted by the National Research Council (CNR).

Within Subproject P6 of the Progetto Finalizzato Sistemi Informatici e Calcolo Parallelo, the INFOKIT research line marked a turning point in the design of information systems, anticipating approaches that are now considered foundational. In response to the growing complexity of information systems and the need to reduce development time, costs, and risks, INFOKIT promoted the paradigm design by reuse. This approach was based on the idea that it was possible to define, catalogue, and reuse standardised design components, adaptable to different application contexts.

Within INFOKIT, we proposed a structured methodological approach to support application engineers in the construction of a Library of Entity-Relationship (E-R) schemas, systematically classified using indexing criteria and clustering techniques [14, 15]. This library served as the basis for identifying and extracting reusable components from selected existing schemas. Reusable components were defined as generic entities, each accompanied by a set of meta-entities. The generic entities were derived through comparative analysis of entities belonging to similar schemas grouped within clusters of the library. The associated meta-entities offered a set of reuse guidelines, indicating how generic entities could be modified, extended, or tailored to meet the requirements of new applications under development.

The INFOKIT initiative demonstrated how publicly funded research can produce innovative methodologies and tools with tangible impact on industrial practice. Italian companies were engaged in pilot projects, validating the approach in real-world settings and contributing to technology transfer. An increasingly close collaboration between universities and industry contributed to the achievement of significant results. At the time, the concept of design by reuse was pioneering; today, it is a foundational principle in the development of information systems, particularly in domains such as software engineering, process modelling, and low-code environments.

2.3 A Conceptual Framework for Requirements Engineering: The F3 Project

The European FP3-ESPRIT3 project F3 (From Fuzzy To Formal) (1992–1994) brought together researchers and practitioners from various European countries to tackle a fundamental challenge in requirements engineering: transforming ‘fuzzy’ (that is, informal, ambiguous, and preliminary) problem statements at the enterprise level into ‘formal’ (precise, validated, and executable) system specifications. The F3 project significantly advanced information system (IS) design, not only by creating a structured pathway from informal business or user requirements to formal, executable system specifications, but also by enriching IS design through business context modelling, multi-view models, traceability, and the reuse of conceptual artefacts. These contributions enhanced the alignment between business needs and system design, improved the quality of system specifications, and enabled faster and more reliable IS development. In particular, they provided the essential groundwork for the consolidation of Requirements Engineering as a distinct and recognised field in information systems.

A comprehensive conceptual framework for requirements engineering was devised, comprising a suite of models representing enterprise objectives, business processes, actors, domain concepts, data, dialogues, and non-functional requirements, thereby modelling both the enterprise and its information system environment [6]. These models clarify both the "why/what" (business goals and requirements) and the "what/how" (system perspective), providing a bridge from the informal, ambiguous world of business to the formal world of system specifications. To enforce the F3 requirements engineering process and to design coherent systems rather than isolated modules, a range of support functionalities was developed including model linkage, traceability, and consistency.

Building on this modelling foundation, a key objective of the project was to capture conceptual assets (domain knowledge, data schema templates, business goals, process patterns) and package them as reusable conceptual components. This approach was intended to promote design-by-reuse across multiple requirements engineering and IS design projects. A major achievement of F3 was the development of a reuse methodology and supporting tool environment for constructing reusable conceptual components that encapsulate recurring patterns in business and information system design [8, 9, 15].

At the heart of the project was the creation of a requirements engineering workbench, conceived as an integrated environment to support engineers throughout the entire process. From the initial gathering of user needs, through their analysis and organisation, to the formalisation of models and the validation of specifications, the workbench provided a structured pathway. Two components proved particularly significant: the Reusable Requirements Library, an archive of validated specifications that enabled the reuse of established knowledge, and the User Interface, designed as the practical access point for engineers and developers. The Reusable Requirements Library, serves as a repository of core enterprise knowledge for a given domain and provides a valuable reference point when developing new applications.

The anticipated benefits of the F3 reuse methodology include:

- Supporting conceptual modelling by providing users with a library of ready-to-use, reusable conceptual components that may suit their requirements.
- Improving the quality of conceptual schemas by leveraging well-defined and proven components from prior IS designs.
- Accelerating the requirements engineering process by reusing previously developed assets and components.

Within the F3 approach, a reusable component is defined as a conceptual artefact encapsulating domain or system invariants that frequently recur in information systems projects—such as E-R schemas, business goal templates, or activity templates. This focus on conceptual artefacts marks a key distinction of F3 compared to the state of the art at the time, when much of the research in software engineering was centred on software code artefacts for reusability.

2.4 *Experimentation of the Reuse Approach on Conceptual Schemas: The AIPA Project*

The validation of the reuse approach developed in INFOKIT and F3 projects was conducted on a set of conceptual schemas developed within the framework of activities promoted by AIPA (Authority for Informatics in Public Administration). The aim was to assess the effectiveness of the approach in public contexts characterised by high semantic complexity, strong standardisation requirements, and institutional relevance.

AIPA's mission was to foster innovation and rationalisation in the information systems of the Italian Public Administration. Over the years, it generated a substantial corpus of conceptual schemas for modelling services, administrative processes, and public archives, providing a rich and structured foundation for experimentation purposes addressing practical challenges in public administrations like heterogeneous systems, variety of legacy databases, need for integration, and shared data semantics. Specifically, our experimentation aimed to:

- Evaluate the transferability of reuse-based design principles in regulated, multi-organizational contexts;
- Construct a library of reusable conceptual components derived from AIPA schemas;
- Analyze the semantic coherence and generalization potential of key concepts;
- Support the design of data architectures for public administration systems.

We contributed a systematic approach to building large-scale schema inventories in public administration contexts by defining the meta-schema of the inventory, structuring the repository, and applying semi-automated techniques to handle scalability—an essential aspect when dealing with large portfolios of systems. Moving beyond manual schema-by-schema analysis, we proposed automated techniques for schema indexing, similarity-based clustering, and schema abstraction [2, 10, 12].

The following activities were conducted during our AIPA experimentation:

- Collection and analysis of E-R schemas developed for public applications (e.g., registry services, protocol management, document handling).
- Application of semantic clustering techniques to identify families of related schemas.
- Derivation of generic entities and definition of meta-entities providing structured guidelines for reuse and adaptation.

- Evaluation of component adaptability across diverse public administration contexts.

Using indexing and similarity metrics, E-R schemas were classified into families. Each family represents a coherent application domain or context within the public administration and serves as the basis for identifying reusable schema components. As pointed out by Parnas, the systematic analysis of a family enables the discovery of common features among its members, which can then be properly normalized into reusable components [11, 13].

A reusable component is thus a normalized version of a schema structure recurring across multiple conceptual schemas within a given family. Once reusable components are identified and normalized within families, made general and independent from application-specific requirements, some of them prove to be transversal, used across several families. These become core components at the upper levels of the inventory conceptual "pyramid" shared across multiple application contexts. This represents one of the key features of the AIPA repository design for our experimentation.

A reusable knowledge base was successfully constructed to support the design of public information systems. The experiment demonstrated the potential of conceptual reuse to streamline information system design, reduce development costs, and improve data modeling consistency in public sector systems. Our schema analysis methods have been seminal; since then, research on large-scale data and metadata analysis techniques has gained dramatic importance for system and application development in the era of big data and cloud computing.

2.5 *Research Journey Reflections*

Looking back on the research journey traced in this chapter, the authors are reminded not only of the methodological advances and institutional frameworks that shaped information systems design, but also of the human dimension that sustained them. The collaborative spirit between researchers, practitioners, and public institutions was never merely procedural, but deeply relational.

The development of reuse-oriented design approaches proposed in ITHACA, INFOKIT, F3 and experimented in AIPA, beyond a technical undertaking, was part of a broader effort to align conceptual modelling with the demands of organizational contexts. This journey emphasizes the value of ongoing dialogue between theory and practice and the role of shared knowledge in defining context-aware information systems.

3 Literacy on the Application of Methods and Related Techniques in the Design of Information Systems

In the 1970s, once the pioneering phase of information system design had ended and software companies in Italy began to expand, the need for an industrial approach to information systems design became evident. During this period, structured methodologies for systems analysis and design spread rapidly.

Initially, these methodologies addressed the more technical activities: programming, logical and physical design, functional analysis, and data analysis. The national programs described in Sect. 2.2 engaging universities, companies, and public administrations, generated significant industrial benefits. However, industrial adoption of these methodologies proceeded slowly due to several limiting factors. First, effective analysis support tools were largely absent: their use was labor-intensive, the resulting artefacts were difficult to maintain, and the integration between analysis outputs and the subsequent technical design and programming phases was weak.

In the 1980s, the rapid development of analysis support tools, combined with the emergence of new conceptual models for data and function analysis, accelerated the adoption of more advanced methodologies. Notable examples include process mapping tools; CASE/CAISE environments for data analysis, data design, and functional analysis; BPM platforms; process mining tools; reverse-engineering tools; and automated documentation systems. The evolution of methods and tools for IT project management further impacted information systems development and maintenance, through collaboration tools, project management tools, and integrated suites for requirements, testing, release, and defect management. Technologies used for system development and maintenance also shaped life-cycle models and adopted methodologies, including new programming languages, macro languages and program generators, data and document management systems, test management software, configuration management platforms, and Robotic Process Automation systems.

In the 1990s, the emergence of the Internet not only as a communication infrastructure but also as a platform for deploying and collaborating on applications profoundly changed information systems design paradigms. The definition—narrow or broad—of "information system" plays a crucial role in shaping industrial design methodologies. These methodologies must extend beyond technological components such as ICT technologies and data, to include organizational and social components: laws and regulations, services, organizational structures and processes, and economic, human, and informational resources. Consequently, methodological frameworks expanded to encompass organizational aspects (process analysis, process reengineering, insourcing/outsourcing), quality of delivered services, quality of the development process (contractual rules), technical aspects (platforms, modularity, distributed systems, web applications), economic factors (feasibility studies, cost-benefit analyses), and social considerations (ethics, ergonomics, accessibility, environmental sustainability).

The six-volume series Sistemi Informativi, published from 2001 onwards and edited by Barbara, together with Carlo Batini and Gaetano Santucci [5], constitutes a comprehensive and timely response to the need for extended industrial methodologies for information systems. The series involved the collaboration of 23 authors from academia, the ICT industry, and end-user organizations.

- The first volume, following an introduction to information systems, examines methodological aspects related to planning interventions and managing systems reengineering projects, as well as those concerning the assessment and diagnostic "check-up" of information systems.
- The second volume describes data and process modelling techniques, with particular emphasis on object-oriented methodologies and the UML language.
- The third volume addresses economic issues: feasibility studies for information systems, cost evaluation criteria, and investment appraisal.
- The fourth volume explores contracts for the supply of ICT goods and services, with a specific focus on outsourcing contracts and on ensuring the quality of services and suppliers.
- The fifth volume covers technological architectures of information systems, distributed system architectures, legacy system management, IT security, and systems and infrastructure management.
- The sixth volume, released a few years later in 2006, illustrates methods and technologies for developing web-based information systems designed to manage large volumes of data and to support collaboration among distributed sites working toward common business objectives.

The organization of an information system into component parts emerging from the six volume series is shown in Fig. 1.

4 Evolution of Data, Process, and Service Design Methodologies (1980–2025)

The six-volume series published in 2001 marks a turning point between two eras: the 1980s and 1990s, when models and methodologies for database design—the primary technology underlying information systems—were consolidated, and the subsequent period, extending to the late 2020s, that has witnessed the publication of innovative books on networked information systems such as [18], a flourishing of research initiatives such as the Multichannel Adaptive Information System (MAIS) project, coordinated by Barbara Pernici, the eGovernment for Mediterranean Countries (eG4M) project, coordinated by Carlo Batini, as well as the publication of university and master-level textbooks co-authored separately by Barbara and Carlo (incidentally, Barbara and Carlo married in 1999) [1, 3, 7]. This body of work led to a significant maturation of models and methodologies for process and service design.

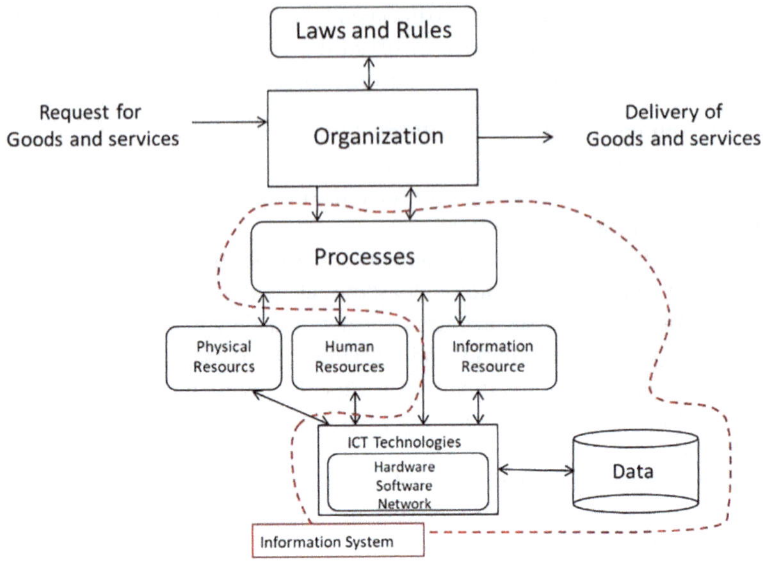

Fig. 1 Information system and organizational system

4.1 Evolution of Data Design Methodologies

Before the introduction of formal modeling methods (before 1980), data design was predominantly implementation-oriented. Developers manipulated file structures, record formats, and DBMS-specific constructs. Semantics remained implicit. This situation constrained maintainability and hindered the long-term evolution of systems.

A turning point occurred (1980s) with the consolidation of E-R modeling and early methodological works later formalized in systematic treatments such as [4]. The conceptual data model is defined as a high-level representation of an organization's information requirements, using entities, relationships, attributes, and constraints, independent of any implementation technology. Based on this model, the conceptual schema is the formal description of a domain's semantics, including real-world objects and their constraints. This innovation responded to the need for stability and technology independence in system design.

The formalization of the relational model enabled the definition of the logical data model, a representation of data in terms of a specific data model—typically relational—independent of physical storage. From it, the logical schema derives, specifying tables, attributes, keys, and normalization constraints as systematic transformations of the conceptual schema. By the late 1980s: conceptual models captured semantics, logical models captured formal structure, physical schemas captured storage, indexing, and optimization. This three-level architecture later informed the evolution of models for processes and services.

4.2 Evolution of Service Modeling

The first methodological treatments of services (e.g., [19]) interpreted services mainly as technical interfaces. Services are conceived as flexible, composable units that respond to variations in context, device capability, and network conditions; e-services constitute the fundamental mechanism enabling multichannel interaction and quality-of-service management. In this context, a web service was defined as a standardized representation of computational functionality accessible via Web protocols such as SOAP and WSDL, enabling machine-to-machine communication. In parallel, the category of e-service emerged in early e-government and ICT literature, defined as a service whose design, delivery, or consumption is mediated by digital technologies and accessed via online channels such as Web portals or mobile platforms. E-services are seen as digital delivery mechanisms through which abstract services are operationalized. They serve as front-end channels for users, while web services represent technology-level components enabling service-to-service integration.

In [19] quality of service is treated as a multi-level, formally modelled set of about 150 non functional QoS dimensions, used to specify, measure, negotiate, and constrain adaptive service provisioning across architectural, functional, context, and channel levels. In this way, QoS constitutes a unifying design principle across all architectural layers—from networking to middleware and service components—and drives the definition of systematic adaptation mechanisms.

The conceptualization of services evolved in works such as [3], where a service is characterized as an activity or set of activities of intangible nature, carried out in an exchange between provider and client, in which value is co-created. This definition moves beyond technical interfaces and emphasizes organizational roles, goals, and user interaction. In analogy with data design, two types of services are distinguished:

- the abstract service, a technology-independent specification of goals, semantics, and constraints;
- the concrete service, the technological realization of an abstract service within a specific platform, with defined operational parameters.

Composite abstract services correspond to conceptual data schemas. Abstract services are described in terms of (i) a name, (ii) a set of functional properties; (iii) a set of service qualities, (iv) a set of non-functional properties, (v) a service data schema, and can be organized according to two conceptual relationships:

- Part-of relationship that holds between a service si (the part) and a service sj (the whole) when the specification of sj has as component part the specification of si.
- Is-a relationship that holds between a service si (child) and a service sj (parent) when si is a specialization of sj; sj inherits all functional and non-functional properties and all part-of relationships of sj.

Quality of service drives in [20] the identification of services bundles and corresponding e-Government projects, implemented by leveraging the cooperative application architectures of public administrations.

4.3 Evolution of Process Modeling

Early analyses such as those found in [19] treated processes as workflow descriptions: procedural sequences of tasks, control flow transitions, and synchronization constructs described by means of the Business Process Modeling Notation (BPMN). Processes are implicitly embedded within the architecture of mobile adaptive information systems, where adaptation and context-awareness require dynamic orchestration of e-services.

A mature conceptualization, articulated in [1], defines a process as the set of activities that, using available resources in an organizational and technological environment, an organization performs to produce a good or a service to realize a business or administrative goal. This definition establishes processes as organizational entities structured around goals and resource usage. The two-level conceptual and logical paradigm in data design is articulated in process design in terms of:

- the public process, defined as the externally visible sequence of interactions, messages, and obligations exchanged with external actors;
- the private process, the internal organizational logic that realizes the public process through decisions, resource allocation, and internal activities.

BPMN, similarly to the E-R model for data, provides a standard to model processes through activities, gateways and events, defining execution order and organisational interactions; it also models message exchanges between organizations via message flows. Public processes expose only the interaction messages with partners, whereas private processes describe the organisation's internal workflow while still coordinating with external actors through BPMN communication constructs. Processes are formally defined and traced across organizational boundaries, with strong emphasis on identification, value-chain alignment, and inter-organizational cooperation. The assessment of process performance (efficiency and effectiveness) and the design of data, applications, and architectures, make clear how process analysis drives IS design. Executable processes are modeled in BPMN, BPEL, or workflow engine languages that correspond to implementation-level constructs, analogous to physical schemas in data design. In the emerging view processes structure organizational functionality and services implement and integrate those processes across enterprise and technological layers. The table shown in Fig. 2 synthesizes the preceding discussion by comparing data, processes, and services across the conceptual, logical, and physical/executable levels.

4.4 Reflections on the Literacy Journey

The evolution of models and methodologies for defining the roles of data, services and processes in information systems illustrates a progressive formalization of the separation of concerns between semantic and implementation layers, and the consequent consolidation of a three-level architecture.

Domain	Conceptual Level	Logical Level	Physical / Executable Level
Data	Conceptual data model; conceptual schema E-R Model	Logical data model; logical schema Relational model	Physical schema; storage structures
Processes	Public process (external semantics) BPMN model	Private process (internal logic) BPMN model	Executable workflow (BPMN/BPEL)
Services	Abstract service (goals, semantics) Conceptual service model	Concrete service (implementation-specific design)	Web service; e-service; other digital service implementations

Fig. 2 Comparative modeling layers for data, processes, and services

Starting from the conceptual evolution in data modeling in the 1980s, these ideas extended to services and processes, generating stable and interoperable design frameworks capable of supporting complex information systems over long time horizons. In conclusions, over four decades, methodologies for data, service and process modeling have converged toward a shared structure based on:

1. a conceptual level, representing meaning, goals, and semantics;
2. a logical level, representing formal structure and organization;
3. a physical/executable level, representing implementation and operational execution.

This unified architecture supports stability, interoperability, and long-term system evolution.

5 Conclusions

This chapter represents a moment of reconnection with a journey that has been characterised by intertwined research, collaboration, and passion for systemic thinking, but also an opportunity for scientific reflection. The contemporary advent of big data, data analytics, and artificial intelligence is not merely a technological development; it is profoundly reshaping the architecture and underlying logic of information systems, prompting a re-examination of their components, capabilities, and design principles.

References

1. Batini, C.: How to design an Information System. Creative Commons Licence (2019). https://boa.unimib.it/handle/10281/248702
2. Batini, C., Castano, S., De Antonellis, V., Fugini, M.G., Pernici, B.: Analysis of an inventory of information systems in the public administration. Requirements Eng. **1**(1), 47–62 (1996)
3. Batini, C., Castelli, M., Comerio, M., Cremaschi, M., Iaquinta, L., Torsello, A., Viscusi, G., et al.: The Smart Methodology for the Life Cycle of Services. Creative Commons Licence (2015)
4. Batini, C., Ceri, S., Navathe, S.B.: Conceptual database design: an entity-relationship approach. Benjamin-Cummings Publishing Co., Inc (1991)
5. Batini, C., Pernici, B., Santucci, G.: Sistemi informativi - Six Volumes. F. Angeli. (2001)
6. Bubenko, J., Rolland, C., Loucopoulos, P., De Antonellis, V.: Facilitating "fuzzy to formal" requirements modelling. In: Proceedings of IEEE International Conference on Requirements Engineering, pp. 154–157. IEEE (1994)
7. Cappiello, C., Fugini, M., Grefen, P.W., Pernici, B., Plebani, P., Vitali, M.: Fondamenti di Sistemi informativi per il Settore dell'Informazione - Seconda Edizione. Politecnico di Milano (2025)
8. Castano, S., De Antonellis, V.: Reuse of conceptual requirement specifications. In: [1993] Proceedings of the IEEE International Symposium on Requirements Engineering, pp. 121–124. IEEE (1993)
9. Castano, S., De Antonellis, V.: The F3 reuse environment for requirements engineering. ACM SIGSOFT Softw. Eng. Notes **19**(3), 62–65 (1994)
10. Castano, S., De Antonellis, V.: Reference conceptual architectures for re-engineering information systems. Int. J. Cooper. Inf. Syst. **4**(02n03), 213–235 (1995)
11. Castano, S., De Antonellis, V.: Engineering a library of reusable conceptual components. Inf. Softw. Technol. **39**(2), 65–76 (1997). https://www.sciencedirect.com/science/article/pii/S0950584996011275
12. Castano, S., De Antonellis, V., Fugini, M.G., Pernici, B.: Conceptual schema analysis: techniques and applications. ACM Trans. Database Syst. (TODS) **23**(3), 286–333 (1998)
13. Castano, S., De Antonellis, V., Pernici, B.: Building reusable components in the public administration domain. In: Proceedings of the 1995 Symposium on Software Reusability, pp. 81–87 (1995)
14. Castano, S., De Antonellis, V., Zonta, B.: Classifying and reusing conceptual schemas. In: International Conference on Conceptual Modeling, pp. 121–138. Springer (1992)
15. De Antonellis, V., Pernici, B.: Reusing specifications through refinement levels. Data & Knowl. Eng. **15**(2), 109–133 (1995)
16. Fugini, M.G., Nierstrasz, O., Pernici, B.: Application development through reuse: the ITHACA tools environment. ACM SIGOIS Bull. **13**(2), 38–47 (1992)
17. Fugini, M.G., Pernici, B.: RECAST: a tool for reusing requirements. In: International Conference on Advanced Information Systems Engineering, pp. 339–364. Springer (1990)
18. Grefen, P.: Beyond E-Business: Towards Networked Structures. Routledge (2015)
19. Pernici, B. (Ed.): Mobile Information Systems: Infrastructure and Design for Adaptivity and Flexibility. Springer (2006)
20. Viscusi, G., Batini, C., Mecella, M.: Information Systems for eGovernment: A Quality-of-Service Perspective. Springer Science & Business Media (2010)

Articulating Information Systems Engineering Research Contributions

Oscar Pastor, John Krogstie, Selmin Nurcan, Steven Alter, Johann Eder, Xavier Franch, Monique Snoeck, and Jolita Ralyté

Abstract This chapter is written in honour to Barbara Pernici, who has been a central figure in the information systems engineering field since the eighties—strongly contributing to its formation and evolution. This chapter presents a framework for articulating the research in the many-faceted field of information systems engineering with the aim to contribute to the ongoing discussions related to understanding and organizing the field of information systems engineering. The framework attempts to accommodate the diverse nature of research contributions in the field of information systems engineering. The framework was inspired by, and is able to characterize, a large set of published papers in the field, and a preliminary evaluation through a set

O. Pastor (✉)
Universitat Politècnica de València, Valencia, Spain
e-mail: opastor@dsic.upv.es

J. Krogstie
Norwegian University of Science and Technology, NTNU, Trondheim, Norway
e-mail: john.krogstie@ntnu.no

S. Nurcan
Université de Paris 1 Panthéon-Sorbonne, Paris, France
e-mail: selmin.nurcan@univ-paris1.fr

S. Alter
University of San Francisco, San Francisco, CA, USA
e-mail: alter@usfca.edu

J. Eder
University of Klagenfurt, Klagenfurt, Austria
e-mail: johann.eder@aau.at

X. Franch
Universitat Politècnica de Catalunya, Barcelona, Spain
e-mail: xavier.franch@upc.edu

M. Snoeck
KU Leuven, Leuven, Belgium
e-mail: monique.snoeck@kuleuven.be

J. Ralyté
Université of Genève, Geneva, Switzerland
e-mail: jolita.ralyte@unige.ch

C. Cappiello et al. (eds.), *Retrospective and Prospective Views on Information Systems Engineering*, https://doi.org/10.1007/978-3-032-19578-4_2

of selected cases is presented. The framework allows researchers and reviewers to identify the contributions of their work. Using the framework to describe a research paper also promotes meaningful discussion among reviewers and readers.

1 Introduction

Information Systems (IS) and Information Systems Engineering (ISE) are well-established disciplines, that are supposed to be well-grounded. Definitions of IS and ISE can be found in many relevant sources. Highly ranked, widely recognized conferences and journals have been established under their umbrella. CAiSE is of particular interest to this chapter. Barbara Pernici is one of the most relevant researchers who established CAiSE as a highly recognized reference for ISE. In her honour, this chapter explores how really well-grounded this discipline is, and how consensus should be reached in a natural way when ISE experts try to identify a relevant and valuable ISE research contribution.

ISE is sometimes considered to be in the shadow of Software Engineering (SE) and IS, but is not a union or intersection of these areas. Surprisingly, what people have in mind when they must precisely define what is ISE, is much more open to discussion that one could expect.

The link between significant ISE and domains as Requirements Engineering, Business Process Management (BPM), AI-based technologies, Data Management, or Conceptual Modeling (CM) is explored in this chapter. In particular, considering the strong CM background of most of the authors, the CM connection is considered in this chapter, debating the role that CM should play in ISE.

Even a conceptual characterization of how ISE is supposed to "engineer" IS is often the subject of long discussions. A good example of this problem is the difficulty in identifying whether the contribution of a paper submitted to CAiSE is really an "ISE contribution".

This chapter, which, as stated above, is written in honor of Barbara Pernici, with whom all the authors have shared challenging discussions during their CAiSE journey, faces all these questions with the purpose of providing a characterization of what ISE is, and what dimensions should be considered when a contribution to ISE must be determined. To start a discussion on how to face the conceptual characterization of such an ISE contribution is our main goal in this chapter. With that discussion, our purpose is to pave the way for creating an ISE manifesto, that could help committees running CAiSE (and other ISE-related venues) decide which papers belong in the conference, which papers belong marginally, and which papers do not belong at all. In this particular context, we address the problem of CAiSE welcoming almost any submission related to IS in some way, needing to use refereeing resources to evaluate those papers, and finding some poorly fitting papers presented because reviewers like them or find them interesting, independent of their relevance to the ISE working domain. The CAiSE CFP already includes relevant guidance.

"Each contribution should explicitly address the engineering or the operation of information systems, clearly identify the information systems problem addressed, the expected impact of the contribution to information system engineering or operation, and the research method used. We strongly advise authors to clearly emphasize these aspects in their paper, including the abstract."

But... what does it exactly mean to be providing a (relevant) contribution to ISE? What dimensions should be considered to delimit a conceptual characterization of such a contribution? One possible use of a future manifesto could be to provide guidance for a cover letter that authors might include to explain briefly why their paper fits into CAiSE. The body of the paper would not waste space with that explanation because it would only be in the cover letter. Another possible use of the manifesto is to address one or more questions that reviewers should answer as part of their review, such as how the paper's subject matter aligns with at least part of the expected subject matter for a CAiSE paper. What exactly is to be considered is what this paper aims to (start to) discuss and characterize.

We want to emphasize that our purpose here is to start such discussion. We are perfectly aware that it is a non-trivial, long-term purpose. We do not want to provide ideas that could become a straitjacket for reviewers or a check-off list for reviewing. The only requirement for papers submitted to CAiSE is that they should fit in some way, and definitely not that they need to conform to an outline or check-off list of the type that some reviewers have used to decide whether a paper qualifies as design science research.

Having in mind to answer the commented questions, this chapter starts in Sect. 2 with a related work that contextualizes what is to be done compared with what has been done, trying to face a similar problem. In Sect. 3, we discuss the definition of IS and ISE, emphasizing the diversity that exists and the need to find their shared, precise understanding. After that discussion, we propose the use of Work System Theory ideas to structure the ISE field and to determine which aspects of ISE are to be considered relevant in order to propose a widely accepted conceptual characterization. With that objective in mind, we propose in Sect. 4 an initial framework to be used to articulate an ISE research contribution. Section 5 will provide an initial validation of the proposed framework by make a characterization of a limited set of selected cases. A final discussion on the concluding remarks will end the chapter.

2 Related Work

The conceptual characterization of a contribution can be viewed as a research goal applicable to various disciplines. What we want to do here in the ISE scope, has already been explored by [1] in the Conceptual Modeling (CM) area. Initially centered around CM, it was soon adapted to CM research [2]. As Fig. 1 shows, a work's contribution in terms of CM research is structured in three main parts: (short) identification of the work, characterization of the working context within CM, and specification of the type of contribution. Three main types of contributions are considered:

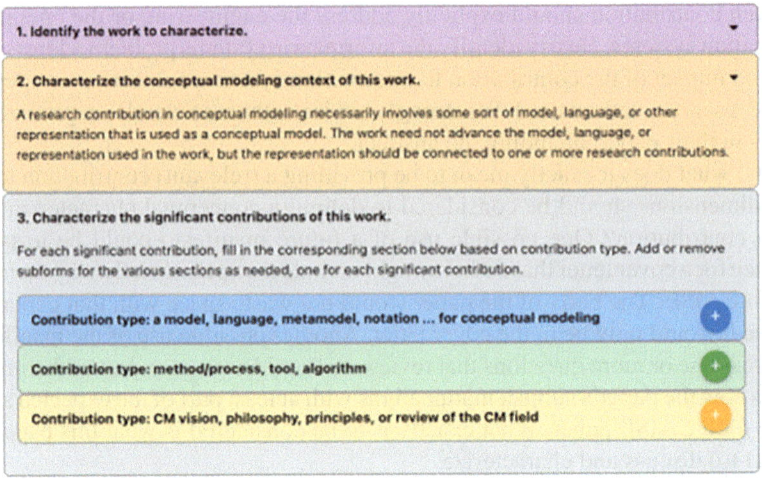

Fig. 1 The proposal for characterizing a conceptual model research contribution. It shows how the idea explored in this chapter has been worked out in the CM context

the CM-based artifact that is contributed, the CM process or method that is proposed, or the CM vision that is discussed. Characterizing the contribution of a particular work implies identifying at least one type, even if, in some cases, more than one type of contribution can be present.

A number of papers have been intended to extend and adapt the proposed framework, and several experiments have been reported, trying to assess the value of the framework application in practice [3]. Extensions to analyze how the use of LLMs could be applied instead of humans have been reported, providing significant results that show the feasibility to design AI-based assistants that can help in the tedious task of applying the framework to big sets of research papers [4]. This chapter explores a different domain, but it shares a similar purpose, and it provides an interesting baseline to compare what we will provide for ISE to what has been explored for the CM scope.

3 Definitions of Information System and Information System Engineering

The notion of Information System (IS) has been defined in many different ways, e.g., 20 divergent definitions cited by Alter [5] and 34 definitions in four categories cited by Boell & Cecez-Kecmanovic [6]. Inconsistencies between **definitions** and **characterizations** of information (e.g., Boell & Cecez-Kecmanovic in [7]) contribute to a surprising lack of clarity about whether and how the IS discipline should treat information as part of an IS. We are not "inventing" this problem. Indeed, rethinking the theoretical foundations of the IS discipline" was tied for first of **21** challenges as a grand challenge for IS research in a Delphi study reported in BISE by Becker et al. in [8]. Moreover, it was ranked third of **21** as having an impact on the discipline if it were solved, and it was ranked 1it can still be argued that a universal, precise, and widely accepted characterization of what an IS is remains open to interpretation, as many different IS-based audiences exist and interpret IS in various open to interpretation because many different IS-based audiences exist, and they interpret IS in different ways. The purpose of this work is to explore a concrete conceptual characterization of what an IS is, and how ISE can subsequently generate valuable and relevant research contributions. How can we articulate such a relevant research contribution? We will answer that question by considering that ISE views IS through Engineering principles, not only based on mathematics and natural science, but also with a focus on creating and evaluating artifacts for improved use in IS.

We are absolutly aware that we don't start from scratch. Trying to base our analysis in widely accepted and influential works, the definition of IS is discussed by Fitzgerald in [9]. Early work that helped define the IS field includes Børge Langefors' infological equation: I = i(D, S, t) where I is the information (or knowledge) produced from the data D, and the recipient's prior experience (world view) S, by the interpretation process i, during the time period t [10]. A key insight here is that given the inherent variety in S, different individuals will infer different information from data, even when the data is simple.

Langefors, being the advisor of both Janis Bubenko and Arne Sølvberg, the founders of CAiSE can also be seen as grandfather of ISE. Langefors was the first chair of the IFIP TC 8 Information systems in 1976. Two working groups were established at the beginning. On the one hand, WG 8.1, "Design and evaluation of information systems", which can be seen as the origin of ISE. The IS field was then defined as focusing on the interaction between the technological elements (hardware, software, etc.) and the social elements (people, processes, organization culture, power and politics, etc.). Key people of this working group were involved in starting CAiSE [11]. On the other hand, the second working group, WG8.2, "Interaction of information systems and the organization", can also be seen as central to the origins of IS and later the Association for Information Systems (AIS), as well as to well-established conferences such as ICIS and ECIS.

From the IS perspective, Langefors' basic principle has been borne out in much subsequent IS research. Other fundamental work outlining the theoretical and conceptual foundations of IS was published by Gordon Davis [12], who clearly identified the man-machine interaction as central to IS. After many years of IS research, it is now well-established that the field of IS focuses on the interaction between technological elements (e.g., hardware and software) and the social elements (e.g., people, processes, organization culture, power, and politics). Ahituv and Neumann [13, 14] initiated the systematic study of information systems by defining an information system as "a set of components (people, hardware, software, data, and procedures) that operate together to produce information that supports the operational and managerial functions of an organization". More recent research by Sidorova et al. [15] analyzed a body of IS research papers published over a 22-year period. They concluded that the

IS discipline focuses on how IT systems are developed and how individuals, groups, organizations, and markets interact with IT. Buckingham [16] offered a key insight in proposing that an information system is a social system involving human activity, and which may or may not involve the use of computer systems. If we look at our that accumulated work, Without a universal and widely accepted definition, we can still be optimistic.

Trying to go further in our "clarification effort", we can wonder what the conceptual foundations of IS and ISE are to go further in our "clarification effort", we can wonder what are the conceptual foundations of IS and ISE. Davis [17] identified three generic approaches to establishing conceptual foundations for a discipline: the intersection approach, which accepts concepts from any field that appear to provide insight; the core approach, which defines the ideas that characterize a discipline and distinguishes it from others; and the evolutionary approach, which combines the core approach with concepts from other fields that, over time, are found to be useful.

In the early years of the field, the intersection approach was predominant in IS. Over time, a core approach has been attempted, but the field has naturally evolved into an evolutionary one as new technologies, such as big data, AI or distributed ledgers, have become part of general use in organizational IS. Davis suggests that the evolutionary approach will become more prevalent in the future. This seems to be clearly the case when considering the diverse components of the definition of the IS field that we have discussed.

However, we still aim to promote the core approach by providing a definition of ISE, along with clarifications of specific phrases within the definition. We also aim to provide a means of discussing the distance between the core of ISE and any specific contribution to knowledge related to ISE. Therefore, the question is not whether a potentially relevant contribution X is a contribution to ISE, but rather, what the conceptual distance is between X and the core. At equal quality levels, a contribution with less distance from the core is more relevant to CAiSE than a contribution that is more distant from the core. This provides a reasonable and useful background to discuss and justify any potential "out-of-scope" decision.

We will examine ISE as "the development, evaluation, and improvement of specifications of systems that process information to support, control, or execute activities that stakeholders recognize and care about". In this context, Steve Alter's work system theory (WST, [18]) might play a central role in designing a framework of reference to characterize research contributions within the scope of ISE.

Without taking it strictly as it is proposed, the WST provides a valid starting point of discussion for establishing guidelines to be followed to characterize the relevance of an ISE contribution. For each of the main WST components -process and activities (with their participants, involved information and technological support), products/services, customers (stakeholders for the IS under analysis) and the environment, the purpose of an ISE contribution must be centered around the identification of tools, methods, conceptualizations, experiences or new ways of thinking where IS practice is influenced by the environment. We propose an initial framework in that direction in the next section to enable the identification and characterization of the ISE contribution of a research work, the central contribution of this book chapter.

If we focus on ISE, the "big" question is what exactly does it mean to add the word "Engineering" to the IS domain. **Engineering** is the practice of using natural science, mathematics, and the engineering design process to solve technical problems, increase efficiency and productivity, and improve systems. The method that incorporates humans and organizations in the engineering design process is particularly important for ISE, even though a link to mathematics in the use of logics, set theory, etc., supporting e.g. modeling approaches can also be central.

Engineering real-world IS requires a coherent design, encompassing human, organizational, economic, societal, and technological aspects. IS are omnipresent in increasingly diverse contexts, including business process management, geographic information systems, health information systems, and digital twins, to name just a few. At the same time, the discipline continually evolves alongside trends in data science, machine learning, process mining, blockchain technology, mobile computing, sustainability, new regulations, cyber warfare, and military conflicts. All these trends influence the development of the ISE field. Each application context and emerging trend can lead to specializations within ISE, necessitating various research traditions and needs. While beneficial, these specializations risk creating silos within the field of ISE. Thus, it is important to prevent such fragmentation. ISE is best viewed as a cohesive design involving multiple aspects of the IS life cycle, from design and development to deployment, operation, maintenance, and evolution. While specific specializations in AI and data management are certainly necessary, they must explicitly position their results within the broader context to engage researchers across different areas and prevent the formation of silos.

The engineering approach also makes use of Design Science Research (DSR), which is focused on a technical artifact in context, as a central research methodology for ISE. However, as seen in the CFP for CAiSE'2025, a wide variety of methods are acceptable, and three types of scientific papers are permitted: technical papers, empirical papers, and exploratory papers. Their detailed description is shown in Fig. 2.

For any of them, contributions should explicitly identify the ISE problem addressed, its expected real-world impact, and the research method used. Furthermore, as mentioned above, research concerning specific specializations within the ISE field can be relevant, but it must always explicitly position its results within the broader context to engage researchers across different areas and avoid silo formation. Both the IS background that is the subject of interest (we would refer to it using the generic term of "IS artifact") and what representation is provided as a proposal of solution are crucial components for the proposal of a framework to characterize a research ISE contribution, which we introduce in the next section.

Technical Papers which describe original insights pertaining to the field of information systems engineering. A technical paper should clearly describe the situation or type of problem tackled, the relevant state of the art, the position or solution suggested and its potential, as well as demonstrate the benefits of the contribution through a rigorous evaluation. There are three kinds of technical papers:

- **Technology-oriented papers**: produce and evaluate some technological artifact (infrastructure, tool, language, or system) in controlled/scoped experiments in lab settings.
- **Method-oriented papers**: produce and evaluate some socio-techno-logical artifact (a method, approach to be used in an information systems engineering context) that needs to be evaluated in a (less controllable) real-world setting.
- **Conceptual and theoretical papers**: deal with ontological, philosophical, semiotic, and mathematical foundations of information systems engineering. These papers typically use a deduction and/or argumentation-based approach to develop a point/contribution as part of their evaluation.

Empirical Papers, which evaluate existing problem situations, including problems encountered in practice, or validate proposed solutions with scientific means, i.e., by empirical studies, experiments, case studies, experience reports, simulations, etc. Scientific reflection on problems and practices in industry also falls into this category. The topic of the evaluation presented in the paper as well as its causal or logical properties must be clearly stated. The research method must be sound and appropriate.

Exploratory Papers, which describe completely new research positions or approaches, in order to face a generic situation arising because of new ICT, new kinds of activities, or new IS challenges. They must precisely describe the situation and demonstrate why current methods, tools, ways of reasoning, or meta-models are inadequate. They must also rigorously present their approach and demonstrate its pertinence and correctness in addressing the identified situation.

Fig. 2 Description of the types of research papers accepted by CAiSE 2025 as explained in its web page

4 Artefact, Representation, Method, Tool and Vision: The Main Dimensions of an ISE Research Contribution

Characterizing the contribution of a research work to the ISE field requires identifying the work under analysis, delimiting its ISE context, and determining its significant contributions.

The first step is to identify the work whose research contribution is being performed. Any standard bibliographical reference style can be used for this purpose.

The second step describes the context of the contribution in relation to ISE concerns, so that its relevance to the field becomes justified. An ISE research contribution must state clearly its IS connection, this is the purpose of this step, showing how to link the work with the ISE domain. We take Alter's World System Theory (WST) approach as a conceptual framework to guide the description of such an ISE-based context. A research contribution in ISE involves technology, information, participants, processes and activities, products or services, and customer, all of which are associated with strategies, infrastructure and environment. The proposal of using WST to structure ISE context involves the identification and specification of the main WST components of the work under analysis: What is the underlying IS? What processes or activities are considered? What are their affected stakeholders and/or technological support? What products/services are the result of the IS management tasks? How customers, infrastructure or business strategies align with them?

Finally, the third component is intended to clarify the type of contribution the work presents. To structure the answer to the previous questions, five main dimensions are considered, each of them intended to characterize a potential IS contribution in the context of the subject matter which is related to IS engineering:

1. The artifact: a description of the aspects of IS that is under the contribution to knowledge
2. The representation of the artifact
3. Methodological approaches to represent, to evaluate, or to make the artifact evolve
4. Means (tools) to support the three above
5. New ways of thinking for the three above.

Novel tools, methods, conceptualization or generalizations, descriptions of real world experiences, or new ways of thinking must be described by one (or several) of the proposed dimensions, by focusing either on the identification of the artifact of the contribution, and/or how it can be represented, and/or on the methodological or experimental/empirical aspects to develop an IS, and/or tool support or new ways of facing the problems under study. By novel we mean that members of the IS engineering community will get new insights from learning about the contribution.

Contributions must demonstrate their intended value to the community. How to manage the different dimensions of ISE according to this vision is initially developed in the subsequent subsections.

(1) **IS as Artifact**. We assume that ISE contributions focus on (aspects of) an IS as central artefact or object of study. The IS as artifact and the implications of the research for the engineering of this artefact must be introduced explicitly. What we mean by "artifact" is either the IS which is engineered, seen as discussed before as a WS whose essential activities are devoted to processing information, i.e., capturing, storing, retrieving, deleting, transmitting, manipulating, and displaying information or a component of it. We consider that this view is compatible with looking at an IS as (i) "a set of components (people, hardware, software, data, and procedures) that operate together to produce information that supports the operation and management functions of an organization" (following [14]), and as (ii) a socio-technical system with human actors performing some of the activities supported by the software tools which are part of the IS. WST provides a conceptual basis to characterize what are the relevant components of the IS that is behind the intended ISE contribution.

An example of a contribution could be a work analyzing the recent use of a new software application in the company to facilitate its adoption. To fall under the scope of ISE, the software application should be an IS, and the contribution of the analysis to understanding how ISE engineering should be done to facilitate the adoption should be clarified.

(2) **Representation of the artifact**. In any engineering domain, the object (product/artifact) to be engineered must first be represented in some way, using appropriate representation techniques (depending on the product under engineering), such as a bridge, a building, a car, or a plane.

In ISE, these representations are also required before the implementation of the IS; they are also extremely useful for handling the evolutions of the IS. Those representations require “ways of modeling” (according to [21]).

To be able to create those representations of what exists and/or happens in the physical world, we need languages or formalisms, or meta-models, etc. We need modeling languages that represent reality through conceptual models.

A research contribution may thus focus on representations of the artefact, for instance, a work that develops and presents the MAPS modeling language.

(3) **Methodological approaches to create, represent, evaluate, or to make evolve the artefact**. Representations are not sufficient if the ways for using or for creating them are unknown or not documented or purely based on tacit and individual knowledge and expertise of IS engineers.

Thus, in ISE methods, “ways of working” [21] are formalised and capitalised to be re-used. They could also be extended when needed, based on the past experiences and learnings of ISE researchers and practitioners. Those “ways of working” are necessary in the entire lifecycle of IS engineering, i.e., not only in the initial development of the IS but in the whole lifecycle if the IS, for its evaluations, and when needed (very often), for its maintenance (corrective or evolutive) until the end of life of the artifact.

For instance, a work that reports the use of MAPS for describing an IS governance method.

(4) **Means (tools) to support the three above**. Software is a fundamental component of an IS. The ISE perspective can be also enhanced when it is supported by specific software. This type of contribution takes into consideration what technology the IS is using in order to operate It can refer to:

- The software components of the engineered IS (artifact).
- Software supporting the creation of conceptual models (e.g., with CASE tools or Model-driven Development tools), languages (e.g., Metaedit) without any guidance about how to do it and often without any specific link to the application domain.
- Software extending the point above with methodological guidelines for the creation of conceptual models; software supporting the transformations of models (e.g., CMP [22]); software supporting the use of an IS project management method (e.g., Kanban) ...

(5) **New ways of thinking**. This refers to completely new research positions or approaches, still without concrete representations of methodological background associated to them. They can face a generic situation arising because of new ICT, new kinds of activities, or new IS challenges. They must precisely describe the situation and demonstrate why current methods, tools, ways of modeling, ways of reasoning, or meta-models are inadequate. They must also rigorously present their approach and demonstrate its pertinence and correctness in addressing the identified situation.

This type of contribution can also group research that presents a vision for the field, a discussion of philosophy or principles, an approach to pedagogy or education in ISE, or an application of ISE to a (mostly) unexplored challenging domain.

For example, a work that explores how LLMs users' experience can affect ISE practice.

5 Preliminary Validation

To show how to use the framework, and make an initial evaluation of its practical use, we analyze two questions and four paper abstracts describing potential submitted CAiSE papers, for which authors are interested in knowing if their work is suitable for a CAiSE submission. We interpret this question as: "is the intented contribution of our research work adequate for CAiSE?". The answer is provided on the basis of the proposed framework. In the two first cases, we introduce the authors's question, and a discussion with an answer. In the latter four cases, we provide the abstract of a paper together with a (short) evaluation that argues on its adequacy in ISE terms. These four cases faces different dimensions of the proposed evaluation framework.

5.1 Case 1

In the first case, authors give the following description: *we are working on explainability for graph neural networks (GNNs). GNNs are widely used in healthcare applications (e.g., biomolecular processing, metabolic graphs) as data are increasingly represented as graphs. Given the sensitivity and high cost of experimentation in this domain, explainability is particularly important: models should provide not only predictions but also justifications that increase user trust. Existing methods typically generate explanations such as "this edge led to this classification." However, after an extensive review of the literature, we found no technique capable of accounting for the absence of nodes—i.e., statements such as "had this node (or these nodes) been present, the prediction would have been substantially different." Developing such techniques first requires suitable benchmarks, yet current datasets and generation strategies do not address this scenario. Constructing examples in which adding a node changes the class is nontrivial. Our contribution is a tool/framework for generating such datasets, representing an initial step toward exploring this new direction.*

Would this work fits within the scope of Exploratory papers? Applying the framework, our answer is "NO". The work is focusing on technological aspects intended to improve explainability for GNN without giving a clear, precise reference of what is the IS that is behind any engineering activity. In other words, the artifact description is absent. There is no answer to the question "What IS is the subject of the contribution of knowledge to ISE" in this work; the article could be seen as a potentially relevant contribution for an audience related to AI, GNN, who could evaluate what technological improvements the proposed solution provides. But it is not delivering any significant value to an ISE audience, that should understand what is the IS that is being improved, how and with which representation (in WST terms, what products/services are being provided, or what processes/activities are being improved, what stakeholders are going to be benefited). The IS as subject of research is unclear, there is no contribution in the dimension of representation, methodological approaches, development tools or vision. We therefore conclude that this paper does not offer an ISE contribution, and is therefore out of scope for CaiSE.

5.2 Case 2

In the second case, authors give this description: *"We are working on predicting antibiotic resistance. As part of our long-term group project, we aim to build an information system for clinicians that predicts whether a given organism (e.g., a bacterium) will be resistant to a specific antibiotic—something largely determined by its genes. To keep the workflow simple for medical users, the input should be the raw genomic sequence. We then apply bakta to extract the organism's gene list. However, this list (1) contains many highly specific genes, which must be grouped to avoid an unmanageable number of distinct features, and (2) does not indicate whether they correspond to known antibiotic-resistance genes (AMR genes). We worked with a dataset that initially contained only AMR genes, and we performed the bakta annotation ourselves (requiring a supercomputer) to assess the feasibility of a more principled grouping strategy and to compare performance. In short, we addressed several challenges in training and deploying an antibiotic-resistance prediction model designed for seamless integration into clinician-facing systems. Except for a few cases, the results are comparable to those obtained using AMR genes alone, and in some instances significantly better—particularly for antibiotics represented by few samples. This suggests that, for these less-studied antibiotics, additional relevant genes remain to be identified. This work fits within the scope of Empirical papers."*

Applying the framework, our answer in this case is "YES". Aspects of a concrete IS is described as subject of research: an IS for clinicians intended to predict which organism will be resistant to a specific antibiotic. The representation of the artifact in the form of the object (product) to be engineered is also described: an antibiotic-resistance prediction model designed for seamless integration into clinician-facing systems. The combination of these two dimensions (both artifact and representation) characterizes a potential ISE contribution, whose practical value is to be established in terms of any evidence provided by the work. We believe that this line of argumentation can be applied to any work to establish its adequacy as an ISE contribution. Our immediate further work is to select the papers of CAISE 25 proceedings in order to make an exhaustive work of conceptual characterization of their intended ISE contributions using the framework that we have presented in this work. With such an experiment, we want to learn how feasible its use is for our purpose, introduce any improvement when required, and providing a tool to be used in the CAiSE scope to guide any discussion oriented to explain when a paper is decided to out-of-scope. An initial analysis of some past CAiSE contributions is found below.

5.3 Case 3 (Tool)

Abstract: *A Tool to Design Resilient Aware Multi-party Business Processes. Today business organizations operate in digital ecosystems that can be conceptualized in terms of multi-party business processes, where co-operation among parties is mandatory. Being every party a potential source of failures with impacts on the entire ecosystem, resilience is a feature that should be enforced by multi-party business processes directly at design-time, to anticipate what should be done in case of possible occurring failures at run-time. In this direction, this paper presents R-CMMN, a modeling tool that implements a maturity model to support process designers in the definition of resilient aware business processes at design-time, using OMG CMMN as modeling notation.*

Evaluation: YES. The IS as artifact is a process-based IS, supporting multi-party business processes in digital ecosystems. In the representation dimension, models using OMG CMMN are used. In the tool dimension, the contribution is R-CMMN, a modeling tool that implements a maturity model to support process designers in the definition of resilient aware business processes at design-time, of which the usability is evaluated.

5.4 Case 4 (Methodological, Tool)

Abstract: *This exploratory paper builds on the EMMSAD 2024 paper "Could a Large Language Model Contribute Significantly to Requirements Analysis?" Eight versions of each of three LLM prompts (for system structure, analysis, and recommendations) were applied to three 3000+ word case studies. Those versions expressed different "treatments" including a control with no RAG augmentation, a version with RAG augmentation based on an analysis template used by MBA and EMBA students, and six other versions based on theoretical approaches such as activity theory, a BPM design space, work system principles, and so on. The LLM responses were somewhat reliable for summarizing system structure, less reliable for summarizing an analysis, and often generic and impractical for recommendations because the LLM did not understand contexts. This new paper adds three new capabilities: (1) RAG augmentation using a knowledge base consisting of "knowledge objects" built on work system theory, (2) application of that knowledge base using chain-of-thought reasoning, (3) inclusion of direct feedback from analysts during an analysis process in order to correct errors and to extend the prompt in new directions. Examples are used to illustrate results from applying those capabilities to 3 disparate case studies.*

Evaluation: YES. The paper is in the domain of "Requirements Engineering" (or "Requirements Analysis" to be more precise). The addressed artifact is any information systems. The paper clearly contributes to a methodological step in the creation of Information System (in particular, the requirements analysis step). The contributed tool is an AI-based Requirements Analysis Assistant. A potential contribution in the "Vision" dimension is that LLMs supported by a knowledge base and under human guidance can contribute to the overall performance in the requirements analysis phase.

5.5 Case 5 (Representation)

Abstract: *Clinical Practice Guidelines (CPGs) are of high value to healthcare because of the evidence-based medical knowledge contained. However, actual CPG compliance is lower than one would expect. It is said that the guidelines are not easy to apply, for a variety of practical reasons. Compliance could be increased by transforming the CPG into an executable format. The question in this research is whether the OMG standard DMN (Decision Modeling Notation) is a suitable representation and what its value is for medical practice. These questions are addressed by a qualitative literature review. Potential ad-vantages of a conceptual decision model notation, but also several limitations and challenges for executable CPGs are identified. The literature research was part of a larger project in which an excerpt of breast cancer guidelines was translated into executable DMN. Main findings: It has been confirmed that the use of decision services implementing the CPGs has a positive effect on policy conformance. DMN is not widely used yet for CPG representation, but it has been applied successfully in a couple of exploratory projects. There is a need for more rigorous evaluation research on decisions services in general.*

Evaluation: Yes. The paper addresses Clinical Practice Guidelines. While there is no automated IS as artifact, the goal of the paper is clearly to target the development of an IS by means of CPGs in an executable format. The main contribution targets the "representation" dimension by evaluation the suitability of DMN as representation for the CPGs.

5.6 Case 6 (Vision)

Abstract: *In order to promote conceptual-model programming (CMP), a set of CMP articles is presented. We hold these articles to be the defining principles for model-complete software development. Essentially, this CMP manifesto asserts that programming activities should be carried out through conceptual modeling. For applications amenable to conceptual-model designs, software developers should never need to write a line of traditional code. Thus, programming is actually conceptual-model programming. To accommodate CMP, conceptual-modeling languages must be executable. They must also be capable of completely deploying both databases and user interfaces and conceptually expressing database access and user interaction. To enable CMP, a conceptual-model compiler must exist to generate underlying code, which could be, but is not necessarily, high-level language code that itself needs further compilation. Important, however, is that model-compiled code is beyond the purview of CMP programmers—both for initially creating the application system being developed and for enhancing or evolving the application system. Thus, application-system development becomes entirely model-driven, and CMP constitutes model-complete software development.*

Evaluation: Yes. The paper presents a vision for the field of software development, grounded in conceptual modeling. It proposes a completely new research position to be applied to any IS design and development, using models as the key artifacts. Authors discuss how current methods and tools fail in generating correct software, and they introduce the CMP proposal as a general view that concrete methods and tools should materialize.

In all the cases, the application of the framework shows useful: it provides a solid, common basis for a discussion intended to determine the contribution of the research works, and their adequacy to CAiSE

6 Concluding Remarks

In this chapter, we analyze how difficult it is to share a universal and precise intuition of what does it mean to contribute to the ISE research domain, and we explore potential frameworks of reference intended to conceptually characterize such a research contribution. We propose an initial, preliminary framework composed by five dimensions, and we make a first attempt to use in practice, having in mind to use it to delimit when a paper submitted for CAiSE is in the scope of the conference (we used CAiSE as conference of reference for the ISE case).

Whereas early work related to ISE conferences and communities has focused more on the role of conferences in the community in general, and CAiSE in particular [19] and people being involved in the community [20], here we focus on the content of the articles to be within (the evolving) scope of ISE.

We are perfectly aware that our framework is a preliminar one. We present our work as a first attempt to explore the problem and looking for valid and practical solutions. The framework has been evaluated using examples of papers, and our shared feedback indicates us that the research is extremely promising, but much further work is to be done to look at the problem more comprehensibly in order to have a framework ready to be used in practice to evaluate the adequacy and relevance of any ISE-related research work.

Let us finish emphasizing once more that we have written this chapter in honour to Barbara Pernici, with whom we have shared fruitful discussion around the topic of the work for years. We want to emphasize our full recognition and appreciation for her brilliant scientific career, that has made possible these challenging discussions, and many more to come in the future. Thanks so much, Barbara.

References

1. Delcambre, L.M.L., Liddle, S.W., Pastor, O., Storey, V.C.: A Reference Framework for Conceptual Modeling. In: Trujillo, J., et al. (ed.) Conceptual Modeling. ER 2018. Lecture Notes in Computer Science, vol. 11157, pp. 27–42. Springer, Cham (2018). https://doi.org/10.1007/978-3-030-00847-5_4
2. Delcambre, L.M.L., Liddle, S.W., Pastor, O., Storey, V.C.: Articulating Conceptual Modeling Research Contributions. In: Reinhartz-Berger, I., Sadiq, S. (eds.) Advances in Conceptual Modeling. ER 2021. Lecture Notes in Computer Science, vol. 13012. Springer, Cham (2021)
3. Panach, J.I., Pastor, Ó., Liddle, S.W., Storey, V.C., Mayr, H.C., Thalheim, B.: Evaluating a Framework of Conceptual Modelling Research. In: Saeki, M., et al. (eds.) Advances in Conceptual Modeling. ER 2024. Lecture Notes in Computer Science, vol. 14932. Springer, Cham (2025). https://doi.org/10.1007/978-3-031-75599-6_16
4. Liddle, S. W., Mayr, H.C., Pastor, O., Storey, V.C., Thalheim, B.: Conceptual modeling: a large language model assistant for characterizing research contributions. Data Knowl. Eng. **161**, 102497 (2025). https://doi.org/10.1016/j.datak.2025.102497
5. Alter, S.: Defining information systems as work systems: implications for the IS field. Eur. J. Inf. Syst. **17**(5), 448–469 (2008)
6. Boell, S. K., Cecez-Kecmanovic, D.: What is an information system?. In: 48th Hawaii International Conference on System Sciences, pp. 4959–4968. IEEE (2015). https://doi.org/10.1109/HICSS.2015.587
7. Cecez-Kecmanovic, D.: What Is 'Information' Beyond a Definition? ICIS (2015)
8. Becker, J., Vom Brocke, J., Heddier, M., Seidel, S.: In search of information systems (grand) challenges: a community of inquirers perspective. Business & Inf. Syst. Eng. **57**(6), 377–390 (2015)
9. Fitzgerald, B. [2402.04200] Information Systems and Software Engineering: The Case for Convergence arxiv.org
10. Langefors, B.: Theoretical analysis of information systems. Studentlitteratur, Lund (1966)
11. Bubenko, J., Rolland, C., Sølvberg, A.: The CAiSE Adventure. In: Bubenko, J., Krogstie, J., Pastor, O., Pernici, B., Rolland, C., Sølvberg, A. (eds.) Seminal Contributions to Information Systems Engineering. Springer, Berlin, Heidelberg (2013). https://doi.org/10.1007/978-3-642-36926-1_1
12. Davis, G.B.: Management Information Systems: Conceptual Foundations, Structure and Development. McGraw-Hill Book Company, New York (1974)
13. Ahituv, N., Neumann, S.: A flexible approach to information system development. MIS Q. **8**(2), 69–78 (1984)
14. Ahituv, N., Neumann, S.: Principles of Information Systems for Management, 2nd edn. W. C. Brown, Dubuque, Iowa (1986)
15. Sidorova, A., Evangelopoulos, N., Valacich, J.S., Ramakrishnan, T.: Uncovering the intellectual core of the information systems discipline. MIS Q. **32**(3), 467–482 (2008)
16. Buckingham, R.A., Land, F.F.: Education for ISE: what does it mean? ITNOW **29**(2), 33–35 (1987)
17. Davis, G.B.: Information systems conceptual foundations: looking backward and forward. In Organizational and Social Perspectives on Information Technology: IFIP TC8 WG8. 2 International Working Conference on the Social and Organizational Perspective on Research and Practice in Information Technology June 9–11 (2000), Aalborg, Denmark, pp. 61–82. Springer US, Boston, MA

18. Alter, S.: Work system theory: overview of core concepts, extensions, and challenges for the future. J. Assoc. Inf. Syst. **14**(2) (2013). https://doi.org/10.17705/1jais.00323
19. Krogstie, J., Pastor, O., Pernici, B.: The Future of CAiSE. In: Bubenko, J., Krogstie, J., Pastor, O., Pernici, B., Rolland, C., Sølvberg, A. (eds.) Seminal Contributions to Information Systems Engineering. Springer, Berlin, Heidelberg (2013). https://doi.org/10.1007/978-3-642-36926-1_37
20. Jarke, M., Pham, M.C., Klamma, R. Evolution of the CAiSE Author Community: A Social Network Analysis. In: Bubenko, J., Krogstie, J., Pastor, O., Pernici, B., Rolland, C., Sølvberg, A. (eds.) Seminal Contributions to Information Systems Engineering. Springer, Berlin, Heidelberg. https://doi.org/10.1007/978-3-642-36926-1_2 (2013)
21. Seligmann, P.S., Wijers, G.M., Sol, H.G.: Analysing the structure of I.S. methodologies, an alternative approach. In: Proceedings of the First Conference on Information Systems, Amersfoort, The Netherlands (1989)
22. Embley, D., Liddle, S., Pastor, O.: Conceptual-model programming: a manifesto. In: Embley, D., Thalheim, B. (eds.) Handbook of Conceptual Modeling. Springer, Berlin, Heidelberg (2011). https://doi.org/10.1007/978-3-642-15865-0_1

Time in Business Process Management: Some Research Activities

Carlo Combi and Giuseppe Pozzi

Abstract Process management aims at representing how to orchestrate the execution of atomic work units to achieve a final goal. Temporal information management considers every piece of data coupled to one or more temporal aspects, whose management requires suitable techniques. The two topics have been widely considered in the literature for some decades, but in separate ways. The overlapping of the two research topics, the management of temporal information in process models, has emerged only within the last decade or so, after some seminal work at the end of the nineties. In this chapter, we examine research activities that encompass both process modeling techniques and the management of temporal aspects of information. As an application scenario, we consider a healthcare process involving patients who undergo pacemaker implantation and periodic follow-up visits.

1 Introduction

Time is the travel companion of mankind, and time never abandons human life but stamps every event for mankind. Literature reports several definitions of time, as well as some difficulties in providing the reader with a precise definition of time: e.g., "Quid est ergo tempus? Si nemo ex me quærat, scio; si quærenti explicare velim, nescio [1]—What, then, is time? If no one asks me, I know; but if I want to explain it to someone who asks, I do not know." In many areas of computer science, e.g., database and information systems, real-time systems, and AI, besides the concept of time, a the temporal dimension of data attracted specific attention, coupling every piece of data with a timestamp which can describe different temporal aspects of that piece of data: when the piece of data starts to be true, or ends to be true, or is stored by

C. Combi
Università degli Studi di Verona, Verona, Italy
e-mail: carlo.combi@univr.it

G. Pozzi (✉)
Politecnico di Milano, Milan, Italy
e-mail: giuseppe.pozzi@polimi.it

C. Cappiello et al. (eds.), *Retrospective and Prospective Views on Information Systems Engineering*, https://doi.org/10.1007/978-3-032-19578-4_3

a computer system, or is removed from a computer system. Several other temporal dimensions can be defined (see, for example, [9, 21]).

Business Process Management (BPM) considers complex organizational processes that require the coordinated execution of simple activities (tasks) by several human or automatic executors (agents), and can be described in terms of workflows. Given a process model, the automatic enactment (execution) of process instances of that process model is supported by suitable software systems, namely process engines or workflow management systems (WFMS). Most process engines rely on database management systems (DBMS), where temporal aspects, which are relevant for the execution of a workflow, are managed explicitly.

Over the last two decades, scientific research has deeply investigated the management of temporal information in process modelling and management (see, e.g. [2, 6, 8, 10, 12, 13, 17–20, 22, 23]).

While far from an exhaustive description of the overall scenario, we consider here some of the major aspects, we investigated in the last years:

i. *temporal modelling of data managed by the BPM/system*: the concepts of valid time and transaction time apply [11] to data managed by the process engine;
ii. *temporal conceptual modelling of the process*: some temporal constraints can be added to the model, to specify temporal requirements and their control over the process [12];
iii. *task scheduling*: additional details and impacts on the correct execution of the process can derive from the actions performed by the scheduler when assigning tasks to executors. The temporal dimension of the organisational model must be properly considered [14];
iv. *temporal architectures of the process engine*: to exploit the advantages of temporal process models, the architecture of the process engine must be adapted [13];
v. *temporal constraints and healthcare process management.* Process models can be successfully deployed in several application domains, e.g., in defining clinical guidelines, whose temporal constraints help to guarantee the correctness and the efficacy of the therapy or of the surgery [7, 8].

In the following sections, we introduce a motivating example, taken from a paper by Casati, Ceri, Pernici, and Pozzi [4], where some temporal issues are implicitly mentioned, even though they are not the main focus of the chapter; next we briefly describe the major features of the research investigations in light of the above aspects.

2 A Motivating Example

As a motivating example, we consider here the process of managing a patient who needs a pacemaker [4]. The process model, i.e. the schema according to which the several instances (cases) are enacted by the process engine, is depicted in Fig. 1 according to the business process modelling notation BPMN. One unique clinical protocol

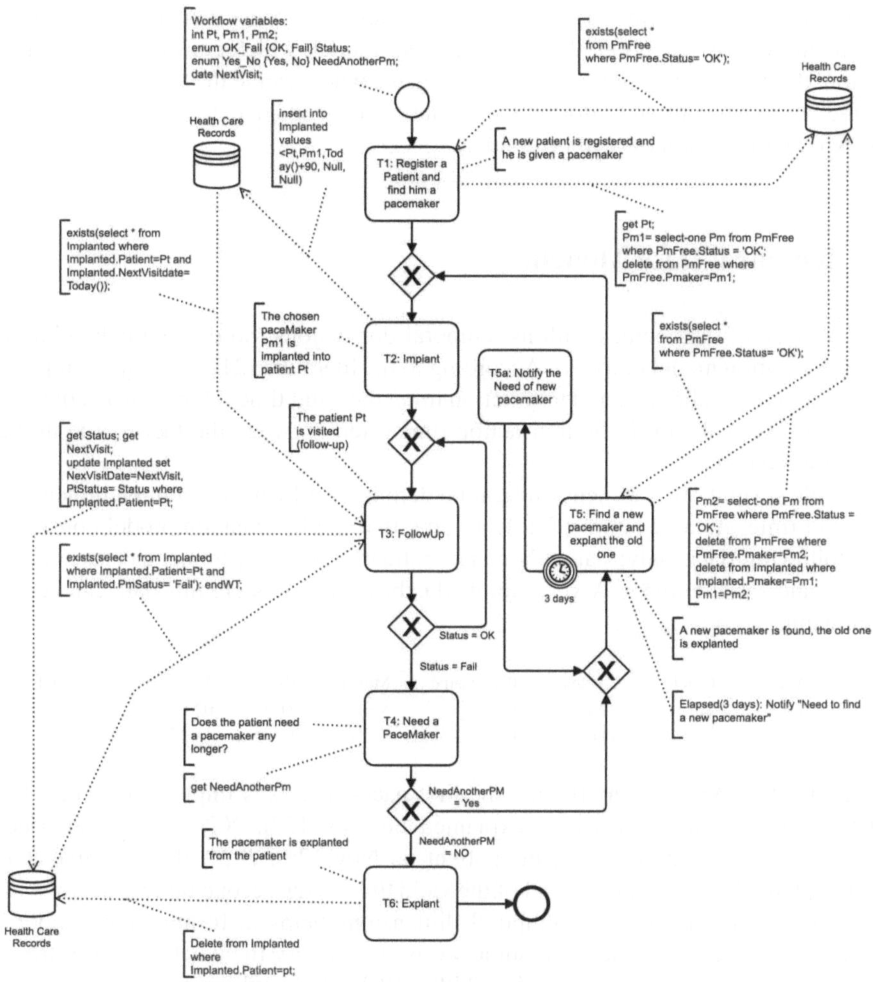

Fig. 1 The BPMN diagram of the process model used throughout the chapter. The process refers to pacemaker implantations. Cylinders depict data stores. Texts depict comments and actions, which in turn can include SQL commands

manages all the patients in the same manner. One case manages the data for one patient; one case can't refer to data from another case, unless via a shared database table.

The patient is registered, and a new pacemaker is found (`T1`). The pacemaker is then implanted (`T2`). After some time, the pacemaker is checked, and the patient enters a follow-up routine (`T3`). If the result of the check-up is OK, the next check-up visit is booked; otherwise, a new pacemaker is required (`T4`). If a new pacemaker is required, the old one is explanted (`T5`) and a new one is implanted. If no pacemaker is needed, the existing one is explanted, and the case ends (`T6`).

The complete description of a process includes the *process* model, which defines the main flow of execution, the *organizational* model, which considers the organization, the roles, the authorizations of the agents who execute the work units (tasks) of the process model, the *information* model, which considers the data managed by every case of the process can be divided.

3 Temporal Data Modelling

Every piece of data comes with its temporal dimensions. So do data belonging to the information model of a case. According to the literature [21], the major temporal dimensions are valid time and transaction time: the valid time refers to when the fact is true in the real world; the transaction time refers to when the fact is true in the database system.

While several other dimensions can be defined, we focus here on the dimension of valid time. As an example, let us assume that the information model considers the following data, only: patient's name, patient's surname, implanted pacemaker model and serial number. A very simple database table to store this data can be the following:

PaceMaker	CaseId	P_Name	P_Surname	Model	SN	VT_Start	VT_End
	27	John	Doe	VVI	00875	02-01-18	11-12-21
	27	John	Doe	DDD	01548	11-12-21	$+\infty$

Table `PaceMaker` reports that the first pacemaker was implanted on Feb 1st, 2018: that pacemaker was then explanted on Nov 12th, 2021. A second pacemaker was implanted on the same patient on Nov 12th, 2021: that pacemaker is still implanted, as the upper bound of the valid time of the second tuple is set to $+\infty$.

A proper management of temporal dimensions helps in formulating temporal queries. As an example, let us assume we want to query the database and retrieve the implanted pacemaker as of May 24th, 2019. The resulting SQL query is the following (where function VALID() explicitly manages the valid time of a tuple):

```
SELECT P_Name, P_Surname, SN
FROM PaceMaker as P
WHERE VALID(P) OVERLAPS 05-24-19
```

Temporal dimensions also affect the process model. It may occur, and often does, that the process model needs to be updated to better align with new requirements from the application domain. As a consequence, the process model is updated, and a new version of the existing process model is released. To ensure the consistent execution of process instances (cases) that have already started but are not yet completed, as well as to initiate new process instances according to the latest process model definition, a temporal query is essential. In detail, the process model to be considered for still-running cases is the one that was valid at the time of case creation. For new cases to be created, the most recent release of the process model is the one to be considered.

Let us assume that the process engine runs supported by two database tables, namely `Process_Model` and `Case`: the first table stores the versions that have been defined for every process model; the second table stores the case identifier, the name of the process model, and the valid time of every case.

Process_Model	Process_Name	Version	VT_Start	VT_End
	PaceMaker	V1	01-01-18	12-31-22
	PaceMaker	V2	01-01-23	$+\infty$

Case	CaseId	Process_Name	Status	VT_Start	VT_End
	27	PaceMaker	running	02-01-18	$+\infty$
	28	PaceMaker	Running	02-03-23	$+\infty$

To correctly detect the version of the process model according to which a running case has to be completed, we apply the following temporally-extended SQL query:

```
SELECT CaseId, Version
FROM Process_Model as PM join Case as C on Process_Name
WHERE VALID(PM) OVERLAPS BEGIN(VALID(C))
```

We observe that the temporal query in the `WHERE` clause requires us to consider the beginning timestamp of the valid time of the current case. The query will return that case 27 runs version 1, and case 28 runs version 2 of the process model named `PaceMaker`.

4 Temporal Process Modelling

To ensure the correctness of the process model, it can include temporal constraints. These additional data help the scheduler of the process engine identify the most appropriate agents, as well as detect any anomalies or delays in the execution of process instances.

Constraints can be defined at the task level, at the task scheduling level, and at the inter-task level. A possible taxonomy of temporal constraints is as follows:

i. *task constraints*: constraints at the single task level relate to task start or end time (timestamp constraint) and to task duration time (duration constraint). The task start time can be either an absolute timestamp (e.g., on May 24th 2002, 16:10:34) or a periodic timestamp (e.g., every Sunday morning at 2:10:05 a.m.); an end time for the task (e.g., on June 7th 2002, 18:30:00) can also be provided, specifying a deadline for that task, no matter when the task started.

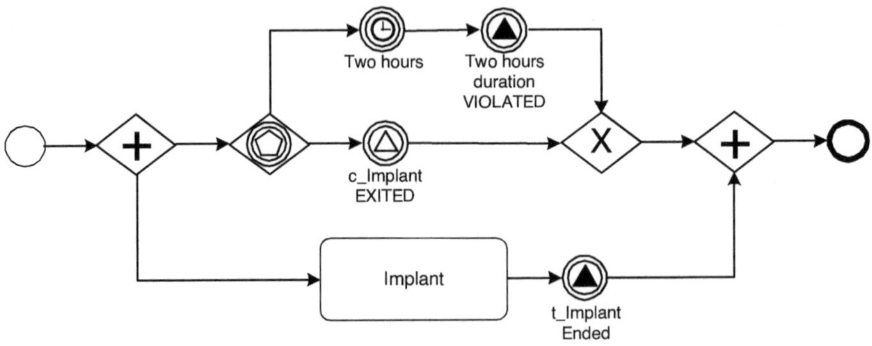

Fig. 2 The task `Implant` embedded in a BPMN subprocess allowing the management of constraints on the maximum duration of a task. Whenever a task requires a `maxTaskDuration` constraint, the subprocess monitors such a constraint

Every task definition in the process model thus includes two main attributes, namely `ExpectedTaskDuration` and `MaxTaskDuration`, which establish acceptable limit values for the duration of each task. We observe that these two attributes semantically are a duration.
As an example, in Fig. 1 a task constraint can require that the task `Implant` has an `ExpectedTaskDuration` of one hour, and a `MaxTaskDuration` of two hours. Such a constraint related to the maximum duration can be, for example, represented through a standard BPMN subprocess [5, 10] as depicted in Fig. 2;

ii. *schedule-task constraints*: these constraints apply when a task ends and the successor task(s), i.e., the next one(s) to be executed, is to be scheduled. The scheduling time plays a key role in the definition of these constraints: e.g., in a distributed or federated environment, the queries performed by the scheduler can require a non-negligible amount of time. The scheduling time can result in even higher values if there is more than one successor task due to a split gateway (to start two or more parallel executions) or more than one predecessor task due to a join gateway (to re-synchronize after two or more parallel executions have ended). We observe that these constraints can indicate that the scheduling time must not exceed the maximum duration expressed by the constraint. However, a task scheduling constraint can also define the minimum duration, thereby introducing a required delay between the end of the predecessor task and the start of the successor task, as dictated by the application domain's requirements.
iii. *inter-task constraints*: these constraints involve different tasks. Typically, an inter-task constraint considers the timestamp of a task and the timestamp of its successor: the constraint can also involve more than one successor due to a split gateway or more than one predecessor due to a join gateway.

The constraint can also be extended to a group of tasks. If we consider a subprocess (grouping several tasks into one unique module), the inter-task constraint defines when the first task of the subprocess has to start, thus starting the entire subprocess itself, or when the last task has to end, thus ending the entire subprocess itself. The above concepts of `ExpectedTaskDuration` and `MaxTaskDuration` apply to the entire subprocess, thus limiting the time span between the beginning of the first task and the end of the last one for that subprocess.

Finally, inter-task constraints can also be extended to arbitrary sequences of tasks. Let us consider a very simple process model where tasks `A`, `B`, `C`, and `D` are sequentially connected (no split, no join, but a straightforward connection). Task, schedule-task, and inter-task constraints can be defined as from above over a couple of subsequent tasks. Additionally, the process designer may also want, for example, to define another constraint limiting to δ the maximum allowed temporal duration elapsed between t_{startB} and t_{endD}: this constraint is an inter-task one that considers one task (`B`) and one successor of one successor of its (`D`). The global effect is similar to that of defining a subprocess including `B`, `C`, and `D`, featuring a `MaxTaskDuration` equal to δ.

Finally, we observe that a process model with temporal constraints opens several issues on the analysis of its correctness, as well as on the satisfiability of the constraints defined. Checks can be performed statically, at process definition time, as well as dynamically, at process execution time (see Sect. 7).

5 Task Scheduling of Temporal Processes

Task scheduling and task assignment to executing agents is a well-known problem [27]. Basically, the scheduler operates to optimize an overall figure of merit, ensuring that all tasks are executed in the shortest possible time and balancing the workload among the various agents within the organization.

Deploying the scheduling policies to process execution reveals several additional problems. The process execution environment can be distributed, where agents, even if within the same organization, are physically located in distinct locations. One additional constraint the scheduler must consider when assigning tasks is that the executing agent must be in the same location as the process being executed. As an example in Fig. 1, the surgeon to implant the pacemaker (task `T2`) must be in the same hospital where the patient is admitted.

Another issue the scheduler must consider is the temporal constraints of the process model. If a task must be completed within a given deadline, the agent to whom the task will be assigned for execution must have a work list that is compatible with the constraint. As an example in Fig. 1, if a patient requires an immediate implantation of a pacemaker and the surgeon needed to implant the pacemaker (task `T2`) is already involved in another surgery intervention, a different surgeon must be selected for the current case.

Since tasks and processes are long-running activities, the availability and unavailability time of every agent also plays a key role in task scheduling. If the expected duration for a task spans over an unavailability interval of the agent, e.g., because of the holidays of that agent, the temporal constraint of the task can be violated: in case of improper task assignment to an agent, the detection of the constraint violation can occur too late, and the recovery of the constraint violation becomes very hard. As an example in Fig. 1, if the scheduled follow up visit is booked for Apr 04th and the surgeon taking care of the follow up of that patient is on holiday from Apr 01st to Apr 08th, a different surgeon must be assigned the follow up visit of that patient for Apr 04th. In this search, the temporal properties suitably managed by a Temporal DBMS are fundamental.

Last but not least, temporal constraints can be defined at different granularity levels, i.e., the temporal granularity can vary from days (Apr 04th) to seconds (Apr 04th, at 11:34:56 a.m.). The finer the granularity, the bigger the scheduling problem.

6 Temporal Architecture for the Process Engine

Process engines manage a vast amount of data and rely on a database management system, primarily based on the relational model. Every piece of data in a process model, as well as in all the instances of running cases, features a temporal aspect. The management of some temporal aspects of a process model is defined at the conceptual model level, i.e. at schema definition time. The management of some other temporal aspects of a process model is defined at run time, only; e.g., workload balancing among agents can be performed only during case enactment.

Besides those typical of the management of standard data, main advantages coming from the adoption of a temporal database system inside a process engine are related to the execution of temporal queries as in schema version management (typically, due to new versions and changes in the process model), selection of the executing agent with load balancing over time, exception management, and temporal data warehouse analysis, to mention few of them only.

Whenever temporal aspects of information need to be managed, two main scenarios can be identified: explicit management, i.e., the application developer considers time as a special data item or attribute along with other traditional data; and management supported directly by the DBMS. In the latter situation, for every information the application developer can refer to the valid time, i.e., the time during which the fact is true in the modelled world [25], that is managed directly by the DBMS itself. Unfortunately, most DBMS do not manage temporal information explicitly.

Figure 3 depicts the typical architecture of a process engine running a DBMS with no support for temporal data management. In Fig. 3, the agent runs the client, which connects to a web server showing the list of tasks assigned to that agent. The `Engine` is the core unit of the process engine: while the engine has several connections with

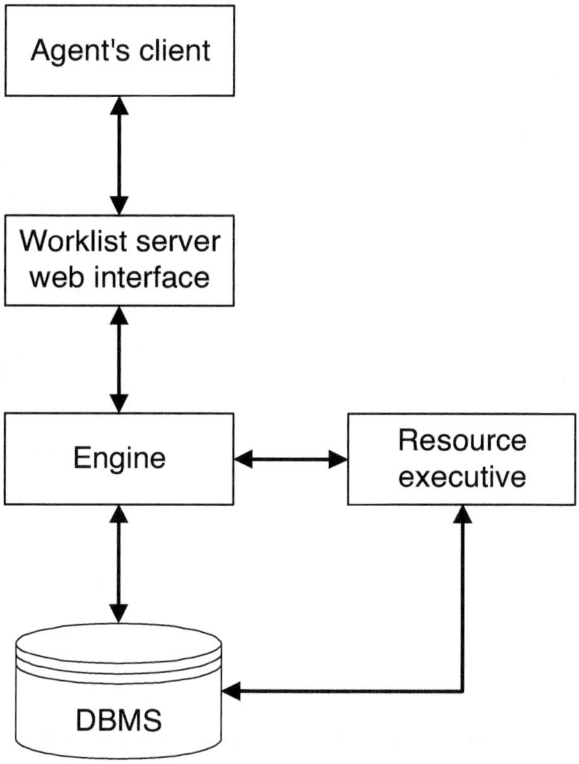

Fig. 3 Typical architecture of a process engine where the DBMS has no support for temporal information management

additional services (not reported in Fig. 3, e.g., the history manager), it connects to the `Resource executive` unit. The `Resource executive` is responsible for task scheduling, thus performing a query over the database. The query considers the workload of each agent, their availability, the expected duration of the task, and the static and dynamic temporal constraints from the process model, among other factors. In case the DBMS comes with no temporal support, all the queries must include direct management of the temporal aspects of every piece of data.

If instead the deployed DBMS comes with a support for temporal data management, its typical architecture is depicted in Fig. 4: the temporal data support management is achieved via an intermediate layer, namely, `TemporalLayer` in Fig. 4 [26].

In Fig. 4, the temporal layer intercepts all the temporal queries and maps them directly to the underlying relational DBMS. It may occur that some temporal queries are hardly mapped to the SQL of the deployed DBMS; thus, some stored procedures need to be invoked. In turn, a stored procedure can issue additional temporal queries, which again need to be handled by the temporal layer as depicted in Fig. 4. Obviously, the stored procedure is strictly dependent on the deployed DBMS, as no standard

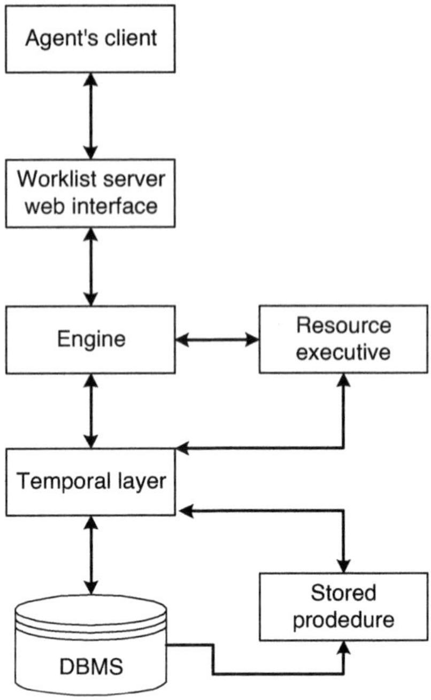

Fig. 4 Typical architecture of a process engine where the DBMS has support for temporal information management

language exists so far for this type of programming. Thus, moving from one DBMS to a different DBMS requires writing the stored procedures from scratch, resulting in no portability.

7 Temporal Constraints and Process Models in Healthcare

Healthcare is a very challenging application domain for process models. The successful completion of a process often depends on the correctness of the temporal aspects modeled at process design time. If temporal constraints cannot be satisfied, the process cannot be successfully and correctly executed. Temporal evaluations and simulations are needed to state whether the specified temporal constraints can be satisfied by some process instances, i.e., the process model is somehow consistent.

Clinical guidelines typically describe, in natural language, the recommended behavior for a medical team, the activities to apply to a patient, and their fulfillment with respect to both the time and the health state of the patient. Clinical guidelines are narrative documents that lack a formal organizational structure. The lack of structure, consistency, and potential ambiguity in these documents could be mitigated by computer systems to enhance clinical practice. Due to the fact that the specification of a guideline can be very lengthy, some information may be spread throughout the document, and the suggested sequence of medical activities can be difficult to comprehend. In this regard, several attempts have been made to develop computer-based systems, called Computer-Interpretable clinical Guidelines (CIGs), to assist healthcare providers in charting a given patient's course through a whole guideline [15].

Clinical guidelines can benefit from process modelling and management techniques. In fact, managing patients, especially those in critical condition, requires much more detail than that specified in a standard process model.

Finding a sound technique for representing guidelines is an important and difficult issue, requiring the modeling of several elements such as actions, patient's information, decisions to be taken, constraints between activities, and temporal properties. In particular, the need to represent and reason with time is crucial when guidelines are used in critical contexts, such as when physicians must schedule different drug regimens within specific temporal intervals and coordinate multiple tasks. Some examples of temporal aspects to be considered are: durations of an activity (e.g., *4 h for a treatment*), instantaneous events (e.g., *heart attack event*), constraints (e.g., *maximum delay of 5 d between the stroke event and the drug administration*), periodic activities (e.g., *radiation therapy from Monday to Friday for 25 d*), required delays (e.g., *clinical analysis must be re-checked after at least 1 day from the first check*). Moreover, there can also be some implicit temporal constraints that must be considered when a guideline is modeled, such as synchronization of activities (e.g., *clinical assessment must be performed by the physician after completing all the tests*), and serialization of activities (e.g., *haematology checks must be performed after glycerol administration*).

7.1 Temporal Contraint Definition

Focusing on temporal constraints, they can be classified as *relative* constraints, *absolute* constraints, *periodic* constraints, and *required delays*.

i. a *relative* constraint limits the time distance (duration) between the starting/ending instants of two non-subsequent tasks. In turn, the *upper bound* constraint denotes the maximum range between the starting or ending execution instant of the first task and the starting or ending execution instant of the last task. A *lower bound* constraint denotes the minimum range between the starting or ending execution instant of the first task and the starting or ending execution instant of the last task.
   An upper bound constraint can model a deadline that corresponds to the maximum allowable execution time for activities. Indeed, if the first activity of the upper bound constraint is the starting timestamp of the case, then the constraint represents the deadline of the last activity of the upper bound constraint.
ii. an *absolute* constraint represents a time interval during which an activity can be performed. Interval bounds are expressed by timestamps: bounds of an *absolute* constraint are independent from the case execution starting timestamp. The span

of the time interval for the *absolute* constraint must be greater than or equal to the maximum duration defined for the corresponding activity.
An *absolute* constraint can also be used to represent a time interval during which an activity cannot be executed: in this case, the key "*not*" must be specified before the specification of the time interval.

iii. a *periodic* constraint represents a periodic time interval during which an activity can be started.

iv. a *required delay* constraint represents the minimal time distance between two non-subsequent activities: this is not a strict temporal constraint because it cannot be violated, as it imposes the process engine to wait until the *required delay* expires.

7.2 Temporal Constraint Verification

The successful completion of a process instance often depends on the correctness of the temporal aspects modeled at process design time. If temporal constraints cannot be met, the process cannot be executed successfully. Temporal evaluations and simulations are needed to state whether the specified temporal constraints can be satisfied by some process instances, i.e. the process model is somehow consistent.

As a process model can contain several alternative or conditional split gateways, one process model can experience many possible and differing execution paths. Consistency must be verified for each of these possible execution paths. The consistency of each of these execution paths can be described as a simple temporal problem (STP), which the literature reports to be a tractable problem when only one granularity is used for expressing the temporal constraints [16]. As for the general case of single-interval constraints given at *different* granularities, Bettini et al. [2] show that checking temporal consistency is a NP-hard problem.

When dealing with a temporal conceptual model, the consistency check of the temporal process model occurs at process design time, and it is, in some sense, "static," as opposed to the "dynamic" consistency checking performed at process execution time. The consistency of a temporal process model at the conceptual level can be interpreted from different perspectives. Indeed, the consistency of the overall process model can be derived from the consistency of every possible execution path, considered separately. However, the consistency of every execution path could not suffice at the conceptual level. A more restrictive view could require, for example, that any duration of a given task allowed by a given temporal constraint is consistent with every execution path (or with most paths of the process model).

We may further refine the constraint checking activities as:

i. *design-time evaluation.* It takes place as the process model has been completely defined. The evaluation aims to verify all temporal constraints, without considering absolute ones. The verification requires converting all temporal constraints to the finest granularity and verifying their satisfiability.

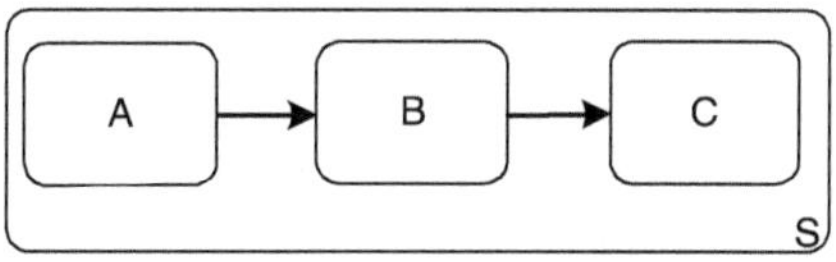

Fig. 5 BPMN graph of a simple subprocess which includes three tasks in a streamline connection

We observe that absolute constraints can't be verified because such verification depends on the starting time of execution, and this data is available only at runtime.

ii. *run-time evaluation.* It runs in parallel with the execution of the process instances, and its aim is to continuously update the active temporal constraint values given the actual times of completed activities. This stage can be divided into two different sub-stages:

   a. *start-time evaluation.* It starts when a starting time for a process instance is given. Its goal is to convert and verify all absolute temporal constraints. These constraints are converted into relative equivalent ones using the process instance starting time. Afterwards, all the constraints (including the new ones) are verified again in the same way as they were in the first stage.
   If all constraints are satisfiable, the schema instance is validated, and its execution can begin at the specified starting time.
   b. *node-by-node evaluation.* As an activity completes, if it is involved in some relative constraints, its actual execution time can compel changes for other activities/delays involved in the same relative constraints. These changes can require the process engine to adjust the allowed duration ranges of some subsequent activities or to increase the delay before or between two subsequent activities to ensure overall constraint satisfaction. On the other hand, some constraints can be relaxed at runtime because certain execution paths are no longer possible due to previously executed alternative/conditional splits.

As an example, let us consider a very simple subprocess `S`. The subprocess includes three tasks, namely `A`, `B`, and `C`, in a streamline connection as in Fig. 5: the obvious sequence of execution is `A`, then `B`, and finally `C`. Let us assume that the temporal process model reports the $\texttt{maxTaskDuration}_{\texttt{A}}$, $\texttt{maxTaskDuration}_{\texttt{B}}$, and $\texttt{maxTaskDuration}_{\texttt{C}}$, for the three tasks, respectively. The process model also reports the $\texttt{maxTaskDuration}_{\texttt{S}}$ for the subprocess. Indeed, subprocesses are first-class citizens, too.

It may occur that the $\texttt{maxTaskDuration}_{\texttt{S}}$ defined for the entire subprocess is smaller than the maximum duration among the durations of every execution path. In the example of Fig. 5, the $\texttt{maxTaskDuration}_{\texttt{S}}$ is smaller than the sum of the `maxTaskDuration` of all the single tasks included in the subprocess.

$$maxTaskDuration_A + maxTaskDuration_B +$$

$$maxTaskDuration_C \leq maxTaskDuration_S$$

A static check of the temporal constraint could fail, and the constraint checking can thus be performed only at runtime.

In more detail, if every task must be completed in 6 min or less and there is a relative constraint stating that the entire subprocess must be completed in 10 min or less, the constraints are satisfiable. If task `A` takes 6 min, the second (`B`) and third (`C`) tasks can't take more than 4 min globally. Therefore, after the completion of `A`, the process engine must determine new ranges of allowed durations for tasks `B` and `C` before assigning them to agents.

Moreiver, if a constraint violation is detected at runtime, a suitable exception management unit is required to properly and timely manage the abnormal event [3], either by signaling it to the responsible agent or by automatically starting a recovery or compensating action, if any is defined.

Finally, while temporal consistency assumes that the process engine can enforce some restrictions on the duration of tasks, over the last 15 years, a significant amount of research on temporal business processes has focused on the concept of *controllability*. In this case, at process design and then process execution times, the BPM system has to verify that the process can be executed without enforcing any given duration of tasks. Durations of tasks are decided by agents and are known only when they are executed. Different techniques and modeling aspects have been addressed to this regard [6, 22–24].

8 Conclusions

In this chapter, we briefly described some of the major research activities we faced in the field of temporal information management for temporal business process modelling and management. As an application domain, we considered a healthcare scenario in which patients require the implantation of a pacemaker.

The healthcare domain still remains a challenging one for the deployment of process modelling and management techniques: some of the major issues still to be faced in a complete manner deal with the temporal constraint definition (and, in particular, the management of constraint violation), the exception management (a patient can experience a sudden change in his/her health status, requiring a special treatment not foreseen in the process model, thus abandoning the expected main flow of execution), as well as the coordinated execution of tasks (a surgical intervention is performed by a team of surgeons and not by one unique executing agent).

Acknowledgements The authors would like to deeply thank Professor Barbara Pernici for inspiring them in the fields of both temporal information management and process modeling, and for providing them with fruitful suggestions and comments.

References

1. Aurelius Augustinus. *Confessiones, XI, 14.* –, –, –
2. Bettini, C., Wang, X.S., Jajodia, S.: Solving multi-granularity temporal constraint networks. Artif. Intell. **140**(1/2), 107–152 (2002)
3. Casati, F., Ceri, S., Paraboschi, S., Pozzi, G.: Specification and implementation of exceptions in workflow management systems. ACM Trans. Database Syst. **24**(3), 405–451 (1999)
4. Casati, F., Ceri, S., Pernici, B., Pozzi, G.: Semantic workflow interoperability. In: Apers, P.M., Bouzeghoub, M., Gardarin, G. (eds.) EDBT, Lecture Notes in Computer Science, vol. 1057, pp. 443–462. Springer, Berlin (1996)
5. Combi, C., Galetto, F., Nakawala, H.C., Pozzi, G., Zerbato, F.: Enriching surgical process models by BPMN extensions for temporal durations. In: Hung, C.-C., Hong, J., Bechini, A., Song, E. (eds.) SAC '21: The 36th ACM/SIGAPP Symposium on Applied Computing, Virtual Event, Republic of Korea, March 22–26, 2021, pp. 586–593. ACM (2021)
6. Combi, C., Gambini, M., Migliorini, S., Posenato, R.: Representing business processes through a temporal data-centric workflow modeling language: an application to the management of clinical pathways. IEEE Trans. Syst. Man Cybern. Syst. **44**(9), 1182–1203 (2014)
7. Combi, C., Gozzi, M., Juarez, J.M., Oliboni, B., Pozzi, G.: Conceptual modeling of temporal clinical workflows. In: TIME, pp. 70–81. IEEE Computer Society (2007)
8. Combi, C., Gozzi, M., Posenato, R., Pozzi, G.: Conceptual modeling of flexible temporal workflows. TAAS **7**(2), 19 (2012)
9. Combi, C., Montanari, A., Pozzi, G.: The T4SQL temporal query language. In: Silva, M.J., Laender, A.H.J., Baeza-Yates, R.A., McGuinness, D.L., Olstad, B., Olsen, Ø.H., Falcão, A.O. (eds.) CIKM, pp. 193–202. ACM (2007)
10. Combi, C., Oliboni, B., Zerbato, F.: A modular approach to the specification and management of time duration constraints in BPMN. Inf. Syst. **84**, 111–144 (2019)
11. Combi, C., Pozzi, G.: Towards temporal information in workflow systems. In: Spaccapietra, S., March, S.T., Kambayashi, Y. (eds.) ER (Workshops), Lecture Notes in Computer Science, vol. 2503, pp. 13–25. Springer, Berlin (2002)
12. Combi, C., Pozzi, G.: Temporal conceptual modelling of workflows. In: Song, I.-Y., Liddle, S.W., Ling, T.W., Scheuermann, P. (eds.) Conceptual Modeling - ER 2003, 22nd International Conference on Conceptual Modeling, Chicago, IL, USA, October 13–16, 2003, Proceedings, Lecture Notes in Computer Science, vol. 2813, pp. 59–76. Springer, Berlin (2003)
13. Combi, C., Pozzi, G.: Architectures for a temporal workflow management system. In: Haddad, H., Omicini, A., Wainwright, R.L., Liebrock, L.M. (eds.) SAC, pp. 659–666. ACM (2004)
14. Combi, C., Pozzi, G.: Task scheduling for a temporal workflow management system. In: TIME, pp. 61–68. IEEE Computer Society (2006)
15. De Clercq, P.A., Blom, J.A., Korsten, H.H., Hasman, A.: Approaches for creating computer-interpretable guidelines that facilitate decision support. Artif. Intell. Med. **31**(1), 1–27 (2004)
16. Dechter, R., Meiri, I., Pearl, J.: Temporal constraint networks. Artif. Intell. **49**(1–3), 61–95 (1991)
17. Franceschetti, M., Eder, J.: Negotiating temporal commitments in cross-organizational business processes. In: Muñoz-Velasco, E., Ozaki, A., Theobald, M. (eds.) 27th International Symposium on Temporal Representation and Reasoning, TIME 2020, Bozen-Bolzano, Italy, September 23–25, 2020, LIPIcs, vol. 178, pp. 4:1–4:15. Schloss Dagstuhl - Leibniz-Zentrum für Informatik (2020)
18. Franceschetti, M., Eder, J.: Determining temporal agreements in cross-organizational business processes. Inf. Comput. **281**, 104792 (2021)
19. Lanz, A., Reichert, M., Weber, B.: Process time patterns: a formal foundation. Inf. Syst. **57**, 38–68 (2016)
20. Lanz, A., Weber, B., Reichert, M.: Time patterns for process-aware information systems. Requir. Eng. **19**(2), 113–141 (2014)
21. Maiocchi, R., Pernici, B.: Temporal data management systems: a comparative view. IEEE Trans. Knowl. Data Eng. **3**(4), 504–524 (1991)

22. Posenato, R., Franceschetti, M., Combi, C., Eder, J.: Introducing agile controllability in temporal business processes. In: van der Aa, H., Bork, D., Schmidt, R., Sturm, A. (eds.) Enterprise, Business-Process and Information Systems Modeling - 25th International Conference, BPMDS 2024, and 29th International Conference, EMMSAD 2024, Limassol, Cyprus, June 3–4, 2024, Proceedings, Lecture Notes in Business Information Processing, vol. 511, pp. 87–99. Springer, Berlin (2024)
23. Posenato, R., Combi, C.: Flexible temporal constraint management in modularized processes. Inf. Syst. **118**, 102257 (2023)
24. Posenato, R., Lanz, A., Combi, C., Reichert, M.: Managing time-awareness in modularized processes. Softw. Syst. Model. **18**(2), 1135–1154 (2019)
25. Snodgrass, R.T. (ed.) The TSQL2 Temporal Query Language. Kluwer (1995)
26. TimeConsult. TimeDB 2.2 (2025). https://www.timeconsult.com/Software/Software.html. [Online; Accessed 05 Dec 2025]
27. Xu, J., Liu, C., Zhao, X., Yongchareon, S., Ding, Z.: Resource management for business process scheduling in the presence of availability constraints. ACM Trans. Manag. Inf. Syst. **7**(3), 9:1–9:26 (2016)

When Data Betrays You: From the Early Web to the Age of AI

Sonia Bergamaschi, Cinzia Cappiello, Tiziana Catarci, Monica Scannapieco, and Letizia Tanca

Abstract High-quality data are essential for reliable information processing and effective decision-making in contemporary socio-technical systems. Poor Data Quality (DQ) can compromise organizational processes and reduce trust in data-driven outcomes, making systematic data quality management a central concern in modern data governance. This chapter examines data quality assessment and improvement as key components of an effective DQ program. Assessment evaluates data against established quality dimensions, such as accuracy, completeness, consistency, and timeliness, while improvement involves corrective and preventive actions, including data cleansing, process refinement, and continuous monitoring. Together, these activities form an iterative cycle that ensures data remain fit for purpose over time. The chapter also discusses new challenges in the field, highlighting the emerging role of generative and agentic AI and the growing fundamental recognition of ethics as a DQ principle. As data increasingly inform decisions with significant human impact, integrating ethical considerations into data quality practices is essential to ensure trustworthy and responsible data-driven systems.

S. Bergamaschi
University of Modena and Reggio Emilia, Modena, Italy
e-mail: sonia.bergamaschi@unimore.it

C. Cappiello (✉) · L. Tanca
Politecnico di Milano, Milan, Italy
e-mail: cinzia.cappiello@polimi.it

L. Tanca
e-mail: letizia.tanca@polimi.it

T. Catarci
Università degli Studi di Roma La Sapienza, Rome, Italy
e-mail: catarci@diag.uniroma1.it

M. Scannapieco
Individual researcher, Rome, Italy
e-mail: monica.scannapieco@gmail.com

C. Cappiello et al. (eds.), *Retrospective and Prospective Views on Information Systems Engineering*, https://doi.org/10.1007/978-3-032-19578-4_4

1 Introduction

High-quality data constitute a critical prerequisite for effective and trustworthy information processing within contemporary socio-technical systems. Failures in maintaining adequate Data Quality (DQ) can negatively affect both organizational operational processes and decision-making. Moreover, in the context of the EU General Data Protection Regulation (GDPR), data quality is a legal obligation that directly conditions the protection of data subjects' rights.

For example, in 2022, the enforcement action issued by the Italian Data Protection Authority (Garante Privacy) against the electricity provider Areti S.p.A. illustrates the foundational importance of data quality in GDPR-compliant data governance frameworks. The Authority's investigation found that Areti's processing activities were compromised by significant inaccuracies and outdated customer information, leading to the erroneous classification of numerous individuals as "customers with pending payments" in their internal integrated information system. These deficiencies in data accuracy and maintenance not only impeded data subjects' ability to switch energy providers in a liberalized market but also produced systemic effects affecting tens of thousands of consumers. Moreover, the inadequacy of Areti's responses to data subject requests and the long retention periods applied to customer data violated the GDPR's accountability requirements.

This case exemplifies how insufficient data quality controls can propagate compliance breaches across multiple regulatory dimensions, ultimately resulting in substantial financial penalties and highlighting the need for robust, continuously monitored data governance mechanisms that integrate data quality as a central pillar.

A comprehensive data quality program necessarily includes systematic assessment and continuous improvement. DQ assessment measures the current state of data assets against predefined quality dimensions (e.g., accuracy, completeness, consistency, timeliness) and, if the quality level is low, an effective DQ program should consider improvement activities that trigger suitable corrective and preventive techniques. Such techniques may involve process redesign, system enhancements, data cleansing, and the implementation of monitoring controls. Together, assessment and improvement form an iterative cycle that embeds data quality into organizational practices, ensuring that data remain fit for purpose over time and resilient to evolving operational, regulatory, and analytical demands.

This chapter will outline practices for assessing and improving data quality and examine emerging challenges and recent developments in the field. We will consider, for example, that the scientific community has recently recognized the importance of **ethics** among the Data Quality principles [15, 39]. In every civilization, ethics is grounded in established principles of right and wrong that dictate the actions humans should take, typically framed in terms of rights, duties, fairness, or specific virtues. When data are used in critical decision-making processes in which human beings are at stake, the behavior of data and algorithms must not only adhere to well-known data quality standards but also ensure that they do not lead to unethical practices in their application.

The chapter is structured as follows. Section 2 presents approaches for modeling DQ requirements and for assessing DQ dimensions, Sect. 3 focuses on data preparation and improvement solutions, while Sect. 4 illustrates the emerging data quality issues in the artificial intelligence era, including ethics as a data quality dimension.

2 Modelling and Assessing Data Quality

This Section introduces the complexity related to data quality representation and assessment by providing specific examples of solutions, i.e., languages, methodologies, and architectural blueprints, which can support data quality management.

In particular, in Sect. 2.1, we present a concrete language to model quality requirements that extends the Unified Modelling Language (UML) with a data quality-specific *profile*. Then, Sect. 2.2 presents examples of issues and methodologies for assessing the quality of Web data sources, as well as data quality dimensions specific to Web data, such as *completability*. Finally, in Sect. 2.3, an example of a concrete architecture for managing data quality in distributed systems is presented.

2.1 Modelling Data Quality in Data and Process Analysis

Data Quality management is inherently complex, and various dedicated methodologies have been developed for this purpose (see, e.g., [41]). When adopting one of these methodologies, a major problem is the lack of a modeling language that supports all phases of the methodology and that is formal enough to allow a unique interpretation of the language constructs, i.e., precise semantics should be defined for it. At the same time, such a language should be easily understood by people without scientific or technical skills; this is because one of the most important activities in designing for quality management is interacting with customers to identify the actual quality requirements. In [35], a *profile* of the Unified Modeling Language (UML) is defined that is compliant with the requirements detailed earlier. The profile is inspired by the IP-MAP framework proposed in [37] and has the advantage of combining data and process analysis to assess data quality. Data are treated as a product, called the Information Product (IP), and the processes that create data are analyzed to identify quality bottlenecks in manufacturing information products.

The Data Quality profile consists of three different models, namely: a Data Analysis Model, identifying which data are of interest, what is their composition and what is their derivation in the context of the production process, a Quality Analysis Model identifying the quality requirements for each data type, and a Quality Design Model modeling data and processes together in order to verify quality requirement satisfaction and to model process-based improvement actions.

In Fig. 1, we show an example of a diagram part of a Quality Analysis Model, related to an information product that is *mailing labels* used by a University to send

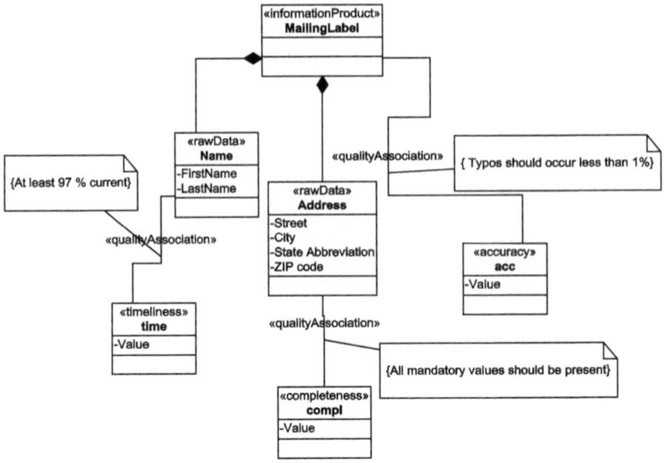

Fig. 1 An example of a quality analysis model

out publications to its alumni. Incorrect or out-of-date mailing labels are a problem for the university, which would like to improve their quality in order to reduce the percentage of undelivered mail due to out-of-date or incorrect mailing labels. In Fig. 1, the accuracy, timeliness, and completeness quality requirements are specified, respectively, on the Quality Data classes Mailing Label, Name, and Address. The interested reader can refer to [35] for the detailed definitions of the meta-model's data and quality constructs (e.g., quality association or information product) shown in the Figure.

In addition to the Quality Analysis Model, the Quality Design Model specifies IP-MAPs, which detail the manufacturing process for an information product. In particular, they show the processes that manage data, as well as how information products are produced from raw and component data. Such a combined process and data analysis allow one to achieve two objectives: (i) to detect quality potential problems and, after having checked the non-conformance to quality requirements, (ii) to introduce quality improvement actions. Let us refer to [35] for the detailed design of IP-MAPs using the UML Data Quality Profile, which is defined purposefully.

2.2 *Assessing Web Data Quality*

Representing the quality of Web data is a highly complex task and depends on the specific Web source. In the following Sects. 2.2 and 2.2, we give two examples showing that, unfortunately, the overall quality of Web data appears to be dramatically poor. Later, in Sect. 2.2, we illustrate how explicitly representing quality of web data, so to be able to govern and improve it.

On Twitter/X's Data Quality

A first example concerns social media data, such as Twitter data (now X's data). As reported in [6], Twitter has been used to examine a wide variety of patterns such as mood rhythms, media event engagement, political uprisings, etc. However,

"Twitter does not represent "all people", and it is an error to assume "people" and "Twitter users" are synonymous: they are a very particular subset. Neither is the population using Twitter representative of the global population. Nor can we assume that accounts and users are equivalent. Some users have multiple accounts, while some accounts are used by multiple people. Some people never establish an account and simply access Twitter via the web. Some accounts are "bots" that produce automated content without directly involving a person."

This shows the relevant data quality issue of *lack of representativeness*, which affects many analyses of Twitter data. In addition, Twitter data are highly unstructured and often lack metadata. This means that large portions of these data cannot be used directly by automated processes, as they are "pointless babbles" [7]. To effectively use this kind of data, it is necessary, on the one hand, to address representativeness issues and, on the other hand, to investigate methods for automatically generating appropriate metadata to describe the data under review.

On the Quality of Deep Web Data

A relevant aspect of Web quality assessment concerns data from the deep Web. The deep Web refers to that portion of the internet not indexed by standard search engines. A significant amount of information on the Web resides on dynamically generated sites, and traditional search engines cannot access this data because these pages are generated only in response to specific search queries. Many websites serve as interfaces to databases, such as e-commerce platforms, airline booking sites, and online bibliographies. The deep Web encompasses all these sites, and as a result, its size is estimated to be many orders of magnitude larger than the surface Web.

In [24], the quality of deep Web data from the stock (55 sources) and flight (38 sources) domains was assessed. The findings revealed poor quality in terms of consistency (70% of data items had multiple values provided) and accuracy (only 70% of the values provided by the majority of sources were correct).

Notably, the study [24] introduces a specific set of quality metrics for Web data. These metrics are outlined below and represent one of the earliest efforts to define a quality assessment framework for Web data. The first dimension to be evaluated is the *redundancy* of data. Specifically: (i) redundancy on objects, i.e., the percentage of sources that provide a particular object, and (ii) redundancy on data items, i.e., the percentage of sources that provide a particular data item.

The further dimension considered is the *consistency* of the data, defined by three measures.

- Number of values. By denoting as $V(d)$ the set of values provided by various sources on d, the number of values reports the number of different values provided on d, that is the size of $V(d)$.
- Entropy. By denoting as $S(d)$ the set of sources that provide data on item d, and $S(d; v)$ the set of sources that provide value v on d, the entropy is

$$\sum_{v \in V(d)} \frac{|S(d, V)|}{|S(d)|} \log \frac{|S(d, V)|}{|S(d)|}.$$

  Intuitively, the higher the inconsistency, the higher the entropy.
- Deviation. For numerical values, by defining v_0 as the dominant value, i.e., the one with the largest number of providers given by $\arg\max_{v \in V(d)} |S(d, V)|$, the deviation from d is:

$$D(d) = \sqrt{\frac{1}{|V(d)|} \sum_{v \in V(d)} (\frac{v - v_0}{v_0})^2}$$

Finally, accuracy is evaluated according to two measures, namely:

- Source accuracy: We compute the accuracy of S as the percentage of its provided values that are consistent with the given gold standard.
- Accuracy deviation: computed as the standard deviation of the accuracy of a source over a period of time. Given that $\mathcal{T}$ is the set of time points in a period, $A(t)$ is the accuracy of the source at time $t \in \mathcal{T}$, and $\bar{\mathcal{A}}$ is the mean accuracy over $\mathcal{T}$, the variety is computed by: $\sqrt{\frac{1}{|\mathcal{T}|} \sum_{t \in \mathcal{T}} (A(t) - \bar{\mathcal{A}})^2})$

The final results of the assessment activity performed according to such measures are quite poor, namely:

- For the stock domain, there is a very high redundancy at the object level, namely, each source provides over 90% of the stocks; for the flight domain, object-level redundancy is lower, namely, only 36% of the sources cover 90% of the flights. It is observed that there is a large redundancy in data items, over various domains: on average, each data item has a redundancy of 66% for stock and 32% for flight.
- There is quite a high inconsistency of values on the same data item: for stock and flight, the average entropy is 0.58 and 0.24, and the average deviation is 13.4 and 13.1 respectively. The inconsistency can vary from attribute to attribute. By choosing dominant values as the true value, precision is 0.908 for stock and 0.864 for flight for the two domains, respectively.
- Accuracy of the sources can vary a lot: on average, the accuracy is about 0.86 for stock and 0.80 for flight.

Completeness of Web Data: The Completability Dimension

Data published in Web information systems can be characterized by temporal evolution. Unlike traditional paper-based media, where information is typically published once and remains fixed, Web information systems are marked by continuously updated content.

For example, consider a university website that lists the courses offered for the current academic year. At any given moment, this list is considered complete, as it includes all courses that have been officially approved. However, additional courses will be added to the list once approved. As a result, it becomes important to understand how this list will evolve over time in terms of completeness. Traditional concepts of completeness offer only a static view. To account for the dynamic nature of completeness in Web information systems, it is relevant to introduce the concept of completability [29]. We consider a function $C(t)$, defined as the value of completeness at the instant t, with $t \in [\texttt{t\_pub}, \texttt{t\_max}]$, where `t_pub` is the initial instant of publication of data and `t_max` corresponds to the maximum time within which the series of different scheduled updates will be completed. Starting from the function $C(t)$, we can define the *completability* of the published data as

$$\int_{t\_curr}^{t\_max} C(t),$$

where `t_curr` is the time at which completability is evaluated and `t_curr` < `t_max`.

Completability, as shown in Fig. 2 can be graphically depicted as an area Cb of a function that represents how completeness evolves between an instant `t_curr` of observation and `t_max`. Observe that the value corresponding to `t_curr` is indicated as `c_curr`; `c_max` is the value for completeness estimated for `t_max`. The value `c_max` is a real reachable limit that can be specified for the completeness of the series of elements; if this real limit does not exist, `c_max` is equal to 1. In Fig. 2, a reference area A is also shown, defined as

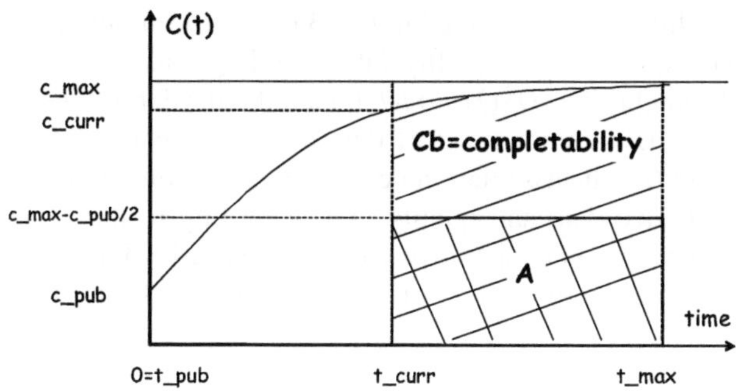

Fig. 2 A graphical representation of completability

$$(t\_max - t\_curr) * \frac{c\_max - c\_pub}{2},$$

that, by comparison with Cb, allows us to define ranges [`High`, `Medium`, `Low`] for completability. With respect to the example above, considering the list of courses published on a university website, the completeness dimension provides information about the current degree of completeness; the completability dimension provides information about how quickly this degree will grow over time, i.e., how quickly the list of courses will be completed.

2.3 *Data Quality Management in Distributed and Cooperative Systems*

When shifting from the Web—where publicly available information is accessed on demand and largely in an unstructured manner—to distributed systems in which participants interact according to predefined rules for sharing data and services, data quality issues can be managed and monitored more rigorously and effectively. Numerous governmental and business contexts illustrate this situation, with organizations increasingly collaborating to deliver services and share data with their customers and partners.

In the context of the *Daquincis*,[1] a novel architecture was proposed for assessing and improving data quality in distributed and cooperative systems (so called Cooperative Information Systems—CISs). The *Daquincis* architecture allows the diffusion of data and related quality and exploits data replication to improve the overall quality of cooperative data. Each organization offers services to other organizations on its own cooperative gateway, and also specific services to its internal back-end systems. Therefore, cooperative gateways interface both internally and externally through services. Moreover, the communication infrastructure itself offers some specific services. Services are all identical and peer, i.e., they are instances of the same software artifacts, and act both as servers and clients of the other peers, depending on the specific activities to be carried out.

The overall architecture is depicted in Fig. 3 (see [36] for details).

Organizations export data and quality data according to a common model, referred to as *Data and Data Quality* (D^2Q) *model*. It includes the definitions of *(i)* constructs to represent data, *(ii)* a common set of data quality properties, *(iii)* constructs to represent them and *(iv)* the association between data and quality data.

In order to produce data and quality data according to the D^2Q model, each organization deploys on its cooperative gateway a **Quality Factory** service that is responsible for evaluating the quality of its own data, see [8] for the detailed design of the Quality Factory.

[1] DaQuinCIS—Methodologies and Tools for Data Quality inside Cooperative Information Systems, a joint research project carried out by DIS—Università di Roma "La Sapienza", DISCo—Università di Milano "Bicocca" and DEI—Politecnico di Milano.

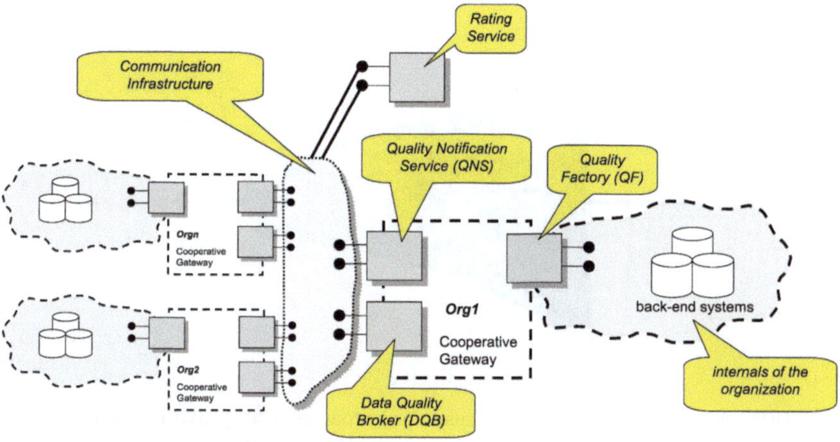

Fig. 3 The *Daquincis* architecture

The **Data Quality Broker** poses, on behalf of a requesting user, a data request over other cooperating organizations, also specifying a set of quality requirements that the desired data have to satisfy; this is referred to as *quality brokering function*. Different copies of the same data received as responses to the request are reconciled, and the best-quality value is selected and proposed to organizations that can choose to discard their data and to adopt higher quality ones; this is referred to as *quality improvement function*.

The Data Quality Broker is, in essence, a peer-to-peer data integration system that allows for posing quality-enhanced query over a global schema, and to select data satisfying such requirements [25].

The **Quality Notification Service** is a publish/subscribe engine used as a quality message bus between services and/or organizations. More specifically, it allows quality-based subscriptions for users to be notified of changes in the quality of data. For example, an organization may want to be notified if the quality of some data it uses degrades below a certain threshold, or when high-quality data are available. Also, the Quality Notification Service is deployed as a peer-to-peer system.

The **Rating Service** associates trust values with each data source in the CIS. These values are used to determine the reliability of the quality evaluation performed by organizations. The Rating Service is a centralized service to be provided by a third-party organization; see [11] for the detailed design of the Rating Service.

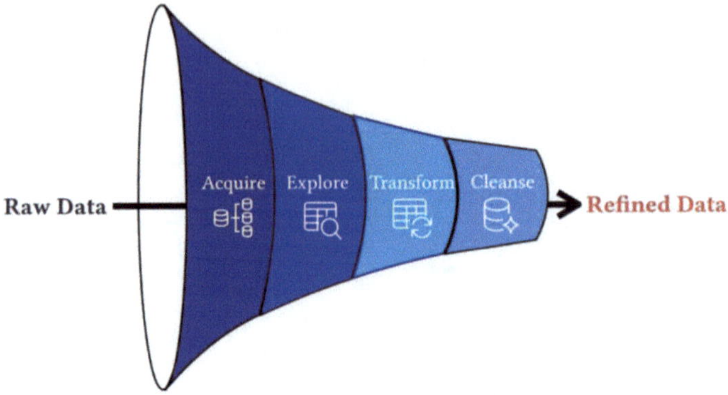

Fig. 4 The four recurring phases of data preparation he four recurring phases of data preparation—(i) acquisition, (ii) exploration, (iii) transformation, and (iv) cleansing

3 Data Preparation and Improvement

3.1 Data Preparation

Data preparation [13, 18, 27] is the process of transforming raw data into formats suitable for analysis. Although often considered a preliminary step, it has long been recognized as one of the most fundamental challenges in data management. Since the early days of statistical computing, researchers have encountered issues of data consistency, formatting, and completeness that must be resolved before meaningful analysis can take place [40].

Despite notable technological advances, industry surveys show that practitioners still spend up to 80% of their time on data preparation rather than analysis [31]. In practice, preparation unfolds as a multi-stage, iterative process grounded in a *divide et impera* logic: complex tasks are decomposed into smaller steps—profiling, cleaning, transformation—that can be composed into end-to-end pipelines. Although workflows vary across domains, most pipelines share four recurring phases: (i) acquisition, (ii) exploration, (iii) transformation, and (iv) cleansing.

3.2 Data Preparation Pipeline Design

In decision-making contexts driven by data and analytics, the availability of high-quality datasets is essential. As a result, data preparation pipelines must be established prior to analysis; however, their design is often complex and frequently depends on trial-and-error approaches. This step is critical because real-world data are commonly noisy, exhibiting errors, inconsistencies, or weakly relevant information that can negatively affect both analytical results and their interpretation.

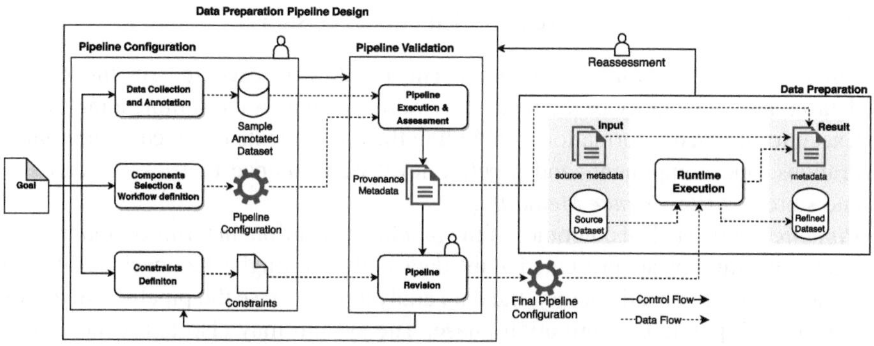

Fig. 5 Data preparation pipeline design process

To mitigate these challenges, data preparation pipelines include components that transform raw data to improve quality and relevance prior to analysis. Equally important is documenting all preparation steps, as provenance information ensures transparency and facilitates data reuse within data-sharing ecosystems.

Given an analytical task, an input dataset to be prepared (e.g., streaming data or batch data collected from one or multiple sources), and a set of available processing tools, the Data Preparation Pipeline Design (Fig. 5) involves identifying the most appropriate sequence of operations, configuring the selected tools, and evaluating the expected quality of the prepared data.

The Data Preparation Pipeline Design is guided by the Goal defined by the data analyst. This goal is specified prior to the pipeline design process and drives all subsequent data preparation steps.

The Data Preparation Pipeline Design consists of two main phases: (i) Pipeline Configuration and (ii) Pipeline Validation.

During the Pipeline Configuration phase, the data analyst carries out the following activities:

- *Data Collection and Annotation*: A representative sample is extracted from the initial dataset. During the annotation step, annotators assess the relevance of individual data items with respect to the predefined goal.
- *Component Selection and Workflow Definition*: The data analyst selects the components to be included in the pipeline from the *Component Library*, which is defined and modeled according to the component model described in [5].
- *Constraints Definition*: The data analyst specifies non-functional constraints related to the performance and quality of the overall pipeline, such as acceptable output volume, processing time and cost limits, and target precision and recall values.

The pipeline configuration phase provides three artifacts: (i) a *Sample Annotated Dataset*, (ii) a *Pipeline Configuration*, and (iii) the list of non-functional *Constraints*. These artifacts serve as inputs to the Pipeline Validation phase, whose objective is to assess the efficiency and effectiveness of the initial pipeline configuration and to refine it when necessary.

The *Pipeline Validation* phase is carried out in two steps:

- *Pipeline Execution and Assessment*: The pipeline is executed on the sample dataset, and the quality of the results is evaluated against the sample annotations. Execution-related information—including the components involved, their configurations, and component- and pipeline-level performance metrics—is captured and stored as *Provenance Metadata*.
- *Pipeline Revision*: The outcomes of the pipeline execution, in terms of both performance and quality, are presented to the data analyst through a feedback dashboard. If the results are unsatisfactory, the data analyst may revise the pipeline by returning to the Pipeline Configuration phase. The system may also assist the analyst by recommending improvement actions, such as component substitution and/or reconfiguration.

When the data analyst is satisfied with the pipeline configuration, the *Data Preparation* phase can be executed on the *Source Dataset*, i.e., the entire data source from which the sample set has been extracted.

The data preparation pipeline processes data and metadata to produce a *refined dataset* for analysis. If the results are unsatisfactory—due to issues such as unrepresentative samples or evolving data characteristics—the pipeline must be redesigned and the process repeated.

The refined dataset produced by the pipeline can be used for a specific analysis or shared within a data ecosystem. To improve both dataset reusability and the transparency of the data preparation process, the refined dataset is enriched with metadata. In particular, three types of metadata are associated with it: (i) **source metadata**, directly provided by the data source and linked to the original dataset; (ii) **execution metadata**, which record information about the execution of the pipeline on the source data items; and (iii) **provenance metadata**, generated during the configuration phase and describing the characteristics of the pipeline. The proposed approach can be used to generate clean datasets from the raw data. Moreover, the availability of provenance metadata associated with the refined dataset allows data analysts to better understand if the data preparation tasks performed are suitable for their analysis.

3.3 Data Preparation for Social Media Data

Social media can provide timely, first-hand information for the real-time analysis of emergencies, such as earthquake detection from tweets [34], or for descriptive analyses of trending topics relevant to crisis management (e.g., Twitter analysis during the COVID-19 pandemic [28]). In these contexts, both data quality and timeliness are particularly critical.

Data preparation aims to improve the quality of raw datasets across diverse scenarios. When data are sourced from social media, extracting relevant information

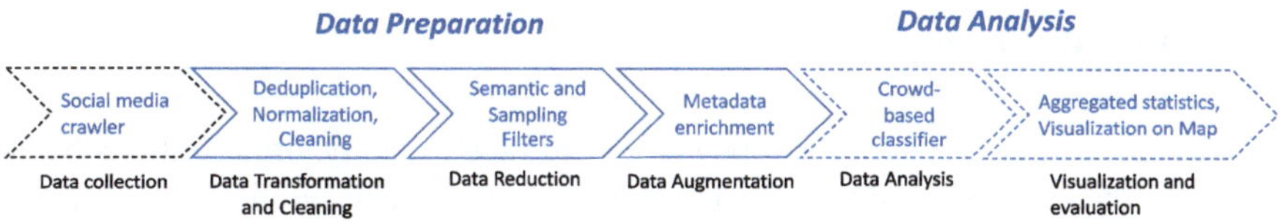

Fig. 6 Example of social media analysis pipeline

becomes particularly challenging [19], as valuable signals are often embedded within a large volume of comments, opinions, support messages, and unrelated content. The distinctive volume, velocity, and variability of social media data call for automated techniques that address different aspects of data understanding to ensure quality control. Moreover, the inherently multimodal nature of social media data necessitates the use of multiple, tailored, and automated AI-based tools, rather than general-purpose or rule-based approaches. In practice, data quality is often ensured through a combination of such tools and human expertise, for instance, by validating extracted information via crowdsourcing platforms [3].

In social media data analysis, as shown in Fig. 6, the collected data first pass through a Data Preparation phase and are subsequently processed in a Data Analysis phase. Data preparation is typically a multi-step and largely automated process, whereas data analysis often requires human interpretation. Nevertheless, the design and configuration of an effective data preparation pipeline remain iterative and resource-intensive.

As depicted in Fig. 6, data preparation for social media data comprises components that can be grouped into three main categories [9]: (i) data transformation, (ii) data reduction, and (iii) data augmentation.

Data transformation includes normalization and cleaning tasks. Normalization refers to the process of converting data into a standard format to ensure representational consistency, whereas cleaning aims to identify and correct errors and anomalies (e.g., anomaly detection and missing-value imputation), resolve conflicts, and remove or modify inappropriate or irrelevant data.

Data reduction encompasses semantic and sampling filters. Semantic filters reduce the number of data items (e.g., images or posts) based on specific content- or metadata-driven selection criteria, such as the presence of food in an image or the availability of geolocation information. Sampling filters, instead, reduce the dataset size according to a predefined reduction rate, which specifies the proportion of data to be discarded.

Data augmentation components generate additional information (e.g., location, topic, or image descriptions) that can be inferred from the available data (e.g., estimating the location of a tweet from its text) or derived through more complex analytical processes.

The design of a social media pipeline, adopting the methodology shown in Fig. 4 and using the components described above, is presented in [5].

4 Data Quality in the AI Era

With the growth of computational power and storage capacity, organizations began to collect data continuously across business, scientific, and public administration domains. This evolution led to the creation of large-scale repositories, from early enterprise data warehouses [10] to modern data lakes [17]. These infrastructures expanded analytical opportunities but also amplified long-standing data-quality challenges across massive and heterogeneous datasets. As a result, data scientists must not only address defects but also reshape data structurally to align with storage models or analytical tasks. Failure to do so may propagate errors through analytical pipelines, producing unreliable insights and biased models [23]. Despite notable technological advances, industry surveys show that practitioners still spend up to 80% of their time on data preparation rather than analysis [31].

Today, data scientists typically adopt two main strategies for implementing preparation pipelines. The first relies on ad hoc programming, often using Python DataFrame libraries such as Pandas [27], which provide flexibility but can lead to brittle or hard-to-reuse scripts. Frameworks such as Bento [27] analyze performance and scalability.

Data preparation plays a key role in achieving strong data management aligned with the FAIR principles—Findability, Accessibility, Interoperability, and Reusability. Its workflows directly influence data and metadata quality, which determine the usability of datasets in modern analytical and scientific contexts. However, the activities required to achieve high-quality standards may become unsustainable due to resource intensity, duplication of efforts, or inefficient processes.

A sustainability-oriented perspective reframes data preparation within a circular-economy mindset. This approach encourages practices that minimize waste, extend the data life cycle, and maximize reuse of both data and preparation artefacts, while supporting FAIR-aligned objectives. It promotes strategies that avoid unnecessary transformations, reduce computational and human-resource consumption, and incentivize long-term maintainability of data assets.

To operationalize this perspective, a recent work proposes an evaluation model that integrates data-quality metrics with sustainability parameters for both human and computational tasks [30]. This model enables practitioners to assess resource footprints, expected quality improvements, and trade-offs among alternative preparation techniques.

By quantifying both quality and sustainability dimensions, the model supports evidence-based decision-making and helps design efficient, reusable, and FAIR-oriented data preparation workflows. The model defines three values, *DQIAssessmentCost*, for evaluating the cost of assessment actions (e.g., for profiling data before data preparation or data exploration), *DQImprovementCost*, for a general assessment of data quality improvement costs in preparation phases for a dataset i, and *DQWaste*, for assessing actions wasting resources.

Modern data-intensive applications increasingly rely on heterogeneous, large-scale, and continuously evolving datasets, requiring data preparation pipelines that remain efficient, adaptive, and sustainable over long operational lifetimes. This shift reflects a broader transition from traditional ETL workflows to ELT architectures, in which raw data is ingested at scale and transformed only when required. Under these conditions, minimizing both *DQImprovementCost* and *DQWaste* becomes a primary objective, motivating selective, incremental, and task-aware data preparation strategies. This perspective aligns with progressive and query-driven approaches explored in prior work on entity resolution [1, 2, 42–45], culminating in systems such as BrewER [46, 47], which evaluate SQL (selection–projection) queries directly over dirty data while returning answers consistent with a fully cleaned dataset. BrewER incrementally resolves only the subset of entities relevant to the final query result, supports stop/resume execution, and enables the reuse of intermediate states across multiple quality levels, thereby avoiding redundant work across analytical iterations.

A central contribution of this work is the formalization of data cleaning and enrichment for dynamic tabular data, especially within Retrieval-Augmented Generation (RAG) pipelines. RAG workflows retrieve semantically relevant content using dense embeddings [14] and pass the retrieved items to a generative model, typically an LLM [12]. However, tabular data indexed for retrieval often originates from diverse sources, exhibits inconsistent schemas, and contains missing or noisy values. Static preprocessing fails to capture the dynamics of data freshness, schema drift, and structural inconsistency, which significantly affect retrieval accuracy and generative quality.

To address this, in [30], data cleaning on demand is positioned as a first-class operator within the RAG retrieval loop. After embedding-based candidate selection, only the retrieved subset is subjected to reconciliation, cleaning, entity resolution, imputation, or outlier removal. This ensures that preparation costs are incurred only for data that contributes to the generated answer, directly reducing *DQWaste*. Extensions such as Self-RAG [4] and Flare [20] introduce autonomous mechanisms to detect insufficient or low-quality retrievals: reflection tokens or confidence thresholds trigger additional retrieval or refinement. These principles are generalized to tabular data, arguing that inconsistencies, missing values, and drops in coherence detected in retrieved relational fragments should trigger targeted enrichment cycles.

More advanced architectures, such as agentic RAG [33], further increase adaptability by incorporating specialized decision-making agents, including general-purpose LLMs, tool-enabled LLMs capable of executing cleaning operations, and independent judge agents that compute data-quality metrics. These agents iteratively retrieve, diagnose, and refine data until (i) a convergence condition is met (coherence or quality thresholds) or (ii) a system-level budget (e.g., API call limits) is exhausted. Techniques such as ToC (Tree of Clarifications) [21] provide structured guidance for iterative refinement, helping agents resolve ambiguities and ensure semantic alignment between user intent and retrieved content.

4.1 Ethics as Data Quality Dimension

Let us now move on to the subject of Ethics: the most common ethical principles are *fairness, transparency*, respect for *diversity*, and, last but not least, respect for *privacy*.

Fairness is defined as a lack of bias, and is further subdivided into the two categories of *Equality*—giving equal support to all—and *Equity*—supporting the weak to put them in the same initial conditions as the others—[22]. *Transparency* is the possibility to interpret the data manipulation process to verify which aspects of the data determine its results. *Diversity* ensures that all the categories of people chosen for a certain opportunity are equally represented in data sets. *Privacy*, the ethical dimension that has been known and considered for the longest time, concerns ways to protect data, algorithms, and models from unauthorised access. However, note that this dimension may conflict with the need for transparency.

Any information extraction process should deliver data to the user in a form that suits the needs of their application, e.g., selecting only the data relevant to a specific goal, aggregating data, as in OLAP queries within Data Warehouses, or analyzing data using statistics or machine learning.

Common selection tasks occur in recommender systems or in selecting candidates for jobs or university admissions. Ensuring diversity in the results can help promote fairness in the selection process, but if the dataset is dominated by a particular category, enforcing diversity may unintentionally exclude members of that majority group, potentially undermining fairness. As for data aggregation, typical aggregate queries used for decision support (e.g., GROUP BY) may yield misleading conclusions: patterns seen in separate subgroups can vanish or even reverse when these groups are combined—a phenomenon known as Simpson's paradox.

For analytical operations, especially when using opaque techniques like deep learning, we still lack a full understanding of which data attributes most influence model outputs. This is a challenge in contexts where data-driven decisions affect people's lives, since we must ensure that neither data nor algorithms introduce bias. As a result, *explanation systems* have become an important area of research.

When integrating social data, each integration step can be subject to different ethical issues. For example, groups of people treated equally across sources can become over- or under-represented as a result of the integration process, leading to unfair decisions or the loss of diversity. Moreover, in the entity resolution and fusion steps, integrating sources, some of which, individually, may or may not apply anonymisation, could result in a dataset that violates privacy. On the other hand, in all integration steps, transparency is crucial, since we can verify compliance with ethical dimensions only by tracing data provenance, explaining intermediate results, and describing where the final data came from. But obviously, this can conflict with privacy.

Last, but not least, right and wrong might be different based on the situation in which we are acting, and the *context* in which these operations are performed may make some ethical dimensions, and the consequent operations, more or less important. Each case is unique and deserves a unique solution; for example, family, financial, legal, and religious factors may strongly influence clinical decisions. As a consequence, *contextual ethics*, at its most fundamental definition, posits that ethical judgments and actions are not absolute or universally applicable, but rather are deeply shaped by the specific circumstances, or context, in which they occur, and this has to be taken into account when applying possible ethical transformations to the data.

A very interesting context is that of *s*ocial media: using such media should be a safe experience, thus ethics, and etiquette (called *n*etiquette in the social context) means maintaining everybody's personal dignity, respect, and privacy [16].

5 Conclusions

This chapter presents a journey through the main contributions to data quality research developed over time, reflecting the evolution of both the field and the research activity of Barbara Pernici. Starting from the foundational work carried out within the DaQuinCIS project, the discussion has progressively addressed increasingly complex data quality challenges, moving from traditional assessment and improvement methodologies to contemporary socio-technical contexts characterized by heterogeneity, volume, and variety.

The chapter highlights that core quality dimensions—accuracy, completeness, consistency, and timeliness—remain central, while their assessment and improvement techniques have evolved to accommodate new data sources and data analytics (e.g., AI-based pipelines).

The later stages of this journey have focused on the impact of generative and agentic AI on data quality management, as well as on the growing integration of ethical and sustainability considerations as fundamental quality principles. This highlights how data quality research and practice must continuously adapt to emerging technologies and societal expectations.

References

1. Altwaijry, H., Kalashnikov, D.V., Mehrotra, S.: Query-driven approach to entity resolution. Proc. VLDB Endow. **6**(14), 1846–1857 (2013)
2. Altwaijry, H., Mehrotra, S., Kalashnikov, D.V.: QuERy: a framework for integrating entity resolution with query processing. Proc. VLDB Endow. **9**(3), 120–131 (2015)
3. Anjum, S., Verma, A., Dang, B., Gurari, D.: Exploring the use of deep learning with crowdsourcing to annotate images. Hum. Comput. **8**(2), 76–106 (2021)
4. Asai, A., Wu, Z., Wang, Y., Sil, A., Hajishirzi, H.: Self-RAG: learning to retrieve, generate, and critique through self-reflection. In: The Twelfth International Conference on Learning Representations, ICLR 2024, Vienna, Austria, May 7–11, 2024, pp. 1–30. OpenReview.net (2024). Accessed: 10 June 2025
5. Bono, C.A., Cappiello, C., Pernici, B., Ramalli, E., Vitali, M.: Pipeline design for data preparation for social media analysis. ACM J. Data Inf. Qual. **15**(4), 42:1–42:25 (2023)

6. Boyd, D., Crawford, K.: Critical questions for big data: provocations for a cultural, technological, and scholarly phenomenon. Inf., Commun., Soc. **15**(5) (2012)
7. Boyd, D.: Twitter: pointless babble or peripheral awareness + social grooming? Apophenia Inc., Technical report (2009)
8. Cappiello, C., Francalanci, C., Pernici, B., Plebani, P., Scannapieco, M.: Data quality assurance in cooperative information systems: a multi-dimension quality certificate. In: Proceedings of the ICDT'03 International Workshop on Data Quality in Cooperative Information Systems (DQCIS'03), Siena, Italy (2003)
9. Chapman, A., Missier, P., Simonelli, G., Torlone, R.: Capturing and querying fine-grained provenance of preprocessing pipelines in data science. Proc. VLDB Endow. **14**(4), 507–520 (2020)
10. Chaudhuri, S., Dayal, U.: An overview of data warehousing and OLAP technology. ACM SIGMOD Rec. **26**(1), 65–74 (1997)
11. De Santis, L., Scannapieco, M., Catarci, T.: Trusting data quality in cooperative information systems. In: Proceedings of the 11th International Conference on Cooperative Information Systems (CoopIS'03), Catania, Italy (2003)
12. Fan, W., Ding, Y., Ning, L., Wang, S., Li, H., Yin, D., Chua, T.-S., Li, Q.: A survey on RAG meeting LLMs: towards retrieval-augmented large language models. In: Proceedings of the 30th ACM SIGKDD Conference on Knowledge Discovery and Data Mining (KDD 2024), pp. 6491–6501. ACM, Barcelona, Spain (2024). https://doi.org/10.1145/3637528.3671470
13. Fernandes, D., et al.: Data wrangling: concepts, tools, and challenges. IEEE Trans. Knowl. Data Eng. (2023)
14. Gao, Y., Xiong, Y., Gao, X., Jia, K., Pan, J., Bi, Y., Dai, Y., Sun, J., Wang, H.:. Retrieval-augmented generation for large language models: a survey (2023). arXiv:2312.10997
15. Firmani, D., Tanca, L., Torlone, R.: Ethical dimensions for data quality. ACM J. Data Inf. Qual. **12**(1), 2:1–2:5 (2020)
16. Geeling, S., Brown, I.: Ethics research in the context of social media. In: Aanestad, M., Klein, S., Tarafdar, M., Han, S., Laumer, S., Ramos, I. (eds.) 31st European Conference on Information Systems - Co-creating Sustainable Digital Futures, ECIS 2023, Kristiansan, Norway, June 11–16, 2023 (2023)
17. Hai, R., et al.: Data lake systems and management: a survey. VLDB J. (2023)
18. Hameed, A., Naumann, F.: Data preparation techniques and tools. ACM Comput. Surv. (2020)
19. Havas, C., et al.: E2mC: improving emergency management service practice through social media and crowdsourcing analysis in near real time. Sensors **17**(12), 2766 (2017)
20. Jiang, Z., Xu, F., Gao, L., Sun, Z., Liu, Q., Dwivedi-Yu, J., Yang, Y., Callan, J., Neubig, G.: Active retrieval augmented generation. In: Proceedings of the 2023 Conference on Empirical Methods in Natural Language Processing (EMNLP), pp. 7969–7992, Singapore. Association for Computational Linguistics (2023). https://doi.org/10.18653/v1/2023.emnlp-main.495
21. Kim, G., Kim, S., Jeon, B., Park, J., Kang, J.: Tree of clarifications: answering ambiguous questions with retrieval-augmented large language models. In: Proceedings of the 2023 Conference on Empirical Methods in Natural Language Processing (EMNLP), pp. 996–1009, Singapore. Association for Computational Linguistics (2023). https://doi.org/10.18653/v1/2023.emnlp-main.63
22. Jagadish, H.V., Stoyanovich, J., Howe, B.: The many facets of data equity. The Workshop Proceedings of the EDBT/ICDT 2021 Joint Conference
23. Krishnan, S., Wang, J., Franklin, M.: Towards reliable data preparation: error detection and correction methods. Proc. VLDB Endow. (2016)
24. Li, X., Dong, X.L., Lyons, K., Meng, W., Srivastava, D.: Truth finding on the deep web: is the problem solved? Proc. VLDB Endow. **6**(2), 97–108 (2012)
25. Mecella, M., Scannapieco, M., Virgillito, A., Baldoni, R., Catarci, T., Batini, C.: The DaQuinCIS broker: querying data and their quality in cooperative information systems. J. Data Semant. **1**(1) (2003)
26. Mehrabi, N., Morstatter, F., Saxena, N., Lerman, K., Galstyan, A.: A survey on bias and fairness in machine learning. ACM Comput. Surv. **54**(6), 115:1–115:35 (2022)

27. Mozzillo, A., Zecchini, L., Gagliardelli, L., Aslam, A., Bergamaschi, S., Simonini, G.: Evaluation of dataframe libraries for data preparation on a single machine. In: Simitsis, A., Kemme, B., Queralt, A., Romero, O., Jovanovic, P. (eds.) Proceedings 28th International Conference on Extending Database Technology, EDBT 2025, Barcelona, Spain, March 25–28, 2025, pp. 337–349. OpenProceedings.org (2025)
28. Negri, V., Scuratti, D., Agresti, S., Rooein, D., Scalia, G., Shankar, A.R., Marquez, J.L.F., Carman, M.J., Pernici, B.: Image-based social sensing: combining ai and the crowd to mine policy-adherence indicators from twitter. In: IEEE/ACM 43rd International Conference on Software Engineering: Software Engineering in Society (ICSE-SEIS), pp. 92–101. IEEE (2021)
29. Pernici, B., Scannapieco, M.: Data quality in web information systems. J. Data Semant. **1**, 48–68 (2003)
30. Pernici, B., Cappiello, C., Bono, C.A., Sancricca, C., Catarci, T., Angelini, M., Filosa, M., Palmonari, M., De Paoli, F., Bergamaschi, S., Simonini, G.: Sustainable quality in data preparation. J. Data Inf. Qual. **17**(4) (2025)
31. Press, G.: Cleaning big data: most data scientists spend 80 of their time on data preparation. Forbes (2016)
32. Purvis, B., Mao, Y., Robinson, D.: Three pillars of sustainability: in search of conceptual origins. Sustain. Sci. **14**, 681–695 (2019)
33. Singh, A., Ehtesham, A., Kumar, S., Khoei, T.T.: Agentic retrieval-augmented generation: a survey on agentic RAG (2025). arXiv:2501.09136
34. Sakaki, T., Okazaki, M., Matsuo, Y.: Tweet analysis for real-time event detection and earthquake reporting system development. IEEE Trans. Knowl. Data Eng. **25**(4), 919–931 (2012)
35. Scannapieco, M., Pernici, B., Pierce, E.M.: IP-UML: a methodology for quality improvement based on IP-MAP and UML. In: Wang, R. (ed.) Advances in Management Information Systems-Information Quality Monograph (AMIS-IQ) Monograph. Sharpe, M.E. (2003)
36. Scannapieco, M., Virgillito, A., Marchetti, M., Mecella, M., Baldoni, R.: The DaQuinCIS architecture: a platform for exchanging and improving data quality in cooperative information systems. Inf. Syst. **29**(7) (2004)
37. Shankaranarayan, G., Wang, R.Y., Ziad, M.: Modeling the manufacture of an information product with IP-MAP. In: Proceedings of the 5th International Conference on Information Quality (ICIQ'00), Boston, MA, USA (2000)
38. Singh, D., Singh, B.: Investigating the impact of data normalization on classification performance. Appl. Soft Comput. **97**(Part B), 105524 (2020)
39. Stoyanovich, J., Howe, B., Jagadish, H.V.: Responsible data management. Commun. ACM **65**(6), 64–74 (2022)
40. Tukey, J.W.: The future of data analysis. Ann. Math. Stat. (1962)
41. Wang, R.Y.: A product perspective on total data quality management. Commun. ACM **41**(2), 58–65 (1998)
42. Firmani, D., Saha, B., Srivastava, D.: Online entity resolution using an oracle. Proc. VLDB Endow. **9**(5), 384–395 (2016). https://doi.org/10.14778/2876473.2876474
43. Papenbrock, T., Heise, A., Naumann, F.: Progressive duplicate detection. IEEE Trans. Knowl. Data Eng. **27**(5), 1316–1329 (2015). https://doi.org/10.1109/TKDE.2014.2359666
44. Simonini, G., Papadakis, G., Palpanas, T., Bergamaschi, S.: Schema-agnostic progressive entity resolution. In: Proceedings of the IEEE International Conference on Data Engineering (ICDE), pp. 53–64 (2018). https://doi.org/10.1109/ICDE.2018.00015.
45. Whang, S.E., Marmaros, D., Garcia-Molina, H.: Pay-As-You-Go entity resolution. IEEE Trans. Knowl. Data Eng. **25**(5), 1111–1124 (2013). https://doi.org/10.1109/TKDE.2012.43
46. Simonini, G., Zecchini, L., Bergamaschi, S., Naumann, F.: Entity resolution on-demand. Proc. VLDB Endow. **15**(7), 1506–1518 (2022). https://doi.org/10.14778/3523210.3523226
47. Zecchini, L., Simonini, G., Bergamaschi, S., Naumann, F.: BrewER: entity resolution on-demand. Proc. VLDB Endow. **16**(12), 4026–4029 (2023). https://doi.org/10.14778/3611540.3611612

Flexible Service Compositions

Danilo Ardagna, Luciano Baresi, Sara Comai, Gianpaolo Cugola, Carlo Ghezzi, Giovanni Meroni, Raffaela Mirandola, Giovanni Quattrocchi, and Chiara Sandionigi

Abstract Our collaboration with Barbara began in the DISCORSO and MAIS projects, which pioneered an integrated framework for designing and managing flexible and adaptive service-based business processes. Anticipating the shift from static Web services to dynamic, service-oriented architectures well before the cloud era, the framework introduced mechanisms for runtime adaptation, QoS-aware service selection, and continuous self-validation. Its design environment combined an extended BPMN model with WebML for human activities. Automated activities were specified through abstract services annotated with functional and QoS requirements. The corresponding BPEL fragments were automatically generated, and the runtime components, including an extended UDDI registry, QoS matchmakers and a Ser-

---

D. Ardagna (✉) · L. Baresi · S. Comai · G. Cugola · C. Ghezzi · G. Quattrocchi
Politecnico di Milano, Milan, Italy
e-mail: danilo.ardagna@polimi.it

L. Baresi
e-mail: luciano.baresi@polimi.it

S. Comai
e-mail: sara.comai@polimi.it

G. Cugola
e-mail: gianpaolo.cugola@polimi.it

C. Ghezzi
e-mail: carlo.ghezzi@polimi.it

G. Quattrocchi
e-mail: giovanni.quattrocchi@polimi.it

G. Meroni
Technical University of Denmark, Lyngby, Denmark
e-mail: giom@dtu.dk

R. Mirandola
Karlsruhe Institute of Technology, Karlsruhe, Germany
e-mail: raffaela.mirandola@kit.edu

C. Sandionigi
Univesité Grenoble Alpes, Grenoble, France
e-mail: chiara.sandionigi@cea.fr

C. Cappiello et al. (eds.), *Retrospective and Prospective Views on Information Systems Engineering*, https://doi.org/10.1007/978-3-032-19578-4_5

vice Selector, mapped abstract specifications to optimized concrete services using mixed-integer linear programming. This foundational work has since evolved into broader research on scalable optimization, dynamic software product lines, advanced monitoring and exception handling, situational computing, and multi-layered service architectures, culminating in new perspectives for AI-driven adaptation.

1 Introduction

Our collaboration with Barbara started long ago within the DISCORSO (Distributed Information Systems for Coordinated Service-Oriented Interoperability) and MAIS (Multichannel Adaptive Information Systems) projects, which aimed to develop a comprehensive framework for specifying and managing flexible and responsive business processes [2, 16].

The research at that time had the ambition to develop solutions to support a significant shift from statically composed Web Services available in the industry to flexible processes that can rapidly adapt to changing business needs. Note that we were well before the *cloud revolution*, and the claim was that since information systems evolved quickly, they required that changes be applied transparently at runtime, not just during conventional maintenance. Moving from closed proprietary systems to open service-oriented solutions, based on public standards, provided the necessary infrastructure for this shift. Since services, which are often complex compositions of other services (processes), may only be selected at runtime, flexible and adaptive solutions were essential to guarantee both the process's functional requirements and its Quality of Service (QoS). This necessity imposed a validation shift, moving away from conventional pre-deployment testing towards *self-validation* and *self-adaptation techniques* that monitor services and trigger corrective actions immediately when problems arise.

The DISCORSO/MAIS framework provided an integrated solution that combined design-time and runtime mechanisms for the design and implementation of flexible and adaptive business processes. The core components included a design environment that used an *extended BPMN editor* [20] and *a WebML editor* [8], and an execution environment that features a *Service Selector* [4], an *extended UDDI registry* [21], a *WS-BPEL engine* [19] and *Process Monitoring components* [5] (see Fig. 1). At that time, our framework was unique in its integration of process model design (incorporating both human-based and automated activities), QoS-based dynamic service selection and optimization, and runtime supervision.

At the design level, an annotated business BPMN description specifies the entire process. The DISCORSO/MAIS framework supported defining processes that include both manual and automated activities: Human-based activities were modeled as web pages through WebML, while automated activities were specified as *abstract* interactions, defined by their functional requirements and QoS constraints. Processes, fragments, and individual service invocations could be annotated with *QoS constraints* (such as cost, response time, reliability, and reputation) and statistics (such as the probability of executing branches and loops). Based on the extended BPMN

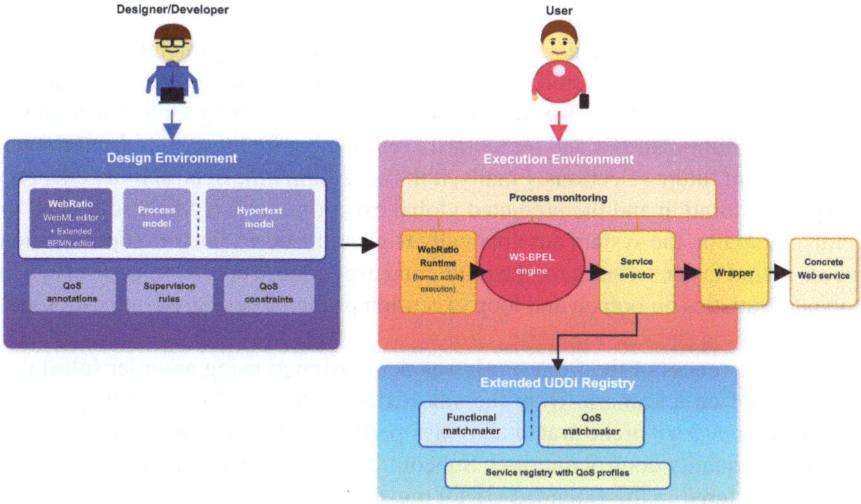

Fig. 1 DISCORSO/MAIS framework

specification, the proposed toolchain automatically generated a WebML hypertext skeleton to control manual activities. The fragments corresponding to automated activities were translated into BPEL (Business Process Execution Language) [20] processes comprising abstract services, with concrete service selection deferred to runtime.

The framework mapped abstract service specifications to concrete services by exploiting the designer-defined QoS annotations. Concrete Web services, along with their QoS profiles, were stored in an *extended UDDI registry*. The registry included a functional matchmaker and a QoS matchmaker. The *Service Selector* used these components to find services that implemented the abstract functional requirements and best fit the specified QoS constraints. Service selection is treated as an optimization problem executed when the process is instantiated and iterated at runtime to account for performance variability and failures. The goal was to maximize the user's average QoS while satisfying local constraints (in a single activity) and global constraints (in a set of activities or the entire process). The framework employed an optimization approach based on mixed-integer linear programming models, which could handle stateful Web services and has been demonstrated to be particularly effective when constraints are severe [4]. If the optimization problem did not yield a feasible solution, the framework attempted to negotiate the QoS parameters with service providers to find a suboptimal solution, thus reducing the failure rate.

The framework oversaw executions and responded to failures or QoS violations. Process monitoring relied on *supervision rules* that contained monitoring assertions and recovery actions. Monitoring Assertions were defined as *pre-* and *post-conditions* that check functional correctness and QoS constraints, specified in a variant of WSCoL [5]. The data for these checks could come from the state of running processes, external remote components, or previously collected persistent data. If anomalies were detected (e.g., a concrete service is faulty or violates a constraint), recovery actions were triggered. These actions could include invoking the *Service Selector* to find a substitute service that satisfies the remaining QoS constraints or notifying the administrator and temporarily removing a faulty service from the registry to prevent future selections. Finally, if the execution time of an activity exceeded its expected duration and the predicted global execution time is likely to exceed the overall constraint, the system automatically triggered a new selection (optimization) process to find faster services for the remaining execution. Supervision was also used to update statistics on branch and loop execution probabilities based on past process runs.

The effectiveness of the framework was demonstrated using an order fulfillment process based on a scenario from the silk-textile district of Northern Italy. In this example, a *converter* orchestrated activities performed by subcontractors (weaving mills, dyers, quality control entities). Subcontractors exposed their services as Web services registered in the extended UDDI registry.

The case study defined global constraints, such as the requirement of two different providers for quality control, an overall process time of less than two weeks, and a total cost under an a priori fixed budget. During the demonstration of the process, a supervision rule was able to detect execution time violations, which triggered runtime reoptimization and negotiation. The system frequently successfully used the available budget to negotiate a faster completion time from subsequent services, ultimately ensuring that global constraints were met.

Building on the seminal contribution of the DISCORSO/MAIS framework, we have since expanded our research in several complementary directions. We improved service selection mechanisms by reducing optimization overhead, enabling more effective management of multiple concurrent process instances (see Sect. 2). We have framed the adaptation problem through dynamic software product lines in Sect. 3. We have incorporated exception handling and integrated it more deeply with advanced monitoring capabilities as discussed in Sect. 4. We have paired it with the situational computing environment, as illustrated in Sect. 5. Additionally, we have extended the idea of flexibility to a multi-layered service architecture and considered flexibility and adaptability at the infrastructure level to dynamically provision resources (Sect. 6). Finally, Sect. 7 briefly discusses the original ideas in the new AI-centered context.

2 Per-Flow Optimal Service Selection

The service selection mechanism implemented in DISCORSO/MAIS was initially extended in [3] where the focus was using a per-flow optimization approach, which distinguishes it significantly from the per-request solutions presented in earlier works [2, 4]. The core innovation of [3] is addressing the challenges that arise when a complex Service-Oriented Architecture (SOA) system handles a sustained traffic of requests for multiple applications concurrently, a limitation explicitly noted in the earlier per-request literature. In this work model, service selection is formulated as a constrained non-linear multi-criteria optimization problem, solved within a broker-based framework. This approach considers multiple BPEL processes (QoS classes) and multiple concurrent requests to the same process simultaneously, optimizing the selection on a per-flow basis. This is achieved by performing the optimization periodically based on a prediction of the request flow for a given time horizon, which allows the system to take into account workload fluctuations and avoid potential instability that occurs when multiple requests are independently assigned to the same "best" service, causing overload and performance degradation. To manage the complexity and scale required to handle concurrent flows, [3] introduces an analytical model where each concrete service is modeled as an M/G/1 queue to indicate system performance, allowing for run-time performance guarantees based on workload predictions. The objective function maximizes a weighted average of QoS scores across all classes, favoring processes characterized by higher importance and/or higher incoming workload. The optimization relies on a heuristic algorithm to provide an initial solution to speed up a commercial solver for the non-linear problem. In comparison, the work described in [4] and the architecture presented in the [2], which introduced the DISCORSO/MAIS framework, primarily focused on the per-request optimization for a single instance of a flexible business process. While the [4] introduced advanced techniques for global optimization, such as loops peeling (which significantly improved performance over previous unfolding solutions) and handling stateful Web service constraints, the goal was finding the optimal execution plan for a single process instance under severe QoS constraints, formalizing the core problem as a Mixed Integer Linear Programming (MILP) model. Furthermore, the earlier DISCORSO work utilized negotiation techniques as a recovery mechanism, specifically when an initially posed per-request optimization problem was found to be infeasible due to stringent resource limits, allowing the system to bargain QoS parameters with service providers. The key limitation addressed by the later [3] per-flow approach is that the per-request optimization inherent to the earlier papers could impose a significant overhead on the SOA infrastructure, especially under sustained traffic, whereas the [3] achieved overall optimization time reductions proportional to the incoming workload, thus outperforming the per-request alternatives even under light load conditions. While the older papers focused on proving the ability to find an optimal solution despite the problem being NP-hard, the [3] paper adapted the formulation to handle dynamic congestion and flow competition, providing a highly efficient and scalable algorithm to identify a local optimum solution for multiple concurrent process instances.

3 Variability Through Product Lines

After the two aforementioned projects, we continued to work on managing the variability of service-based processes and tried to conceive a more structured and precise framework to manage it.

To this end, Baresi et al. [10] explore how modern software systems, increasingly required to operate in dynamic, unpredictable environments, can be engineered to support runtime variability in a principled and reliable way. Traditional Software Product Lines (SPLs, [22]) were conceived to manage variability among products belonging to the same family, but their mechanisms assume that all variation decisions are made at design or deployment times. In many contemporary domains, such as smart homes, mobile computing, self-adaptive systems, and service-based applications, requirements often emerge only at runtime, making static variability mechanisms inadequate. This motivated the shift toward Dynamic Software Product Lines (DSPL, [10]), which extend SPL principles to enable features to be activated, deactivated, or reconfigured while the system is running.

The state of the art preceding this work included multiple attempts to support runtime variability, but none offered a complete and scalable solution. Some research mapped features directly to individual services, trying to use Service-Oriented Architecture (SOA) principles for variability management [14]. Although SOA's loose coupling and late binding offered promise, the mapping of features to atomic services proved too simplistic for real-world systems. Other approaches explored aspect-oriented programming [13] as a way to implement features, dynamically weaving aspects into running systems. Although expressive, these approaches often became unmanageable in large systems, as a single feature could require many aspects, and their composition introduced significant complexity and performance penalties. Additional research explored context-awareness as a means of selecting variants at runtime. However, these solutions lacked the ability to modify running process instances, handle complex multi-operation features, or manage the separation between variability specification and runtime execution.

In this context, the paper argues for a convergence between DSPLs and SOA as a means of pushing the adaptability frontier. SOA provides a mature technological foundation for distributed, loosely coupled, and dynamically bindable systems. However, languages such as BPEL, commonly used to orchestrate services, lacked intrinsic support for runtime modification. Standard BPEL engines did not allow changes to deployed workflows, nor do they allow active process instances to be migrated to new variants. Only partner service substitution is possible, and even that becomes difficult when selecting among many potential services or when dealing with complex fragments rather than single invocations.

The work identifies this gap between SOA's technological potential for dynamism and the need for structured runtime variability, as a key barrier to progress. It proposes bridging this gap using two complementary technologies: the Common Variability Language (CVL) to model variability [27], and Dynamic BPEL (DyBPEL) to implement runtime adaptations [5]. CVL provided a structured, model-driven way to represent variability independently of the specification of the base system. It supports feature models, constraints, variation points, and reusable libraries of variant fragments, enabling designers to express optional or alternative functionality cleanly and formally. DyBPEL, on the other hand, extends the widely used ActiveBPEL engine through aspect-oriented programming, allowing the system to intercept execution and apply changes on the fly. The combination creates a DSPL in which feature-level design decisions are modeled symbolically in CVL, while DyBPEL ensures that changes can be safely and correctly applied to executing process instances.

An example of smart home automation was used to illustrate the feasibility of this integration. A BPEL base model contains the mandatory heating control logic, monitoring temperature and energy consumption through partner services, and adjusting the heater accordingly. Optional features, such as lighting control or alarm control, are modeled as reusable process fragments in a CVL library. CVL substitutions specify how these fragments should be integrated into the base model, including the addition of partner links, message-handling activities, and structured process blocks. The feature model formally expresses constraints such as exclusions (the alarm feature conflicts with automatic light activation).

When a designer selects a configuration, CVL's product realization mechanism determines the required substitutions and communicates them to DyBPEL, which applies these changes at runtime through a coordinated mechanism. A repository stores pending changes, process versions, and the number of running instances. The coordinator component determines where execution must pause to ensure safe application of changes, which must occur outside transactional scopes and at points where partner interactions are not in progress. Using aspect-oriented interceptors, DyBPEL monitors process execution and applies structural modifications directly to the internal representation of active instances. The engine also updates the definition of deployed processes so that future instances follow the new configuration. This approach enables both forward application of new variants and reversion of previously applied substitutions when features are unticked due to conflicts or changing requirements.

The evaluation carried out also evaluated the performance, showing that the migration of the definition of the process takes around 0.13–0.15 s, while adapting the running instances takes on the order of a hundredths of a second. Although interception introduces overhead, the results indicate that runtime adaptability is feasible for many application contexts. The assessment highlights that aspect-oriented interception is intrusive and may require optimization, but emphasizes that the separation enabled by CVL keeps variability manageable even as systems scale.

From a state-of-the-art perspective, the innovation lies in unifying a rigorous variability modeling language with a runtime adaptation mechanism capable of modifying running service compositions. Previous DSPL approaches did not support runtime modification of active workflow engines, nor did they offer a clean separation between feature modeling and execution. Earlier SOA-based dynamic systems lacked the ability to reason about variability structurally, and aspect-based DSPLs lacked scalability and maintainability. CVL provides the modeling discipline needed to ensure that variability remains understandable and analyzable, while DyBPEL operationalizes those variations with fine-grained, instance-level flexibility.

This work can be seen as a promising step toward broadly applicable runtime-adaptive systems. By demonstrating that CVL's expressive modeling can be combined with a dynamic execution environment such as DyBPEL, the work shows that DSPLs and SOAs can reinforce each other, overcoming limitations that have hindered both fields. The model-driven separation of base behavior and variants supports clarity, analyzability, and maintainability, while DyBPEL enables the responsiveness required in modern adaptive systems. The approach is not limited to BPEL; other business process languages could be used.

The work provided one of the first comprehensive demonstrations of how DSPL concepts can be grounded in real SOA execution technologies, contributing significantly to the state of the art in dynamic, context-aware, software product line engineering.

4 GSM-Based Monitoring of BPMN Processes

The problem of monitoring the execution of business processes (or service composition) required additional attention. We both continued to extend the monitoring capabilities to identify more detailed violations, and we studied more flexible ways to encode and implement business processes when BPEL became obsolete.

Meroni et al. [17] provides an appropriate summary of these two dimensions. The work proposes a systematic technique to translate BPMN process models into an extended version of the Guard-Stage-Milestone (GSM) notation [11], called E-GSM, with the ultimate goal of enabling robust, data-aware, and deviation-tolerant monitoring of complex business processes.

BPMN is widely used to model the intended behavior of a process using an imperative and prescriptive control-flow style. However, when such models are used at runtime, they exhibit a major limitation: any deviation from the prescribed sequence of tasks is interpreted as a fatal exception that halts the execution, even though the real-world process may continue executing. Declarative approaches such as GSM, instead, do not enforce a fixed execution order but describe admissible states and transitions. This makes declarative specifications highly suitable for monitoring, since they allow deviations to be detected without stopping process executions. The goal was then to bridge these worlds by automatically converting BPMN models into E-GSM specifications that preserve control-flow intent in a descriptive way to support more flexible execution and enable a monitoring engine that reports deviations, classifies their severity, and continues tracking the evolving process even when violations occur.

The approach extends standard GSM by introducing two key concepts in E-GSM: *Process Flow Guard*s and *Fault Logger*s. In classical GSM, a *Stage* encapsulates a unit of work and is opened and closed by *Data Flow Guard*s and *Milestone*s, respectively, which are event-condition-action rules based on internal or external events. E-GSM augments this structure with *Process Flow Guard*s that capture the expected ordering among activities as expressed in the original BPMN control flow. Unlike imperative execution semantics, these guards are not used to enforce an order but to evaluate compliance: when a *Stage* is activated through one of its *Data Flow Guard*s, its *Process Flow Guard*s check whether such activation conforms to the intended sequence. If the check fails, the *Stage* is marked as out-of-order. *Fault Logger*s, instead, signal that an activity has been executed incorrectly or encountered an exceptional condition. Together, these extensions allow a monitoring engine to distinguish between correct, out-of-order, incorrect, and skipped activities.

E-GSM defines a rich *Stage* lifecycle organized around three orthogonal dimensions: outcome, compliance, and status. The outcome indicates whether a *Stage* completed regularly or experienced an internal fault. Compliance describes whether a *Stage* respects the expected control flow or has been triggered out-of-order or skipped. Status identifies whether the Stage is unopened, opened, or closed according to the activation of its guards and milestones. This tri-dimensional lifecycle offers a nuanced understanding of how a process progresses and where deviations occur. By combining these dimensions over all Stages, the monitoring engine can compute a severity level for the entire process instance. For example, if all *Stage*s follow their prescribed order and no fault occurs, the severity is None; if the control flow is violated but all activities finish successfully, the severity is Low; if tasks are executed incorrectly, severity increases; and if activities are skipped or executed despite faults, the severity becomes Medium-high or High. This allows organizations to identify deviations not only but also assess their impact on the overall business outcome.

The translation from BPMN to E-GSM is based on a structured set of thirteen transformation rules that operate on well-formed workflow nets. For basic elements, activities become atomic *Stage*s equipped with *Data Flow Guard*s and *Milestone*s that represent the beginning and completion of the activity. Events become *Stage*s with guards and milestones triggered by the corresponding occurrences. Boundary events generate either *Fault Logger*s (for non-interrupting exceptions) or additional *Milestone*s and guards (for interrupting boundary events). These element-level rules ensure that BPMN's activity semantics and exception-handling constructs are preserved in the declarative model.

Composite control-flow patterns, including sequence, parallelism, conditional branching, inclusive branching, and loops, are translated by means of specific translation rules. Sequence blocks are translated into enclosing *Stage*s whose nested *Stage*s must close in a prescribed order, imposed only descriptively through *Process Flow Guard*s. Conditional exclusive branches are translated into *Stage*s whose guards evaluate branch conditions but do not enforce them, allowing the system to detect when an "impossible" branch is taken. Loop blocks produce a pair of *Stage*s: one representing the loop's internal iteration and one representing continuation beyond the loop. Because declarative models do not enforce iteration counts, these loop stages are re-opened and evaluated as many times as needed. The are also specific rules for handling interrupting and non-interrupting boundary events, which require distinguishing between flows that must stop normal behavior and flows that may continue in parallel. Exceptional-flow translation is carefully designed to preserve BPMN semantics while maintaining freedom for the declarative engine to detect misuse of exception handlers or unexpected continuation of regular flows.

Having defined the full translation, the validation of the approach was carried out by implementing a prototype translator using ATL [12] and applying it to a complex real-world logistics process. The case involves a pharmaceutical shipment transported by multiple carriers, during which tasks such as loading, inventory check, rail transfer, warehouse storage, and final delivery may generate sensor data from a smart shipping container. The declarative E-GSM monitoring engine, running on the container, observes sensor readings and explicit messages to infer which stages are active and whether they occur in compliance with the modeled process. Three execution scenarios illustrate the monitoring capabilities. In a correct execution, all *Stage*s proceed in the expected order, all milestones are reached correctly, and the overall severity is None. In a catastrophic execution, temperature sensors detect that goods were spoiled during storage; despite this, subsequent stages are executed anyway, leading to multiple violations and a severity of High. In a recoverable, but troublesome execution, missing goods are not reloaded, and the container is shipped prematurely, resulting in out-of-order *Stage*s and an eventual severity of Medium. These examples demonstrate how E-GSM-based monitoring can reveal not only the occurrence of deviations but also their business relevance, supporting accountability among involved parties.

The approach was also confronted against related work on translating imperative models into declarative ones, artifact-centric modeling, and conformance checking. Although prior approaches also generate GSM models [9], they typically use control flow prescriptively or only reconstruct artifact lifecycles [18]; in contrast, E-GSM uses control flow information strictly for deviation detection. Similarly, E-GSM differs from classical conformance checking by enabling runtime log-free detection of deviation severity rather than post-execution analysis.

In conclusion, the work opened new avenues to both declarative process monitoring and flexible monitoring capabilities, and demonstrated that E-GSM offers an effective middle ground between prescriptive BPMN models and flexible declarative monitoring. By translating BPMN into E-GSM, organizations can take advantage of the clarity of BPMN's modeling and the robustness of GSM's monitoring. The resulting monitoring system can track real-world executions and detect various deviations.

5 Service Selection and Allocation in Situational Computing

The service selection mechanisms originally introduced in the DISCORSO framework were subsequently extended and generalized in the work by Sandionigi et al. [23], which advances the applicability of service-oriented principles to the domain of pervasive and situated computing. This extension addresses the limitations of traditional Service-Oriented Computing (SOC) approaches when applied to environments characterized by high dynamism, heterogeneity, and severe resource constraints.

This research direction was motivated by the rapid evolution of communication and mobile technologies, which has enabled the emergence of pervasive applications operating within large-scale, continuously changing ecosystems. These ecosystems—now commonly conceptualized as the computing continuum [24]—comprise billions of heterogeneous devices, including smartphones, embedded systems, and intelligent sensors. Within such environments, applications must be inherently context-aware, dynamically adapting their structure and behavior based on situational attributes such as spatial context, device availability, and network conditions. Consequently, service selection processes must be sensitive to context and capable of reconfiguring at runtime to ensure functional and non-functional requirements are met.

In the extended model, services may execute on a wide spectrum of computational platforms, ranging from cloud servers to laptops, mobile phones, and sensor nodes, each exhibiting distinct capabilities and constraints. As in DISCORSO/MAIS, applications are specified as abstract workflows using a BPEL-like orchestration formalism, with concrete service bindings deferred to runtime. This late-binding mechanism supports continuous self-adaptation as the underlying infrastructure evolves.

A central contribution of Sandionigi et al. is the explicit incorporation of execution locality into the service selection problem. While conventional SOC relies exclusively on remote execution, pervasive computing environments introduce the possibility of dynamic code deployment onto proximate devices. The optimization problem must therefore jointly determine (i) which concrete service implementation to select and (ii) where to execute it—remotely or on a local device. This is achieved through decision variables that encode the execution location, thereby capturing the trade-off between remote execution and dynamic deployment.

The introduction of local execution necessitates the explicit modeling of energy consumption as a primary optimization constraint. This consideration is essential in pervasive environments where devices are often battery-powered and computationally constrained. Moreover, environmental parameters such as network bandwidth, device mobility, and available energy are highly variable, requiring continuous monitoring and runtime reoptimization to maintain QoS guarantees and avoid performance degradation.

Sandionigi et al. extended QoS-aware service selection beyond the relatively stable and resource-rich enterprise settings targeted by DISCORSO, adapting it to the volatile, resource-limited, and context-dependent landscape of pervasive mobile computing. By introducing energy-aware, context-sensitive optimization and explicit reasoning about execution locality, this contribution broadened the scope of dynamic service selection and significantly enhances its applicability across the computing continuum.

6 Dynamic Resource Management

Although dynamism and flexibility have been key characteristics of service compositions at the application level of years, the *cloud* has broadened the scope and made the community to reconsider these characteristics at all levels of the service hierarchy.

If we consider the infrastructure level, one key dimension of flexibility refers to the dynamic provisioning of computing resources. The interpretation is two-fold: one can see available resources as the artifacts that must be composed (provisioned) dynamically, but we can also see them as the enablers that allow for the efficient and flexible execution of service composition at the application level.

Although Baresi et al. [6] was one of the first papers to propose efficient means to manage resources (CPU cores) dynamically, this section addresses the same problem in the context of big data applications, that is, batch processes. DynaSpark [7] proposes a novel solution to dynamic resource management through a control-theoretic loop. The work addresses a fundamental limitation of Apache Spark [1]: its resource assignments are static. Once executors are created at application startup, their CPU cores and memory allocations remain fixed until completion. This means that Spark cannot respond to runtime disturbances, workload variance, data skew, or the competitive presence of concurrently running applications. As a result, traditional Spark clusters frequently waste resources through over-allocation or fail to meet deadlines because of under-allocation. DynaSpark overcomes these limitations by introducing a fine-grained, per-stage, dynamically adjustable resource management system built on containerization and feedback control.

A key design decision is to move from the traditional Spark executor model per-application to a *per stage executor model*. When a stage becomes ready for execution, DynaSpark launches one containerized executor per worker node, each dedicated exclusively to that stage. Containers are regulated through Linux control groups, which allow assigning fractional CPU quotas and dynamically adjusting them on sub-second timescales. This vertical elasticity is central: unlike Spark, which can only change the number of executors at coarse time intervals, DynaSpark can modify CPU allocation dozens of times per minute, aligning resources to the precise progress needs of each stage.

Memory management is also treated dynamically. Although JVM heap memory cannot be resized at runtime, DynaSpark introduces dynamically adjustable off-heap memory to support multiple applications running simultaneously. A centralized memory manager redistributes the off-heap capacity among running applications whenever a new application arrives. This ensures that the system maintains enough memory to execute tasks without excessive spilling while preserving fairness among applications whose memory demands were not known in advance.

To determine how many resources a stage should receive, DynaSpark relies on a two-layer adaptation mechanism. The first layer is a heuristic planner that decomposes the global application deadline into individual per-stage deadlines. Profiling information—such as the nominal records-per-second throughput for each stage, the amount of data to be processed, and estimated stage complexity—serve as input to this heuristic. By weighing each stage's remaining workload against the total unfinished work, the planner assigns stricter deadlines to heavier stages and more flexible deadlines to lighter ones. These deadlines translate into initial estimates of required CPU cores per executor, but because profiling cannot capture runtime disturbances or dynamic conditions, these values are only approximate.

The second and more sophisticated layer consists of local controllers. Each executor is equipped with a controller that actively adjusts CPU allocation in real time. The goal of each controller is to ensure that the executor's progress matches a desired progress trajectory derived from the stage deadline. Instead of simply finishing "before" the deadline, DynaSpark dictates a continuous expected progression curve: at every control period, the executor should have completed a certain percentage of its assigned data. This transforms the problem into one of continuous tracking rather than last-minute correction.

The control loop is built on a simplified, yet expressive, dynamic model of execution progress. The system assumes that if CPU allocation is held constant, the progress rate converges to a steady-state value defined by a nonlinear function of allocated cores and disturbances such as memory pressure, garbage collection overhead, or data skew. To make the control problem tractable, the authors approximate this with a Hammerstein model consisting of static nonlinearity followed by a first-order linear dynamic response. This captures the intuition that giving an executor more CPU does not instantly change its progress rate, but rather influences it over a short transient period. The local controller observes the actual progress rate at each 0.5-second interval and compares it to the desired rate. The discrepancy produces an error signal that feeds a discretized PI (Proportional-Integral) controller. The proportional term reacts to immediate deviations in the rate, while the integral term corrects slow, accumulated errors caused by disturbances or modeling inaccuracies.

A major challenge in this environment is that CPU resources are quantized and bounded: a controller may request a negative amount of CPU (which must be clamped to zero) or more CPU than is available on the worker. To maintain stability, the controller employs an anti-windup mechanism that prevents integral error from growing uncontrollably when outputs saturate. This ensures that once resources become available again, the controller quickly returns to correct behavior instead of overshooting wildly. Because the control loop runs so frequently and the container-based actuators respond nearly instantaneously, the system can maintain progress tracking precision within a few percent even under significant runtime disturbance.

When multiple applications compete for the resources of the same worker, a higher-level layer of coordination is required. DynaSpark introduces distributed supervisors at each worker node to arbitrate between competing local controllers. Each controller reports its desired CPU allocation, and the supervisor applies a contention-resolution strategy whenever cumulative requests exceed available cores. Strategies include earliest-deadline-first (either allocating all or only requested resources to the most urgent application), proportional sharing based on requests, and proportional sharing based on nominal processing rates, which recognizes that some applications benefit more from additional CPU than others. A tunable parameter determines whether supervisors simply honor controller requests or opportunistically saturate all available resources to accelerate execution.

The experimental evaluation confirms the benefits of dynamic control. With homogeneous datasets, deadlines are met with average errors below 3% and, in many cases, below 1%. Even when deadlines are set equal to Spark's fastest achievable execution time, DynaSpark's controllers maintain close tracking with only small violations due to reduced executor overhead. More importantly, resource usage drops dramatically: even with strict deadlines, DynaSpark often uses 10–20% fewer CPU resources than Spark; with relaxed deadlines, savings exceed 50%. Under data skew, Spark suffers from long tails caused by straggling tasks, whereas DynaSpark reassigns CPU cores dynamically to slow executors. Though progress estimation becomes noisier, deadline errors remain acceptable and resource savings increase further. In multi-application scenarios, Spark's FIFO scheduling causes severe deadline violations, while DynaSpark consistently or closely approaches all target deadlines under a variety of contention strategies.

In summary, the work demonstrates an interesting solution for efficient resource management for batch process executions. The solution, based on containers and control theory, can continuously match resources to performance requirements. The result is a system that meets deadlines more reliably, uses fewer resources, and handles concurrency and data variability much more effectively.

7 Conclusions and Future Work

Over the past decade, the center of gravity in software research and industrial innovation has shifted markedly from service-oriented architectures toward Artificial Intelligence (AI), culminating in the rapid rise of agentic AI as the new dominant paradigm. AI has become a pervasive enabling technology in nearly all sectors, and among its emerging directions, agentic AI has gained exceptional momentum in both the industrial and academic spheres. Recent market analyzes estimate that the global agentic AI market will grow from USD 7.06 billion in 2025 to USD 93.20 billion by 2032, representing an extraordinary 44.6% compound annual growth rate [15]. Agentic AI systems comprise coordinated assemblies of heterogeneous computational agents—typically Large Language Models (LLMs) and Small Language Models (SLMs)—that collaborate to solve complex, multi-step tasks. In these systems, an orchestrator must determine not only which agent performs each subtask, but also how that agent is configured, including its inference algorithm and tuning parameters, an ability enabled by test-time computation [25, 26]. In particular, recent evidence shows that appropriately configured small models can outperform large, general-purpose models while consuming dramatically fewer computational and energy resources, further expanding the design space of viable agent configurations.

From a conceptual standpoint, this emerging landscape mirrors, almost one-to-one, the challenges originally addressed in the domain of flexible Web service selection. In both settings, systems must dynamically choose among heterogeneous components—each with different performance profiles, reliability characteristics, and resource demands—to satisfy global constraints involving time, cost, or energy budgets. As in the DISCORSO/MAIS framework, where runtime service binding, QoS guarantees, and continuous monitoring were essential to achieve robust behavior in dynamic environments, agentic AI systems bring an equally stringent set of requirements. Multi-step reasoning pipelines are sequential and delay-sensitive; thus, the weakest-performing step can propagate errors downstream, while resource-intensive choices early in the pipeline may render later steps infeasible under strict latency or energy budgets. Consequently, the selection of agent configurations under test-time compute constraints is fundamentally an optimization problem structurally equivalent to flexible service composition—now transplanted into a far more computationally intensive and rapidly evolving technological context.

Seen through this lens, the trajectory from service-oriented computing to agentic AI does not represent a rupture but rather a continuity of core research themes: dynamic component selection, runtime adaptation, global budget satisfaction, and the orchestration of heterogeneous computational units. What has changed is the scale, complexity, and societal impact of these systems. Whereas early frameworks addressed tens or hundreds of services, contemporary agentic AI systems must navigate vast pools of models, inference algorithms, and parameterized behaviors, operating under tight constraints on execution time, energy consumption, and accuracy propagation. The optimization formulations introduced in [25] spanning max–min robustness, multiplicative accuracy modeling, and resource-constrained configuration selection extend the foundational ideas reported in this chapter into the domain of intelligent, autonomous reasoning systems. As the field continues its rapid expansion, the lessons from flexible service selection offer a principled foundation for designing the next generation of adaptive, efficient, and reliable agentic AI architectures across the computing continuum. And although each of us has followed different research paths over the years, the experience of those years has remained part of our common scientific heritage, shaping how we reason about adaptability and system design.

References

1. Apache Software Foundation. Apache spark (2017). http://spark.apache.org
2. Ardagna, D., Baresi, L., Comai, S., Comuzzi, M., Pernici, B.: A service-based framework for flexible business processes. IEEE Softw. **28**(2), 61–67 (2011)
3. Ardagna, D., Mirandola, R.: Per-flow optimal service selection for web services based processes. J. Syst. Softw. **83**(8), 1512–1523 (2010)
4. Ardagna, D., Pernici, B.: Adaptive service composition in flexible processes. IEEE Trans. Softw. Eng. **33**(6), 369–384 (2007)
5. Baresi, L., Guinea, S.: Self-supervising bpel processes. IEEE Trans. Softw. Eng. **37**(2), 247–263 (2010)
6. Baresi, L., Guinea, S., Leva, A., Quattrocchi, G.: A discrete-time feedback controller for containerized cloud applications. In: Proceedings of the 24th ACM SIGSOFT International Symposium on Foundations of Software Engineering, FSE, pp. 217–228. ACM (2016)
7. Baresi, L., Leva, A., Quattrocchi, G.: Fine-grained dynamic resource allocation for big-data applications. IEEE Trans. Softw. Eng. **47**(8), 1668–1682 (2021)
8. Ceri, S., Fraternali, P., Bongio, A.: Web Modeling Language (WebML): a modeling language for designing Web sites. Comput. Netw. **33**(1), 137–157 (2000)
9. Eshuis, R., Van Gorp, P.: Synthesizing data-centric models from business process models. Computing **98**(4), 345–373 (2016)
10. Hallsteinsen, S., Hinchey, M., Park, S., Schmid, K.: Dynamic software product lines. Computer **41**(4), 93–95 (2008)
11. Hull, R., Damaggio, E., Fournier, F., Gupta, M., (Terry) Heath, F., Hobson, S., Linehan, M., Maradugu, S., Nigam, A., Sukaviriya, P., Vaculin, R.: Introducing the guard-stage-milestone approach for specifying business entity lifecycles. In: Web Services and Formal Methods, pp. 1–24. Springer Berlin Heidelberg (2011)

12. Jouault, F., Allilaire, F., Bézivin, J., Kurtev, I.: ATL: A model transformation tool. Sci. Comput. Program. **72**(1–2), 31–39 (2008)
13. Kiczales, G., Lamping, J., Mendhekar, A., Maeda, C., Lopes, C., Loingtier, J.-M., Irwin, J.: Aspect-oriented programming. In: European Conference on Object-oriented Programming, pp. 220–242. Springer (1997)
14. Krut, R., Cohen, S.: Service-oriented architectures and software product lines-putting both together. In: 2008 12th International Software Product Line Conference, pp. 383. IEEE (2008)
15. Marketsandmarkets. Agentic AI Market (2025)
16. Maurino, A., Mussi, E., Modafferi, S., Pernici, B.: The MAIS framework for composite web services. Int. J. Interoperability Bus. Inf. Syst. **6**, 32–64 (2007)
17. Meroni, G., Baresi, L., Montali, M., Plebani, P.: Multi-party business process compliance monitoring through iot-enabled artifacts. Inf. Syst. **73**, 61–78 (2018)
18. Meyer, A., Weske, M.: Activity-centric and artifact-centric process model roundtrip. In: International Conference on Business Process Management, pp. 167–181. Springer (2013)
19. Standard OASIS. Web services business process execution language version 2.0 (2007). http://wwwoasis-open.org/committees/tc_home.php?wg_abbrev=wsbpel
20. OMG: Business Process Model and Notation (2014). https://www.bpmn.org. Accessed: 11 Dec 2025
21. Plebani, P., Pernici, B.: URBE: Web Service Retrieval Based on Similarity Evaluation. IEEE Trans. Knowl. Data Eng. **21**(11), 1629–1642 (2009)
22. Pohl, K., Böckle, G., Van Der Linden, F.: Software Product Line Engineering: Foundations, Principles, and Techniques, vol. 1. Springer (2005)
23. Sandionigi, C., Ardagna, D., Cugola, G., Ghezzi, C.: Optimizing service selection and allocation in situational computing applications. IEEE Trans. Serv. Comput. **6**(3), 414–428 (2013)
24. Sedghani, H., Ardagna, D., Matteucci, M., Fontana, G.A., Verticale, G., Amarilli, F., Badia, R.M., Lezzi, D., Blanquer, I., Martin, A., Wawruch, K.: Advancing design and runtime management of AI applications with AI-SPRINT (position paper). In: IEEE 45th Annual Computers, Software, and Applications Conference, COMPSAC 2021, Madrid, Spain, July 12–16, 2021, pp. 1455–1462. IEEE (2021)
25. Sedghani, H., Filippini, F., Sadat Seyedi, Z., Spahiu, B., Ciavotta, M., Ardagna, D.: Optimizing agentic AI applications under budget constraints (2025). arXiv:XXXX.YYYYY
26. Snell, C., Lee, J., Xu, K., Kumar, A.: Scaling llm test-time compute optimally can be more effective than scaling model parameters (2024). arXiv:2408.03314
27. Haugen, Ø., Wasowski, A., Czarnecki, K.: Cvl: common variability language. In: Proceedings of the 16th International Software Product Line Conference, vol. 2, pp. 266–267 (2012)

From Adaptive Information Systems to Modern Service Architectures: The Legacy of the MAIS Project

Devis Bianchini, Andrea Maurino, and Enrico Mussi

Abstract The MAIS (Multichannel Adaptive Information Systems) project represents one of the earliest and most comprehensive attempts to reconceptualize services as adaptive, context-aware, and composable entities. Developed in the early 2000s, MAIS anticipated several shifts that later defined modern service-oriented architectures (SOA), cloud-native systems, and adaptive middlewares. This chapter reconstructs the intellectual trajectory of MAIS, outlines its principal methodological and architectural contributions, and situates them within the broader evolution of service modeling. Through the lens of MAIS, we trace a line from UML-based service design and QoS-driven selection to the dynamic, reflective, and context-aware architectures that influence today's microservice ecosystems and service meshes. The chapter analyses the role of the MAIS initiatives in shaping this trajectory and discusses the long-lasting impact of the conceptual tools, modeling approaches, and architectural patterns introduced within the project.

1 Introduction

The early 2000s marked a turning point in the design of distributed information systems. As mobile devices proliferated, network heterogeneity increased, and organizations began exposing functionalities as services, the community faced a rising need for architectures capable of adaptation, quality-aware composition, and context-sensitive delivery [1]. Traditional enterprise systems struggled to manage variability in devices, channels, user preferences, and service-level expectations [2]. Service-

D. Bianchini (✉)
University of Brescia, Brescia, Italy
e-mail: devis.bianchini@unibs.it

A. Maurino
University of Milano Bicocca, Milan, Italy
e-mail: andrea.maurino@unimib.it

E. Mussi
Sense Reply, Turin, Italy
e-mail: e.mussi@reply.it

C. Cappiello et al. (eds.), *Retrospective and Prospective Views on Information Systems Engineering*, https://doi.org/10.1007/978-3-032-19578-4_6

Oriented Architectures (SOA), still in its infancy and mostly tied to Web Services and static orchestration models, needed conceptual and technological innovation to remain adequate for emerging challenges [3].

It is in this context that the MAIS (Multichannel Adaptive Information Systems) project [4] emerged as a landmark initiative in Italy and Europe. Guided by a consortium of researchers from Politecnico di Milano, University of Milano-Bicocca, University of Brescia, University of Roma "La Sapienza", The University of Roma Tre, the University of Lecce, and CEFRIEL, MAIS sought to weave together complementary research threads—requirements engineering, quality-of-service modeling, workflow design, dynamic service selection, and reflective architectures—into a unified framework for adaptive service-based applications [4].

This chapter examines the contribution of MAIS to the modeling of services and to the broader conceptual evolution of service-oriented architectures. Our goal is not to summarize the large amounts of publications that, stemming from the MAIS project, brought novelties in the research field of service-oriented architectures, but to reconstruct the conceptual arc such publications belong to: how MAIS reframed the notion of a "service", how it operationalized adaptation, and how it anticipated several developments that would become mainstream only a decade later. In this sense, we will demonstrate the far-sighted vision of the MAIS project, a push toward integration across layers of abstraction, bridging conceptual modeling with operational concerns, and embracing the complexity of distributed socio-technical systems.

In this chapter, we will provide the vision that forms the basis of the MAIS project, as well as the conceptual foundation that has been built upon this vision. The chapter will also provide an overview of the MAIS methodological contributions, and the principles of the reflective architecture proposed in the project. The final aim of this chapter is to stimulate the discussion about the legacy left behind the MAIS project.

2 The Vision and Context of the MAIS Project

At the time of the MAIS project, service-oriented technologies were rapidly maturing. Standards such as WSDL [5], SOAP [6], and BPEL [7] had begun to formalize interfaces, messaging, and orchestration. Yet, these early technologies shared three major limitations.

- **Lack of adaptivity:** service workflows were largely static; once deployed, changes to channels, devices, or execution conditions could not be incorporated at runtime.
- **Limited treatment of Quality of Service (QoS):** QoS parameters, when modeled at all, were often declarative but not actionable. Few methodologies allowed QoS to influence service selection or adaptation.
- **Minimal consideration of context:** context information—device capabilities, network conditions, user profiles, geographic location—was external to the service ecosystem.

Mobile users, multichannel access, and new wireless technologies made the limitations of classical architectures all too evident. MAIS emerged precisely as an attempt to expand the conceptual model of services so that they could be *context-aware*, *quality-sensitive*, *composable*, and *continuously adaptable* [8]. MAIS researchers' work has consistently bridged organizational process modeling, cooperative information systems, and software architecture, with strong emphasis on model-driven approaches and quality-centric design. The project embraced the belief that: (i) services should be modeled not only through their functionality, but also through their behavioral, contextual, and quality characteristics; (ii) adaptation must be a built-in design concern, not an afterthought; (iii) and the methodology must cover the entire lifecycle, from requirements to runtime governance.

Through MAIS, these principles were not only articulated, but also operationalized in tools, languages, and prototypes.

3 The Conceptual Foundations of Service Modeling in MAIS

MAIS introduced a holistic vision of service modeling that extended far beyond the contemporary SOA practice. Its conceptual foundations can be grouped into four core pillars: *abstract services vs concrete services representation*, *multichannel modeling*, *QoS-driven specifications*, and *context integration*. This holistic vision is reflected in the dual modeling perspective adopted by MAIS, which explicitly distinguishes between the service provider view and the service requester view, as illustrated in Fig. 1a and b. Figure 1a illustrates the conceptual model of an e-service from the service provider's perspective. It identifies the main elements characterizing a service offering, including the provider, the functional description of the service, its exposed operations, input and output parameters, and pre- and post-conditions. The model highlights how these elements are hierarchically organized to describe what the service offers and how it can be invoked, independently of specific execution contexts. Figure 1b depicts the conceptual model of an e-service from the service requester's perspective. It emphasizes how user profile, operational context (e.g., location, device, and network conditions), and quality preferences contribute to the formulation of a service request. Functional and non-functional requirements are integrated in this model to support ontology-based service discovery and QoS-aware service selection.

3.1 Abstract and Concrete Services

One of the conceptual pillars introduced by the MAIS project is the distinction between *abstract* and *concrete services* [9]. Rather than treating a service as a mono-

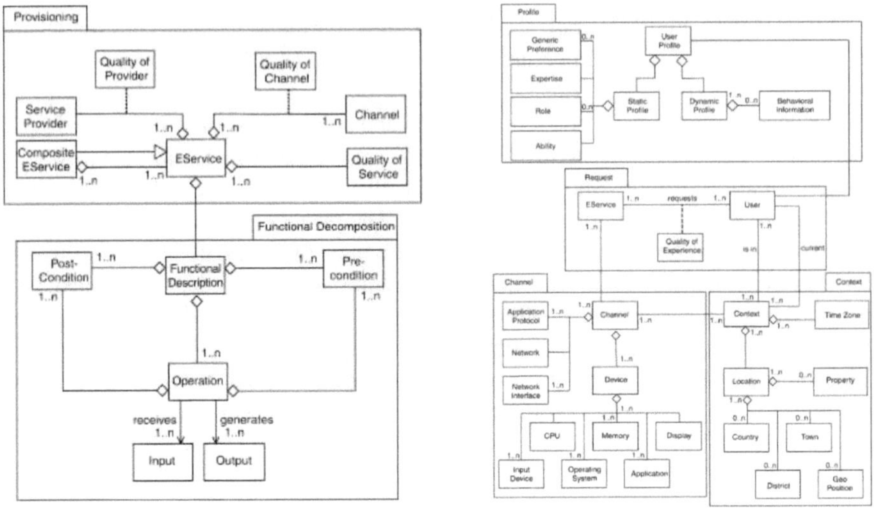

(a) (b)

Fig. 1 Conceptual modeling perspectives in the MAIS framework: **a** service provider perspective, describing the structure and capabilities of an e-service; **b** service requester perspective, capturing user context, preferences, and QoS requirements that drive service discovery and selection

lithic unit defined simultaneously by its interface and its implementation, MAIS proposes to model the two aspects separately:

- **abstract services** capture the essence of a functionality (what the service is supposed to do, which operations it offers, and which quality-of-service characteristics it must satisfy); crucially, they do so without committing to any specific provider, protocol, or technical realization;
- **concrete services**, by contrast, correspond to actual, deployable Web services offered by real providers; these implement the abstract description, but add all the details that matter at execution time—endpoint locations, communication protocols, concrete QoS guarantees, pricing models, and other operational characteristics.

This seemingly simple distinction had far-reaching implications. By decoupling the specification of a service from its implementation, MAIS opened the door to late binding, allowing the choice of which concrete service to invoke to be postponed until runtime. It also made dynamic substitution possible: if a service became unavailable or failed to meet the required QoS levels, another compatible concrete service could take its place without altering the rest of the system. From a more global perspective, the separation provided a natural foundation for optimization-based selection of services, where multiple concrete candidates are evaluated against user goals, QoS constraints, or broker revenue metrics before deciding which one best fits the situation.

Equally important was the role this separation gave to brokers. In MAIS, brokers can negotiate with providers, mediate QoS expectations, and even adjust their choices based on contextual factors or changing user requirements. This transforms service execution from a static, predefined mapping into an ongoing negotiation—an adaptive process responsive to both environment and objectives [10].

Looking back, this modeling strategy anticipated many practices that later became standard in cloud-native ecosystems. Today's service discovery mechanisms, auto-scaling systems, sidecar proxies, and API gateways all rely on the idea that interfaces must remain stable, while implementations evolve dynamically. The abstract-concrete service dichotomy in MAIS captured this insight long before it took hold in mainstream architectures, offering a conceptual blueprint for the decoupled, flexible, and resilient service infrastructures that now define modern distributed systems.

The distinction between abstract and concrete services in MAIS naturally invites comparison with the abstract and concrete layers of the WSDL specification. At first sight, the two pairs appear similar: both introduce a conceptual separation between essential description of a service and its operational realization. Yet, when examined more closely, the purposes they serve and the kinds of knowledge they encapsulate diverge quite profoundly.

Abstract part of the WSDL specification was designed primarily as a way to describe what a Web service "looks like" from an interface perspective (its operations, messages, and data structures), while remaining agnostic with respect to transport protocols or message encodings. This separation was motivated by a desire for portability: the same interface could, in principle, be bound to different protocols or deployed in multiple environments. Its concrete portion then adds the necessary details—bindings and endpoints—to make the service invocable in a specific technological configuration.

MAIS adopts the terms "abstract" and "concrete," but the concepts carry a much broader and more ambitious meaning. An abstract service in MAIS does more than define operations: it expresses the *capability* needed by an application, together with its expected quality levels, constraints, and contextual assumptions. It is deliberately left open with respect to which provider will supply that capability, which communication channel will be used, and even which device or network conditions will be present at runtime. Concrete services, in contrast, correspond to the actual offerings available from providers, complete with QoS guarantees, costs, access protocols, and the contextual factors that influence their execution.

This richer interpretation reflects the fundamental aim of MAIS: not merely to prescribe how a service should be called, but to allow the system to choose *dynamically* among alternative implementations, negotiate their quality, and adapt to variations in context or availability. The distinction is therefore operational, not solely descriptive: it enables late binding, substitution, optimization, and runtime adaptation—capabilities that were simply beyond the scope of WSDL structural design.

A useful way to appreciate this difference is to observe how the two models anticipate different futures. While WSDL laid the technical groundwork for interoperable service invocation, MAIS foreshadowed the adaptive, context-aware architectures that are now central to cloud-native computing. Concepts such as service discovery,

Table 1 Comparison of abstract/concrete concepts in WSDL and MAIS

Aspect	WSDL abstract/concrete	MAIS abstract/concrete
Primary purpose	Structural separation of interface versus binding	Adaptive service design, optimization, substitution
Abstraction level	Technical (operations and protocols)	Conceptual (capabilities, QoS, context, goals)
Runtime behavior	Static binding (usually resolved at deploy time)	Dynamic binding based on QoS, availability, context
QoS modeling	Not part of WSDL abstract interface	Core part of abstract service definition
Context awareness	None	Explicitly modeled and used for selection
Service substitution	Not directly supported	Fundamental mechanism (compatibility classes)
Negotiation with providers	Out of scope	Built-in to MAIS runtime logic

policy-driven routing, autoscaling, and the decoupling of interfaces from implementations, today embedded in service meshes and API gateways, are philosophically aligned with the MAIS notion of abstract and concrete services. The project articulated this vision long before such mechanisms became mainstream.

Table 1 summarizes the key differences between the two interpretations. In summary, while both WSDL and MAIS use a two-level representation of services, the similarity is superficial. WSDL abstraction is syntactic and structural: it describes *how* a service can be invoked once chosen. MAIS abstraction, instead, is semantic and dynamic: it describes *what capability is needed* and leaves open *which implementation will best satisfy that need under current conditions*.

Multichannel Service Modeling

Another particularly innovative aspect of the MAIS vision was the decision to elevate channels—the combination of devices, networks, protocols, and interfaces through which a service is accessed—to the status of first-class elements in service modeling. In the provisioning perspective defined by the project, services were not conceived as abstract functionalities floating above the technological landscape; rather, each service was explicitly linked to the specific channels on which it could be delivered. This simple, but powerful shift repositioned the execution environment as an intrinsic part of the service itself, not a technical footnote [11].

This perspective was groundbreaking at a time when the digital ecosystem was becoming increasingly heterogeneous. The variety of devices available to users was rapidly expanding: PDAs, early mobile phones, laptops, and embedded systems offered vastly different interaction modalities and computational capabilities. A service that behaved elegantly on a desktop browser could become unwieldy or even unusable on a small mobile screen. MAIS recognized that these differences were not mere implementation wrinkles, but factors that fundamentally shaped how a service should be presented, how it should behave, and what level of quality it could realistically guarantee. Content, interaction patterns, and even the service's overall business logic might need to adapt depending on the capabilities and limitations of the device in use.

Equally challenging was the variability inherent in the networks connecting these devices. During the early 2000s, connectivity spanned a patchwork of evolving standards—GPRS, UMTS, WiFi—each exhibiting different bandwidth profiles, latency characteristics, and reliability constraints. For many services, especially those requiring timely delivery or rich content, these differences directly influenced whether QoS requirements could be met. MAIS confronted this head-on by making network characteristics part of the formal service description, acknowledging that the feasibility and quality of service delivery depend as much on the communication substrate as on the service's own implementation.

By treating channels as a core modeling dimension, MAIS anticipated a conceptual evolution that would later become central in edge computing and multi-access architectures. Today, we routinely expect services to modulate their behavior depending on where they run, which network they traverse, and how resource-constrained the client device may be. Adaptive streaming protocols, multi-access edge computing platforms, and device-aware APIs all embody principles that MAIS articulated well before they became mainstream. The project's insight—that the service must adapt to the environment, and not the other way around—remains one of its most enduring contributions.

3.2 Quality of Service as a Modeling Construct

Another major contribution of the MAIS project was its comprehensive treatment of Quality of Service (QoS) as a central, structuring element in the design and operation of service-based systems. Rather than relegating QoS to a peripheral annotation or a deployment-time concern, MAIS approached it as a first-class modeling construct—something that should permeate every phase of the lifecycle, from high-level conceptualization to runtime adaptation [12].

To make this possible, the project introduced a *QoS registry*, a structured vocabulary of quality dimensions and metrics that could be consistently applied across services, channels, and user contexts. This registry served as the foundation for a coherent integration of QoS attributes into several methodological components. In the *UML models* extended by the project, QoS descriptors appeared alongside functional specifications, ensuring that quality expectations were captured early and explicitly in the design.

These attributes then played a central role in *negotiation procedures*, where users, providers, and brokers could express and reconcile their respective objectives. QoS also fed directly into *service selection algorithms*, allowing the system to choose among alternative concrete services on the basis of measurable performance, cost, or reliability characteristics rather than relying on static bindings or developer intuition.

At runtime, QoS assumptions influenced *workflow adaptation rules*, which determined whether a channel switch, a service substitution, or a renegotiation should occur when conditions changed. Even the *reflective middleware* developed within MAIS depended on QoS metrics to observe system state, trigger adaptations, and manage trade-offs between user satisfaction and resource consumption.

What emerges from this integrated treatment is a vision of QoS not as an afterthought, but as a guiding principle. Dimensions such as availability, performance, cost, reliability, and usability were not simply recorded as descriptive metadata; they shaped the structure of services, informed the behavior of the runtime platform, and ultimately determined how the system responded to evolving contexts. By elevating QoS to this level of prominence, the MAIS project anticipated many of the concerns that would later dominate cloud computing, SLA-driven architectures, and autonomic systems. It also underscored a deeper insight: in adaptive service ecosystems, *quality is as fundamental as functionality*.

3.3 Modeling Context: Location, Device, Network, User Profile

Equally transformative was the way in which MAIS modeled the *request* side of service interaction. The project moved well beyond the simplistic notion of a user as a static endpoint issuing service calls. Instead, it developed an elaborate, multidimensional representation of *user context*, capturing details that had rarely been treated systematically in service-oriented models at the time [13].

This perspective embraced the idea that a user's situation is shaped not only by who they are, but also by where they are and *under what conditions* they seek to access a service. Thus, MAIS incorporated *geographic and temporal context*, recognizing that location, time zones, and mobility patterns fundamentally influence which services can be reached or offered effectively.

It also gave careful attention to *device and network capabilities*, acknowledging that the quality and form of service delivery depend heavily on the processing power, display characteristics, communication interfaces, and connectivity available to the user. A PDA connected over GPRS and a laptop on a WiFi network may request the same logical service, yet the experience—and feasibility—of delivering that service can differ dramatically.

In addition, the request perspective modeled *user profiles, preferences, and expertise*, enabling the system to adapt its behavior not just to technical constraints, but also to human ones. Preferences could shape quality negotiations, interaction flows, or service variants, while expertise levels could determine how much guidance or simplification was needed in the user interface or process structure.

MAIS went even further by incorporating *available and fallback channels*, anticipating situations where the currently used channel might degrade or fail. The framework allowed the system to reason about alternative ways of reaching the user, supporting seamless transitions between channels as conditions evolved. Finally, the notion of *service priority and urgency* introduced a semantic layer that could influence routing, scheduling, or adaptation strategies—an especially valuable feature for mobile and safety-critical scenarios.

This nuanced decomposition of user context was highly innovative, and its influence can be seen in a wide range of later research. Context-aware middleware, pervasive and ubiquitous computing frameworks, adaptive human-computer interaction systems, and mobile user modeling all draw on principles that MAIS helped articulate: that context is multifaceted, dynamic, and deeply consequential for how services should be designed, selected, and delivered.

4 Methodological Contributions of the MAIS Framework

A unified lifecycle for service engineering. One of the most remarkable achievements of the MAIS project lies in the completeness of its methodological vision. At a time when research on service-oriented systems often addressed isolated phases of the lifecycle—focusing either on design methods, or on runtime composition, or on Quality-of-Service issues—MAIS brought these elements together into a coherent end-to-end framework. The project proposed a lifecycle that extended seamlessly from the earliest conceptual stages to the fine-grained decisions taken at runtime [15].

Requirements analysis Within this lifecycle, requirements analysis played a pivotal role. It was here that functional and non-functional requirements, user goals, and service-level expectations were first articulated, not as abstract desiderata, but as concrete drivers shaping the subsequent modeling process.

Design phase The design phase then operationalized these requirements by introducing extensions to UML capable of capturing abstract services, QoS constraints, user profiles, and the multi-channel characteristics that distinguished MAIS from other contemporary approaches.

Deployment During deployment, the framework supported the transformation of high-level service descriptions into executable artifacts. This included partitioning workflows across distributed engines, generating variants of BPEL specifications, and mapping conceptual models to the actual infrastructures in which services would run.

Run-time execution Finally, the run-time use and negotiation phase brought the adaptive capabilities of MAIS into full view. Here, dynamic service selection, QoS renegotiation, revenue evaluation between broker and providers, and context-sensitive adaptation came together to ensure that services remained aligned with both system conditions and user expectations.

This holistic vision, spanning the entire lifecycle, was unusual at the time and remains rare even today. Few projects have attempted to integrate conceptual modeling, formal optimization, architectural reflection, and runtime adaptation within a single methodological framework.

Enhanced UML for service design. Central to the MAIS methodology was the enhancement of UML as a modeling language for services. Instead of relying solely on UML's traditional constructs, the project enriched the language with concepts that captured the dynamic and adaptive nature of service-based systems.

Among these were *Abstract Interaction Units*, which provided a structured way to represent user-service interactions independently of specific devices or channels; *QoS annotations*, aligned with the evolving OMG profiles, which made quality properties an explicit part of model semantics; and *context and adaptation specifications*, enabling designers to embed contextual variability directly into the system blueprint.

Through these extensions, MAIS positioned itself as a precursor to later forms of model-driven development for services. Many of the ideas introduced here—such as variability modeling, capability-based design, and architecture-level QoS annotations—would later resurface in Web Service modeling frameworks, domain-specific languages, and architecture description languages.

QoS-driven optimization and negotiation. Another area where MAIS broke new ground was its rigorous formalization of service selection. Rather than relying on simple rules or heuristics, the project framed the problem as a *Mixed-Integer Linear Programming (MILP)* optimization task. This allowed service selection to incorporate complex constraints and trade-offs, including QoS requirements, costs, and performance expectations. But the innovation did not stop there. MAIS also introduced:

- formal negotiation protocols between brokers and providers;
- utility functions capable of balancing broker revenue with user satisfaction;
- dynamic cost-benefit analyses to determine when improving QoS would be worthwhile.

These ideas anticipated many mechanisms that would later become central in cloud and service ecosystems: from SLA negotiation frameworks used by cloud providers, to the elastic resource allocation algorithms that underpin today's scalable infrastructures, to the pricing models that drive modern service marketplaces.

Workflow partitioning for mobility and distribution. In addressing mobility and device heterogeneity, MAIS recognized that traditional, centralized *workflow execution models* were insufficient. The project developed a set of workflow partitioning rules that could transform a monolithic workflow into a collection of federated workflows distributed across multiple engines.

These transformations relied on *graph-transformation systems*, a formal approach that ensured both confluence and termination while preserving the semantics of the original workflow. This meant that workflows could be decomposed intelligently, with different portions executed on different devices or nodes, depending on their capabilities and roles.

Such an approach anticipated modern distributed orchestration frameworks, including those used in IoT ecosystems, mobile workflows, and container-native process engines. Even today, the idea of decomposing and distributing workflow execution to better exploit heterogeneous environments remains an active area of research and practice.

Adaptation rules for runtime evolution. Perhaps the most distinctly adaptive aspect of MAIS was its rule-based mechanism for runtime evolution. The project devised an event-condition-action system that allowed workflows to respond dynamically to changes in the environment.

Events could be triggered by: (a) degradation of QoS; (b) channel failure; (c) shifts in user or system context; (d) service unavailability. When such events occurred, the system could invoke a variety of adaptive actions, including: (i) switching channels; (ii) substituting one service for another; (iii) suspending parts of a workflow; (iv) renegotiating QoS with providers.

These mechanisms foreshadowed many of the principles later embodied in autonomic computing, self-healing architectures, and modern service meshes. Systems like Envoy and Istio, for example, perform traffic shifting and routing adjustments based on policies that are conceptually similar to MAIS's event-driven adaptation rules.

5 The Reflective Architecture

MAIS embodied its modeling and methodological innovations in a reflective runtime architecture [16], which stands as one of the project's most visionary and enduring contributions. While many contemporary systems treated runtime execution as a fixed interpretation of design-time decisions, MAIS imagined an architectural substrate capable of observing, reasoning about, and modifying its own behavior as conditions evolved. This commitment to reflection was not an add-on, but a natural extension of the project's broader goal: to create service ecosystems that could adapt gracefully to variability in context, QoS, and user needs.

Reflection as a middleware principle. At the heart of this architecture were *reflective objects (R_Objects)*, specialized entities designed to expose both the functional characteristics of a component and the non-functional qualities associated with its execution. Through these objects, the system could not only *observe* QoS attributes—

such as performance or availability—but could also *modify* them when appropriate, adjusting configurations or reallocating resources to meet changing demands. The architecture further provided mechanisms to *aggregate or decompose* QoS information (through mapUp and mapDown functions), allowing the system to understand quality at multiple levels: from individual devices to composite services.

This reliance on *computational reflection* consistently emphasized the importance of making system internals explicit, observable, and controllable. Reflection in MAIS was not merely theoretical; it served as a practical foundation for adaptivity, enabling the middleware to react autonomously to deviations in context or quality.

Multi-layered reflection. MAIS advanced this reflective approach by articulating a *multi-layered architecture* that separated low-level concerns from higher-level abstractions. The *Base Reflective Layer* was tied directly to the physical and infrastructural components of the system—devices, operating systems, networks—and provided fine-grained visibility into their capabilities and current conditions. Above it, the *Extended Reflective Layer* consolidated these observations, combining and abstracting QoS properties so that they could be meaningfully interpreted by applications and service composition mechanisms.

This layering was essential because it allowed the system to treat context not as an amorphous collection of sensor readings or metadata, but as a structured entity with well-defined relationships. By mediating between the concrete realities of the infrastructure and the conceptual models used at the application level, MAIS created a coherent pathway through which adaptations could be planned and executed. This architecture foreshadowed later developments in context-aware middleware and autonomic computing.

Integration with service selection and composition. The power of the reflective architecture became most evident when integrated with MAIS mechanisms for *service selection and composition* [14]. Reflection enabled the system to perform *dynamic evaluation of QoS*, constantly assessing whether the services selected at design time or earlier runtime phases continued to meet user expectations and system constraints. It also made it possible to enforce *global QoS constraints*, ensuring that the behavior of composite services adhered to overarching quality objectives.

Whenever these constraints were at risk, the reflective layer facilitated the *optimal recomposition of services*, identifying alternative implementations or channels capable of delivering the required performance. Moreover, the same mechanisms supported *negotiation with providers*, enabling the broker to engage in informed trade-offs between cost, quality, and availability based on real-time data.

In effect, the reflective architecture served as the *nervous system* of MAIS—constantly monitoring, interpreting, and coordinating the various components that made adaptive behavior possible. Through reflection, MAIS transcended the conventional boundaries of service-oriented systems, offering an anticipatory glimpse into the autonomic and self-aware architectures that would emerge in the following decade.

6 Historical Impact and Lesson Learned

Looking back at the MAIS project from the vantage point of today's service ecosystems, it becomes clear that its contributions were not merely incremental, but profoundly anticipatory. MAIS emerged at a moment when service-oriented computing was still consolidating its foundations, yet the project was already exploring ideas that would only enter mainstream practice many years later. Its impact spans conceptual, methodological, architectural, and community dimensions, leaving a legacy that continues to resonate in contemporary research and industrial practice.

Influence on Service-Oriented Computing. MAIS early recognition of the importance of flexibility and adaptivity placed it ahead of much of the service-oriented computing landscape of its time. Concepts that are now considered essential in cloud-native and distributed systems (late binding, dynamic service discovery, QoS-aware composition, context-awareness, and runtime adaptation) were explicitly studied, modeled, and operationalized within MAIS long before they became widespread.

The project treated services not as static endpoints, but as dynamic, contextual, and negotiable entities. Its work on adaptive selection and QoS-driven behavior laid the groundwork for later research on Web Service selection algorithms, pervasive computing frameworks, autonomic systems, and self-healing architectures. From today's perspective, MAIS stands as one of the earliest efforts to articulate what would later be called adaptive service ecosystems.

Contribution to Model-Driven Engineering. Another area in which MAIS left a significant mark is model-driven engineering. By integrating UML with QoS annotations, context models, and abstract service descriptions, the project inspired new research on model-driven service engineering and variability modeling. The methodology's emphasis on transformation—from conceptual models to service orchestration artifacts—prefigured practices that later became common in BPMN extensions, SysML extensions for service modeling, and domain-specific languages. This model-driven line of research remains active and influential. Many current tools and modeling frameworks for service-based and cyber-physical systems incorporate ideas that trace directly back to the representational strategies pioneered within MAIS.

About Cloud and Microservice Architectures. Perhaps the most striking aspect of MAIS's legacy is its intellectual continuity with the architectures that dominate today's cloud-native landscape. Even though the project preceded cloud computing's rise, it implicitly anticipated many of its defining characteristics: contract-based interfaces, dynamic selection of implementations, adaptive routing, runtime negotiation, infrastructural observability, and distributed orchestration. Table 2 illustrates this continuity by juxtaposing some of MAIS key conceptual innovations with their modern counterparts in cloud and microservice ecosystems.

This alignment is not coincidental. Many of the mechanisms that underpin today's highly dynamic, observable, and scalable distributed systems embody principles that

Table 2 Some of MAIS key conceptual innovations and their modern counterparts in cloud and microservice ecosystems

MAIS concept	Later cloud/microservice equivalent
Abstract versus concrete service	API contracts versus deployable microservices
Broker-based optimization	Service registries, load balancers
QoS negotiation	SLA frameworks in cloud providers
Adaptation rules	Resilience patterns, circuit breakers
Reflective middleware	Sidecar proxies, service meshes
Workflow partitioning	Distributed orchestration (e.g., Temporal, Zeebe)

MAIS articulated more than a decade earlier. The project's reflective architecture, in particular, anticipated the shift toward runtime introspection, policy-driven adaptation, and programmable control planes that now characterize service meshes.

Impact on the research community. Beyond its technical innovations, MAIS left a lasting imprint on the research community itself. It generated over a decade of sustained research, inspired collaborations across Italian and international institutions, and contributed to methodological and architectural standards. Perhaps most importantly, it helped educate a generation of researchers who would go on to shape the fields of service modeling, adaptive middleware, and distributed systems.

Impact on the industrial community. Industrial community has also benefit from the results of MAIS project as many of its contributors, including students who elaborated MAIS concepts in their master thesis, are now successful professionals who work in software areas where service modeling, QoS, and context awareness are pivotal (e.g., cloud computing, IoT)

Lessons learned for modern service modeling. Reflecting on MAIS also offers a set of enduring lessons—principles that remain relevant as service ecosystems grow increasingly complex, heterogeneous, and context-dependent.

- **Services are socio-technical entities.** They exist within a web of users, devices, networks, and organizations, and their behavior must be understood in this full socio-technical context.
- **Adaptation must be designed deliberately.** Systems become adaptive not by accident, but through explicit modeling of variability, the definition of policies and rules, and the presence of architectures capable of enacting change.
- **Quality of Service is fundamental.** Real-world service ecosystems cannot operate on functional correctness alone; performance, availability, reliability, and cost must be tightly integrated into both design and operation.

- **Context matters.** Modern distributed systems, from IoT platforms to edge computing infrastructures, continue to confront the same contextual variability that MAIS addressed head-on.
- **Abstraction enables flexibility.** The separation between abstract and concrete services is now a cornerstone of microservices and API-driven development, validating MAIS's early insight.
- **Runtime is as important as design time.** In dynamic environments, decisions about service selection, negotiation, and adaptation cannot be frozen at deployment; they must evolve continuously.

Together, these lessons reveal why MAIS remains a touchstone in the history of adaptive service systems. It did not merely contribute to existing paradigms—it helped shape the conceptual vocabulary that would define the generations of service architecture that followed.

7 Conclusions

The MAIS project represents a moment in the history of service-oriented computing, where bold conceptual integration occurred. It unified modeling, architecture, optimization, and context-awareness in a way that foreshadowed many later developments. Model-driven design, quality-aware systems, and adaptive architectures provided not only the scientific foundations of MAIS, but also a broader research philosophy: that dealing with complexity requires both rigorous formalism and deep awareness of real-world contexts.

As we look at today's service ecosystems (cloud-native platforms, microservices, IoT infrastructures, edge computing environments), we can trace conceptual lineages back to the ideas articulated and refined in MAIS. This chapter has attempted to reconstruct that lineage, discussing the main impacts left by researchers of the MAIS project on the service-oriented architectures.

Acknowledgements The authors wish to thank all researchers and collaborators of the MAIS Project for their significant contributions. Their collective effort across the involved institutions, as documented in the MAIS project book [4], has been essential to the ideas and perspectives presented in this chapter.

References

1. Papazoglou, M.P., van den Heuvel, W.-J.: Service-oriented architectures: approaches, technologies and research issues. VLDB J. **16**, 389–415 (2007). https://doi.org/10.1007/s00778-007-0044-3
2. Kjaer, K.E.: A survey of context-aware middleware. In: Proceedings of the 25th Conference on IASTED International Multi-Conference: Software Engineering, pp. 148–155 (2007)

3. Alonso, G., Casati, F., Kuno, H., Machiraju, V. (eds.): Web Services: Concepts. Architectures and Applications. Springer, Berlin Heidelberg (2004)
4. Pernici, B. (Ed.): Mobile Information systems. Lecture Notes in Computer Science (LNCS 3855). Springer Berlin Heidelberg (2006). https://doi.org/10.1007/3-540-31008-8
5. Christensen, E., Curbera, F., Meredith, G., Weerawarana, S.: Web Services Description Language (WSDL) 1.1, W3C Note, NOTE-wsdl-20010315, World Wide Web Consortium (2001). https://www.w3.org/TR/2001/NOTE-wsdl-20010315
6. Gudgin, M., Hadley, M., Mendelsohn, N., Moreau, J., Frystyk, H.: SOAP Version 1.2 Part 1: Messaging Framework, 2nd edn.. W3C Recommendation, REC-soap12-part1-20070427. World Wide Web Consortium (2007). https://www.w3.org/TR/soap12-part1/
7. Alves, A., Arkin, A., Geng, X., et al.: Web Services Business Process Execution Language Version 2.0 (WS-BPEL 2.0). OASIS Standard, OASIS-WSBPEL-V2.0. Organization for the Advancement of Structured Information Standards, April 11 (2007). https://docs.oasis-open.org/wsbpel/2.0/OS/wsbpel-v2.0-OS.html
8. Baresi, L., Bianchini, D., De Antonellis, V., Fugini, M.G., Pernici, B., Plebani, P.: Context-aware composition of e-services. In: Proceedings of the 4th International Workshop on Technologies for E-Services (TES 2003), Berlin, Germany, pp. 28–41, September 8 (2003)
9. Bianchini, D., De Antonellis, V., Pernici, B., Plebani, P.: Ontology-based methodology for e-service discovery. Inf. Syst. **31**(4–5), 361–380 (2006)
10. Menascé, D.A., Dubey, V.K.: Utility-based QoS brokering in service oriented architectures. In: Proceedings of the 4th International Conference on Service-Oriented Computing (ICSOC), Chicago, IL, USA, pp. 248–253, December 4–7 (2006)
11. Adorni, M., Arcelli, F., Ardagna, A., Baresi, L., Batini, C., Cappiello, C., Comerio, M., Comuzzi, M., De Paoli, F., Francalanci, C., Losi, P., Grega, S., Maurino, A., Modafferi, S., Pernici, B., Raibulet, C., Tisato, F.: The MAIS approach to web service design. In: Proceedings of the 10th International Workshop on Exploring Modeling Methods for Systems Analysis and Design (EMMSAD 2005), Porto, Portugal, June 13–14, pp. 1–12 (2005)
12. Kritikos, K., Pernici, B., Plebani, P., Cappiello, C., Comuzzi, M., Benbernou, S., Brandic, I., Kertész, A., Parkin, M., Carro, M.: A survey on service quality description. ACM Comput. Survey **46**(1), 1:1–1:58 (2013)
13. Plebani, P., Cappiello, C., Comuzzi, M., Pernici, B., Yadav, S.: MicroMAIS: executing and orchestrating Web services on constrained mobile devices. Softw. Pract. Exper. **42**(9), 1075–1094 (2012)
14. Calvanese, D., De Giacomo, G., Lenzerini, M., Mecella, M., Patrizi, F.: Automatic Service Composition and Synthesis: the Roman Model. IEEE Data Engineering Bull. **31**(3), 18–22 (2008)
15. Mussi, E., Maurino, A., Modafferi, S., Pernici, B.: Configuring and executing adaptive service-oriented applications. In: Proceedings of the 4th International Conference on Service-Oriented Computing (ICSOC), Chicago, IL, USA, pp. 248–253, December 4–7 (2006)
16. Maurino, A., Modafferi, S., Pernici, B.: Reflective architectures for adaptive information systems. In: Proceedings of the First International Conference on Service Oriented Computing (ICSOC), Trento, Italy (2003)

Barbara Pernici and the Evolution of BPM: From the Early BPM Conferences to Today's Research and Practice

Fabio Casati and Mathias Weske

Abstract In the early 2000s, Business Process Management (BPM) was still finding its identity. After the founding conference, the BPM 2004 conference in Potsdam and the BPM 2005 conference in Nancy were decisive moments: they framed BPM as a discipline that combines process modeling and analysis, service-oriented architectures, and data-driven analysis, not just formal verification and workflow automation. BPM 2004 was edited by PC Co-Chairs Jörg Desel, Barbara Pernici, and Mathias Weske, while BPM 2005 was edited by Wil van der Aalst, Boualem Benatallah, Fabio Casati, and Francisco Curbera. Later reflections on "A Decade of BPM Conferences" explicitly recognize these volumes as formative for the field's research agenda. Barbara was very important in this development. From that starting point, Barbara's own research has consistently pushed BPM toward quality-aware, adaptive, and sustainable information systems—ideas that are now standard in both research and industry.

1 Setting the Agenda

As PC Co-Chair of BPM 2004, Pernici helped curate a program that made three bold statements about what BPM should be. First, it made explicit process models the central artefact to represent behaviour in information systems. The proceedings emphasise formal and goal-oriented business process modeling, including work on semantics of process notations and domain-specific process models. This line feeds directly into the notion of process-aware information systems, where systems are

F. Casati
Servicenow, Zurich, Switzerland
e-mail: fabio.casati@servicenow.com

University of Trento, Trento, Italy

M. Weske (✉)
Hasso Plattner Institut, University of Potsdam, Potsdam, Germany
e-mail: mathias.weske@hpi.de

C. Cappiello et al. (eds.), *Retrospective and Prospective Views on Information Systems Engineering*, https://doi.org/10.1007/978-3-032-19578-4_7

designed around executable process models, as codified in the influential textbooks by Weske [7] and Dumas et al. [5].

Second, BPM 2004 elevated process mining from a curiosity to a core research direction, with papers on mining process models and social networks from event logs. Today's process mining tools and the broader movement toward data-driven process analysis trace a straight line back to that decision to give process mining its own dedicated space. Third, the conference gave serious attention to process evolution and quality, including work on structural conflicts between process types and running instances, and cohesion/coupling metrics for workflow designs—early, influential steps toward treating processes like high-quality software artefacts rather than static flowcharts. This agenda resonates with foundational work on workflow evolution by Casati, Ceri, Pernici, and Pozzi [4], which formalised how running workflow instances can be migrated when schemata change.

The proceedings of BPM 2005, edited by PC Co-Chairs van der Aalst, Benatallah, Casati and Curbera, built on this foundation and pushed harder into service-oriented and formally grounded BPM. The proceedings highlight formal semantics for workflow patterns, transformations from BPEL to Petri nets, and service interaction patterns—work that underpins today's soundness checking, model-checking, and execution semantics for BPMN in commercial tools. Just as important, BPM 2005 introduced a stronger industrial program and co-located workshops, signalling that BPM was not merely an academic niche but a discipline with growing impact on real-world information systems.

From this Desel–Pernici–Weske/van der Aalst-Casati era, BPM emerges as a field that blends process modeling, process analysis, process mining, and service computing. Against that backdrop, Barbara Pernici's own technical contributions start to define how BPM systems should behave under real-world constraints.

2 Quality of Service and Optimisation

One of Pernici's most influential BPM-related papers is "Global and Local QoS Guarantee in Web Service Selection" (with Danilo Ardagna), published in the BPM 2005 Workshops [2]. This work tackles a problem that industry was only beginning to articulate: if a business process is implemented as a composition of web services, how do we guarantee end-to-end quality of service (QoS)—such as latency, availability, and cost—while choosing among many possible providers?

Their answer is elegant and powerful: they formulate service selection as a mixed-integer linear programming problem that simultaneously enforces local QoS constraints on individual services and global constraints on the entire process.

In practice, this line of work helped shifting BPM thinking from "Will the process run?" to "Will the process deliver the promised level of service?" Modern orchestration and workflow platforms that integrate service level agreements (SLA), cost-performance trade-offs, or automatic choice among service providers are, conceptually, walking the path that Pernici helped lay out.

3 Self-Healing BPM

Pernici then pushes the idea one step further: if we can express QoS objectives formally, systems should not only select services optimally but also repair themselves when things go wrong. In "Self-healing Systems and Web Services: The WS-Diamond Approach", presented at the BPM 2008 Workshops [6], she introduces an architecture for self-healing, QoS-aware web-service-based systems.

WS-Diamond includes monitoring, diagnosis, and automatic recovery strategies, closing the loop between design-time QoS models and runtime adaptation. Instead of viewing a process as a fixed script, it is treated as a managed, adaptive entity that can rebind services, switch paths, or trigger compensations in response to failures and degradations. This anticipates today's language of autonomic computing, self-healing microservice orchestrations, and resilient BPM: concepts like circuit breakers, dynamic re-routing, and automated failover in process-aware systems sit squarely in the space she helped define.

In the broader BPM narrative, this turns processes from static blueprints into living systems. Combined with the early BPM conferences' focus on formal models and process mining, Pernici's work contributes to a vision in which processes are specified, analysed, monitored, and automatically adjusted—a lifecycle now familiar in both research and industrial BPM platforms.

4 Energy-Aware and Sustainable Processes

Long before "Green IT" became a mainstream slogan, Barbara Pernici was pushing BPM research toward energy-aware, sustainable process design. In work such as "Active Energy-Aware Management of Business-Process Based Applications" [1] and "First-Step toward Energy-Aware Adaptive Business Processes" [3], she and her co-authors propose frameworks where business processes are designed and managed with explicit consideration of energy consumption and environmental impact, alongside performance and QoS.

These papers extend the optimisation and adaptation ideas from her earlier QoS work into a new dimension: processes and services carry annotations for energy costs; resource allocation and service selection become multi-objective optimisation problems balancing QoS, cost, and energy. The vision is prescient: in a world now concerned with data-centre energy, carbon footprints, and sustainable digital transformation, BPM is increasingly asked not only to make work fast and reliable but also responsible. Contemporary research on Green BPM and energy-aware process optimisation explicitly cites these contributions as early, foundational work.

5 From Early BPM to Today's Research and Practice

If we follow the thread from BPM 2004 and 2005 to today, three continuities stand out. And in all three, Barbara Pernici's influence is clearly visible:

- *Process-aware, analyzable systems.* The early conferences established that BPM would stand on rigorous models, formal semantics, and process mining. Pernici's editing of BPM 2004 helped crystallise that agenda, and her later work shows how those models can be used at runtime to manage QoS, energy consumption, and resilience.
- *Quality- and contract-driven BPM.* By treating QoS and SLAs as first-class elements in service composition, her research helped move BPM beyond control-flow toward contract-aware processes that are optimised and monitored against explicit objectives. Today's enterprise BPM suites and cloud workflow engines routinely integrate SLA dashboards, optimisation policies, and adaptive routing inspired by that thinking.
- *Adaptive, sustainable process-centric infrastructures.* Her work on self-healing and energy-aware processes positioned BPM at the intersection of autonomic computing and sustainability well before those themes became mainstream. The current push toward resilient, green, and data-driven BPM—both in research and industry—stands on ground she helped prepare.

Taken together, the trajectory from the BPM 2004 Desel–Pernici–Weske and the BPM 2005 van der Aalst–Benatallah–Casati–Curbera conference volumes to today's BPM landscape is not just a story of the field maturing. It is also a story of Barbara Pernici's consistent vision: that business processes should be not only formally well-founded, but also trusted to meet their promises, capable of healing themselves, and mindful of the resources they consume. That vision has quietly but powerfully shaped how BPM is taught, researched, and implemented in industry today—and it is exactly what makes her work so worth celebrating.

References

1. Ardagna, D., Cappiello, C., Lovera, M., Pernici, B., Tanelli, M.: Active energy-aware management of business-process based applications. In: Towards a Service-Based Internet. ServiceWave 2008, Lecture Notes in Computer Science, vol. 5377, pp. 183–195. Springer (2008)
2. Ardagna, D., Pernici, B.: Global and local QoS guarantee in web service selection. In: Business Process Management Workshops, Lecture Notes in Computer Science, vol. 3812, pp. 32–46. Springer (2006)
3. Cappiello, C., Fugini, M.G., Gangadharan, G.R., Ferreira, A.M., Pernici, B., Plebani, P.: First-step toward energy-aware adaptive business processes. In: On the Move to Meaningful Internet Systems: OTM 2010 Workshops, Lecture Notes in Computer Science, vol. 6428, pp. 6–7. Springer (2010)
4. Casati, F., Ceri, S., Pernici, B., Pozzi, G.: Workflow evolution. Data & Knowl. Eng. **24**(3), 211–238 (1998)

5. Dumas, M., Rosa, M.L., Mendling, J., Reijers, H.A.: Fundamentals of Business Process Management, 2nd edn. Springer (2018)
6. Pernici, B.: Self-healing systems and web services: the WS-Diamond approach. In: Business Process Management Workshops, Lecture Notes in Business Information Processing, vol. 17, pp. 440–442. Springer (2009)
7. Weske, M.: Business Process Management: Concepts, Languages, Architectures, 4th edn. Springer, Berlin, Heidelberg (2024)

Vanilla-Converter: A Tool for Converting Camunda 7 BPMN Models into Camunda 8 Models

Dragana Sunaric, Charlotte Verbruggen, Dominik Bork, and Gerti Kappel

Abstract As modeling languages evolve, so do modeling tools. Sometimes this evolution comes with compatibility issues, challenging organizations to co-evolve models created with previous tool versions to remain valid and usable in the new editor. Currently, organizations need to prepare for the end-of-life of Camunda 7, a widely used BPMN modeling tool in practice. Since manual model migration remains complex and prone to error due to fundamental differences between the two platforms, automated model migration would be a huge benefit. In this chapter, we present *Vanilla-Converter*, a command-line tool that facilitates the migration of BPMN models from Camunda 7 to Camunda 8. Vanilla-Converter automates the transformation process, supports a wide range of BPMN elements, and produces a transformed model and a detailed transformation log indicating automatic changes and remaining manual tasks. The tool's effectiveness is demonstrated through three case studies with real industrially used Camunda 7 models, confirming its ability to convert these models into valid and executable Camunda 8 models.

1 Introduction

As information systems are constantly evolving, it is important to maintain the corresponding models to avoid loss of information and rework. Castano et al. [11] present a set of techniques for the classification and analysis of schemas, with the aim to

D. Sunaric · D. Bork (✉) · G. Kappel
TU Wien, Vienna, Austria
e-mail: dominik.bork@tuwien.ac.at

D. Sunaric
e-mail: dsunaric@gmx.at

G. Kappel
e-mail: gerti@big.tuwien.ac.at

C. Verbruggen
TU Wien, Business Informatics Group, Vienna, Austria
e-mail: charlotte.verbruggen@tuwien.ac.at

C. Cappiello et al. (eds.), *Retrospective and Prospective Views on Information Systems Engineering*, https://doi.org/10.1007/978-3-032-19578-4_8

address challenges such as schema reuse and analysis of legacy systems. Additionally, reuse of existing models or model fragments supports quality and consistency while reducing modeling effort. Casati et al. [10] present a method for workflow development that leverages model reuse and includes strategies for mapping activity diagrams to commercial workflow systems. In the domain of model evolution, researchers investigate how to handle existing instances of models as the models evolve. Casati et al. [9] present an approach for handling evolution of workflow schemas.

In the field of business process automation, BPMN has established itself as the de facto standard [12, 15]. Enterprises benefit from using a tool like Camunda [3] to execute and control processes modeled using BPMN [13]. Although BPMN is widely accepted, tool-specific variants and extensions of the standard are common [6, 19]. This is particularly relevant in the context of the announced end-of-life for Camunda 7 in 2030 [1], which is driving many organizations to migrate to Camunda 8.

The migration from Camunda 7 to Camunda 8 presents a significant challenge due to the fundamental architectural and operational differences between the two platforms. Camunda 7 is a monolithic, thread-based workflow engine typically embedded within Java applications, whereas Camunda 8 is a cloud-native, distributed system built on Zeebe, relying on external workers and event-driven execution semantics [4]. While some open-source initiatives, such as VanillaBP [5], attempt to promote engine-agnostic BPMN modeling through architectural patterns like hexagonal architecture, tooling specifically focused on automating the migration from Camunda 7 to Camunda 8 remains scarce. A further complication arises from the fact that, despite both versions relying on the BPMN standard for process definitions, each version extends the standard with incompatible, engine-specific elements. As a result, direct reuse of Camunda 7 models in Camunda 8 is not possible, forcing organizations to find ways to migrate their existing models.

Building on the goals of the VanillaBP [5] initiative, this chapter presents a command-line tool designed to bridge the gap between Camunda 7 and Camunda 8 by automating the transformation of BPMN models. The tool facilitates a more efficient and error-free migration process, reducing manual effort, enhancing model consistency across platforms, and supporting model reuse.

In the remainder of this chapter, we will first introduce the Vanilla-Converter tool in Sect. 2, focusing on the mapping between the Camunda 7 and Camunda 8 model representations. The extensive evaluation with real industrial models is discussed in Sect. 3. A discussion in Sect. 4 and concluding remarks in Sect. 5 wrap up this chapter.

2 Vanilla-Converter Overview

Vanilla-Converter is a command-line application designed to transform Camunda 7 BPMN models into corresponding models that are compatible with Camunda 8. It processes Camunda 7 `.bpmn` files, applies a set of transformation rules, and outputs

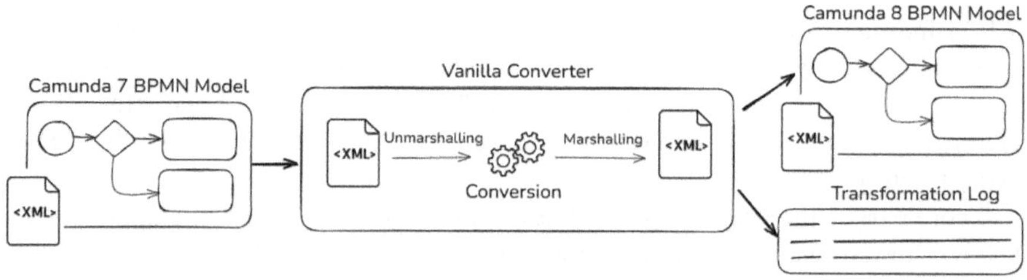

Fig. 1 Overview of the Vanilla-Converter model transformation

updated models suitable for use with Camunda 8. Alongside the converted model, the tool generates a detailed transformation log that documents which elements were automatically converted and highlights remaining manual tasks for elements that require user intervention. Figure 1 shows an high-level overview of the tool.

2.1 *Usage*

The Vanilla-Converter is operated through a simple command-line interface. Users can convert either a single BPMN file or batch-convert all BPMN files within a specified directory:

- To transform a single BPMN file:

```
java -jar vanilla-transformer.jar /path/to/your/file.bpmn
```

- To transform all BPMN files in a directory:

```
java -jar vanilla-transformer.jar /path/to/your/
    files
```

The tool stores transformed BPMN files by appending the suffix `-transformed` to the original filenames and saving them in the same directory as the input files. During execution of the transformation, a detailed transformation log is produced, documenting both the automatically applied changes and any remaining manual tasks. This log is output to the console and persisted in the file `logs/transformation.log` for further inspection.

2.2 *Transformation and Mapping Table*

The Vanilla-Converter accepts Camunda 7 `.bpmn` files as input and processes them directly at the XML level. To enable structured access and manipulation, the BPMN XML is unmarshalled into a Java object graph using JAXB (Java Architecture for

XML Binding). Although both Camunda 7 and Camunda 8 provide model APIs for working with BPMN files, these APIs are not compatible across versions and therefore cannot be used for transformation. As a result, our tool performs all conversions by operating on JAXB-generated classes that directly mirror the BPMN XML structure.

A core part of the project involved developing custom XML Schema Definitions (XSDs)[1] for the Camunda 7 and Camunda 8 BPMN dialects. Because Camunda does not publish official schemas [14], these XSDs were constructed manually based on the documentation and the structure of BPMN files exported by each system. They provide the foundation for unmarshalling, validating, and processing BPMN models.

The transformation logic is implemented as a depth-first traversal of the BPMN XML tree. During this traversal, each Camunda 7 element is mapped to its Camunda 8 counterpart. The following excerpts illustrate typical mappings performed by the converter. A comprehensive mapping table documenting the supported element conversions is provided in the project's GitHub repository [18].

Example 1: Mapping Service Tasks Service Tasks using a `camunda:delegateExpression` in Camunda 7 are translated into Camunda 8 job worker definitions. The converter extracts the delegate expression and embeds it as a `zeebe:taskDefinition` type in the transformed model:

```
<bpmn:serviceTask id="Service-Task-2"
    name="DelegateExpression"
    camunda:delegateExpression="${SomeDelegateExpression}">
</bpmn:serviceTask>
```

Listing 1 Camunda 7 Service Task using a delegate expression

```
<bpmn:serviceTask name="DelegateExpression" id="Service-Task-2"
    >
    <bpmn:extensionElements>
        <zeebe:taskDefinition type="SomeDelegateExpression"/>
    </bpmn:extensionElements>
</bpmn:serviceTask>
```

Listing 2 Converted Camunda 8 Service Task with job worker definition

Example 2: Mapping Conditional Sequence Flows Camunda 7 allows conditions on sequence flows to be expressed using JUEL *e.g.*, `$false`. Camunda 8, however, requires FEEL expressions, which use a leading = instead of JUEL syntax. The converter rewrites such expressions accordingly:

```
<bpmn:sequenceFlow id="Flow_1" sourceRef="src" targetRef="
    target">
    <bpmn:conditionExpression xsi:type="bpmn:tFormalExpression"
    >
    ${false}
     </bpmn:conditionExpression>
</bpmn:sequenceFlow>
```

Listing 3 Camunda 7 conditional sequence flow using JUEL

```
<bpmn:sequenceFlow id="Flow_1" sourceRef="src" targetRef="target"
    >
    <bpmn:conditionExpression xsi:type="bpmn:tFormalExpression">
```

[1] The custom XML Schema Definitions created in this project are available in the projects GitHub repository at https://github.com/dsunaric/vanilla-converter/tree/main/src/main/resources/schema.

```
        =false
    </bpmn:conditionExpression>
</bpmn:sequenceFlow>
```

Listing 4 Converted Camunda 8 conditional sequence flow using FEEL

Example 3: Mapping Multi-Instance Loop Characteristics Multi-instance constructs in Camunda 7 rely on the `camunda:collection` and `camunda:elementVariable` attributes. Camunda 8 replaces these with a `zeebe:loopCharacteristics` extension element. The converter performs this structural mapping automatically:

```
<bpmn:multiInstanceLoopCharacteristics
    camunda:asyncBefore="true"
    camunda:collection="${collection}"
    camunda:elementVariable="${element}"
    isSequential="true"/>
```

Listing 5 Camunda 7 sequential multi-instance configuration

```
<bpmn:multiInstanceLoopCharacteristics isSequential="true">
    <bpmn:extensionElements>
        <zeebe:loopCharacteristics
            inputCollection="= collection"
            inputElement="element"/>
    </bpmn:extensionElements>
</bpmn:multiInstanceLoopCharacteristics>
```

Listing 6 Camunda 8 equivalent multi-instance configuration

Once the transformation is complete, the modified Java object graph is marshalled back into a valid Camunda 8 BPMN file using JAXB. The resulting model is syntactically well-formed and fully compatible with the Camunda 8 engine.

2.3 Transformation Log

As part of the transformation process, Vanilla-Converter generates a detailed transformation log that provides transparency and traceability for each applied transformation. This log documents both the automated transformations performed by the tool and any remaining manual tasks that must be addressed by the user. These manual tasks are necessary not only to achieve syntactic compatibility with Camunda 8, but also to ensure the resulting process model is fully executable and semantically valid within a real-world application context. Additionally, the log includes optional suggestions for further disambiguating or improving the model in Camunda 8.

The transformation proceeds hierarchically, traversing the BPMN model from outer to inner elements, similar to a depth-first traversal of a tree. The log reflects this traversal structure, making it easier for users to understand the transformation context of nested elements.

The log output uses the following standardized messages:

- *MAPPING* indicates that the transformation of a specific BPMN element has begun.
- *FINISHED MAPPING:* marks the successful completion of an element mapping.
- *NO MAPPING NEEDED:* denotes elements that are structurally and semantically compatible between Camunda 7 and Camunda 8 and therefore do not require transformation.
- *TODO* flags elements where manual intervention is required to complete the migration. These tasks are typically essential for the correct execution of the model in Camunda 8.
- *TODO (OPTIONAL)* highlights optional tasks where user action may improve the model or resolve potential ambiguities but may not be strictly required.

An excerpt from a representative transformation log is shown below:

```
MAPPING: bpmn:event with id=Event_0j8p
MAPPING: bpmn:throwEvent with id=Event_0j8p
MAPPING: bpmn:eventDefinition with id=
    MessageEventDefinition_1nr2ae9
TODO: manually configure Jobworker for Message Event Definition
     with id=MessageEventDefinition_1nr2ae9
FINISHED MAPPING: bpmn:eventDefinition with id=
    MessageEventDefinition_1nr2ae9
MAPPING: bpmn:delegateExpression configureJobType into zeebe:
    taskDefinition
MAPPING: camunda:expression configureJobType into FEEL
    Expression Language
TODO (OPTIONAL): set retries=?? in zeebe:taskDefinition Element
TODO (OPTIONAL): adapt zeebe:taskDefinition type for Event with
     id=Event_0j8p to select correct JobWorker
FINISHED MAPPING: bpmn:throwEvent with id=Event_0j8p
FINISHED MAPPING: bpmn:event with id=Event_0j8p
```

This structured output enables users to quickly identify which parts of the model have been successfully transformed and which require manual completion, thereby supporting a more reliable and efficient migration process.

2.4 Supported BPMN Elements

The Vanilla-Converter supports the majority of BPMN elements that are commonly used in executable Camunda 7 process models. In terms of tasks, the converter fully handles Service Tasks, Send Tasks, User Tasks, Receive Tasks, Manual Tasks, and Business Rule Tasks. Gateway support includes Exclusive, Parallel, Inclusive, and Event-Based Gateways, all of which can be translated into their Camunda 8 equivalents without requiring manual adjustments. Among higher-level control-flow constructs, Embedded Subprocesses, Event Subprocesses, and Call Activities are supported, as are the Sequential and Parallel Multi-Instance Markers and the Compensation Marker. These elements map cleanly to Camunda 8 and can therefore be transformed automatically.

Table 1 Overview of the BPMN modeling language concepts and their support in the Vanilla-Converter tool. The notation is as follows: ✓ indicates support, ✗ indicates lack of support, ○ marks elements that Camunda 8 does not implement, and "–" denotes constructs that are not part of the BPMN standard

Type	Start			Intermediate			End	
	Normal	Event sub process	Event sub process non-interrupt	Catch	Boundary	Boundary non-interrupt	Throw	Normal
None	✓	–	–	–	–	–	–	✓
Message	✓	✓	✓	✓	✓	✓	✓	–
Timer	✓	✓	✓	✓	✓	✓	–	–
Conditional	○	○	○	○	○	○	–	–
Link	–	–	–	✓	–	–	✓	–
Signal	✓	✓	✓	✓	✓	✓	✓	✓
Error	–	✓	–	–	✓	–	–	✓
Escalation	–	✓	✓	–	✓	✓	✓	✓
Termination	–	–	–	–	–	–	–	✓
Compensation	–	✗	–	–	✓	–	–	✓
Cancel	–	–	–	–	○	–	–	○
Multiple	○	○	○	○	○	○	○	○
Multiple parallel	○	○	○	○	○	○	○	○

A small number of elements are not yet handled by the converter itself. Currently, the Script Task is the only BPMN element that remains unsupported.

In addition to tool limitations, several BPMN constructs cannot be executed by Camunda 8 at all and must therefore be refactored or removed during migration. These include the Complex Gateway, the non-multi-instance Loop Marker, Transaction Subprocesses, and the Ad-Hoc Marker (the latter being introduced only in Camunda 8.7 and not available in earlier engine versions such as 8.6 used in this evaluation) [2]. Although these constructs are valid within the BPMN 2.0 standard, Camunda 8 does not yet provide execution semantics for them.

A detailed overview of supported and unsupported BPMN event types is provided in Table 1. The table distinguishes between elements that are directly supported by the converter, elements unsupported by Camunda 8, and constructs that do not exist in the BPMN 2.0 specification.

When encountering BPMN elements that have been deprecated or are no longer supported in Camunda 8—such as Conditional Events or Cancel Events—the tool identifies them during transformation and logs a corresponding warning. This ensures that modelers are made aware of semantic gaps introduced by the platform change.

3 Evaluation

To assess the effectiveness and practical applicability of the Vanilla-Converter, we conducted an evaluation based on two real-world BPMN process models from different application domains. These cases allow us to examine how well the tool handles a broad spectrum of Camunda 7 modeling constructs, how accurately it produces Camunda 8–compatible models, and to what extent manual intervention remains necessary.

3.1 Case Study 1: Taxiride Blueprint

The first case study is based on the TaxiRide Blueprint process model [17] from the VanillaBP [5] ecosystem. The TaxiRide Blueprint is designed to be executable on both Camunda 7 and Camunda 8 using the same Spring Boot implementation, which makes it a suitable benchmark for evaluating the correctness of model migration. The objective of this case study is to convert the provided Camunda 7 process model[2] included in the project. Figure 2 shows the graphical representation of the original Camunda 7 process.

Process Description and Model Characteristics

The original process consists of two swimlanes: one representing the Taxi Service, which contains all executable logic, and a Customer swimlane, which serves only as a descriptive perspective without any technical execution semantics. As this case study focuses on the behavior of the workflow engine, the analysis is restricted to the executable Taxi Service lane.

The Camunda 7 version of the process model contains a representative variety of BPMN constructs that together form a meaningful benchmark for migration. The executable part of the model includes one *Start Event*, six *End Events* (four none end events, two message end events), six *Service Tasks*, one *User Tasks*, two *Boundary Events* (both interrupting), one *Intermediate Event*, one *Subprocess*, and three *Multi-Instance Markers*.

These elements reflect typical workflow patterns used in service orchestration, including job worker invocation, exception handling through boundary events, multi-instance execution, and message-based interaction. As such, the TaxiRide process provides a suitable foundation for assessing how well the Vanilla-Converter transformation tool maps Camunda 7 modeling constructs and engine-specific extensions into their Camunda 8 equivalents.

---

[2] TaxiRide Blueprint Camunda 7 BPMN model available at https://github.com/dsunaric/vanilla-converter/blob/main/src/main/resources/examples/taxiride-blueprint/TaxiRide-c7.bpmn.

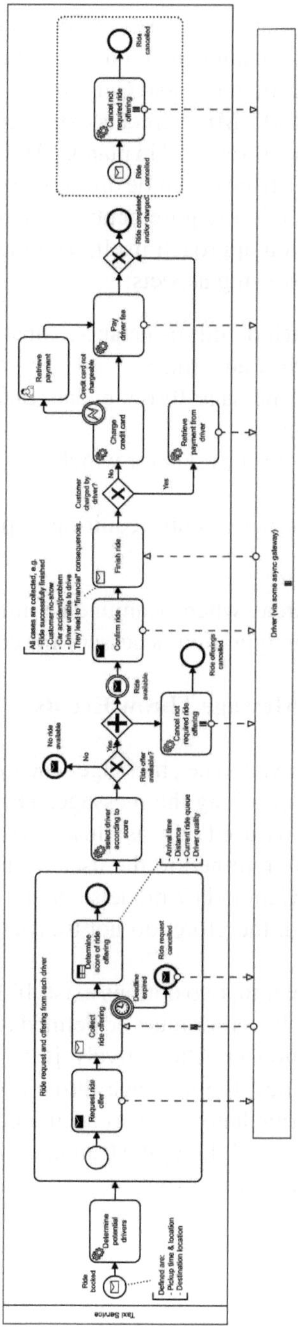

Fig. 2 TaxiRide Blueprint Camunda 7 process model. A high-resolution version of the model is available at GitHub

Conversion Outcome

The transformation log shows that the majority of BPMN elements could be mapped automatically without requiring manual intervention, indicating a high degree of syntactic compatibility between Camunda 7 and Camunda 8. In total, the converter processed and attempted to map 130 XML elements extracted from the original `.bpmn` file. Out of these, only 10 elements resulted in manual TODOs that require user input. These TODOs stem exclusively from semantic differences between the two workflow engines—such as stricter execution requirements in Camunda 8—rather than from limitations of the transformation approach itself. The manual TODOs identified in this case study concern the following aspects:

- **Multi-Instance Configuration**: multi-instance constructs that require explicit input and output mappings in Camunda 8.
- **Job Worker Assignment**: message throw events that must be associated with explicitly defined job workers.
- **Error Code Specification**: error events for which a proper `errorCode` must be configured manually.
- **Message Correlation**: message events requiring explicit correlation keys (see Sect. 3.2).

These TODOs highlight areas where Camunda 8 introduces stricter execution semantics, making explicit configuration necessary for correct runtime behavior.

Job Worker Definitions for Message Throw Events

In Camunda 8, message throw events (i.e., message send events) require an associated job worker responsible for dispatching the message. This differs from Camunda 7, where such events are frequently used only as illustrative markers intended to signal that a message is conceptually returned to the user, without any executable implementation. As a result, many Camunda 7 models contain message throw events that have no operational effect and, therefore, do not translate directly into Camunda 8 semantics.

To ensure a valid transformation, two options exist: If the event is intended to trigger actual execution logic, a job worker must be defined for the message throw event in the Camunda 8 model (Option 1). Alternatively, if the event is purely descriptive and has no executable semantics, the message throw event should be transformed into a none end or none intermediate event to accurately reflect its intended non-functional role (Option 2). Listing 7 shows the Camunda 7 representation of the *Ride available* intermediate message throw event.

```
<bpmn:intermediateThrowEvent id="Event_0j8pq10" name="Ride
    available">
    [...]
    <bpmn:messageEventDefinition id="
    MessageEventDefinition_1nr2ae9" messageRef="Message_0oj1z6"
    />
</bpmn:intermediateThrowEvent>
```

Listing 7 Camunda 7 intermediate message throw event for “Ride available”.

In the predefined Camunda 8 model included in the TaxiRide Blueprint project, this event has no executable meaning and is therefore represented as a none intermediate throw event (Option 2). This version is shown in Listing 8.

```
<bpmn:intermediateThrowEvent id="Event_0j8pql0" name="Ride&#10;
    available">
    [...]
</bpmn:intermediateThrowEvent>
```

Listing 8 Predefined Camunda 8 representation of the “Ride available” throw event (none event).

Since the Vanilla-Converter aims to preserve the original semantics as closely as possible, it does not automatically simplify message events into none events. Instead, it keeps the message throw event and introduces a placeholder job worker configuration, as shown in Listing 9. This ensures that the resulting model is syntactically valid while explicitly highlighting the need for manual clarification.

```
<bpmn:intermediateThrowEvent name="Ride&#10;available" id="
    Event_0j8pql0">
    <bpmn:extensionElements>
        <zeebe:taskDefinition type="configureJobType"/>
    </bpmn:extensionElements>
    [...]
    <bpmn:messageEventDefinition xmlns="" MessageRef="
    Message_0oj12z6" d="MessageEventDefinition_1nr2ae9"/>
</bpmn:intermediateThrowEvent>
```

Listing 9 Converted Camunda 8 version of the “Ride available” message throw event with placeholder job worker.

The transformation log further indicates this unresolved configuration, as shown in Listing 10. The converter explicitly generates a TODO reminding the modeler to define a suitable job worker or to reconsider the event’s semantics (line 3 in Listing 10).

```
1 MAPPING: bpmn:event with id=Event_0j8pql0
2 [...]
3 TODO: manually configure Jobworker for Message Throw Event with
    id MessageEventDefinition_1nr2ae9
4 [...]
5 FINISHED MAPPING: bpmn:throwEvent with id=Event_0j8pql0
```

Listing 10 Transformation log entry for the “Ride available” message throw event.

This example illustrates a typical manual task in the transformation process: determining whether a message throw event requires executable logic in Camunda 8 or whether it should be simplified to a none event to reflect its conceptual purpose.

Multi-Instance Loop Characteristics

The Vanilla-Converter supports the transformation of multi-instance loop characteristics as long as the Camunda 7 model specifies both an input collection and an element variable. These two attributes are essential, as they define how individual iterations of a multi-instance activity are parameterized during execution.

Listing 11 shows a typical Camunda 7 representation of a `multi-instance loop` element. The corresponding Camunda 8 version generated by the converter is shown in Listing 12. In simple cases—such as the one illustrated here—Camunda 7 and Camunda 8 use structurally similar XML representations, allowing the conversion to be largely straightforward.

```
<bpmn:multiInstanceLoopCharacteristics camunda:asyncBefore="true"
     camunda:collection="${collection}" camunda:elementVariable="
    ${element}" isSequential="false" />
```

Listing 11 Camunda 7 multi-instance loop XML representation

```
<bpmn:multiInstanceLoopCharacteristics isSequential=" false">
    <bpmn:extensionElements>
      <zeebe:loopCharacteristics inputCollection="= collection"
    inputElement="element" />
    </bpmn:extensionElements>
</bpmn:multiInstanceLoopCharacteristics>
```

Listing 12 Camunda 8 multi-instance loop XML representation generated by the converter

In the TaxiRide Blueprint case study, however, the predefined Camunda 8 model uses additional input parameters to populate the loop variables and iteration context. These parameters are not explicitly contained in the Camunda 7 model and therefore cannot be inferred automatically. As a result, manual adjustments may be required after conversion to correctly configure the input collection, element variable, and related loop parameters so that the multi-instance behavior matches the intended execution semantics of the original model.

This highlights a common migration consideration: while multi-instance constructs may appear syntactically similar across engine versions, their operational semantics—particularly regarding variable scoping and iteration metadata—may still require manual refinement.

Error Code Configuration

Camunda 7 allows error events to reference a BPMN error definition without specifying an explicit error code, as the engine tolerates missing codes and often resolves errors based on exception types or error messages at runtime. In Camunda 8, however, every BPMN error must define a concrete `errorCode`, which serves as the routing key for matching thrown errors to boundary events and subprocess error handlers [7].

In the TaxiRide Blueprint case study, the original Camunda 7 model defines the error *CreditCardCannotBeCharged* without an error code, as shown in Listing 13.

```
<bpmn:error id="Error_1qhp7a3" name="CreditCardCannotBeCharged" /
    >
```

Listing 13 Camunda 7 error definition without an error code.

The predefined Camunda 8 model uses the name of the error element as an error code (Listing 14).

```
<bpmn:error id="Error_1qhp7a3" name="CreditCardCannotCharged"
    errorCode="CreditCardCannotCharged" />
```

Listing 14 Predefined Camunda 8 model with error element as error code.

During transformation, the Vanilla-Converter inserts a placeholder `errorCode` (Listing 15), along with a corresponding TODO in the transformation log (Listing 16).

```
<bpmn:error name="CreditCardCannotBeCharged" errorCode="
    AddErrorCode" id="Error_1qhp7a3"/>
```

Listing 15 Vanilla-Converter created Camunda 8 model with a TODO 'AddErrorCode' to define an error element.

```
MAPPING: bpmn:error with id=Error_1qhp7a3
TODO: set correct Error Code for bpmn:error with id=Error_1qhp7a3
FINISHED MAPPING: bpmn:error with id=Error_1qhp7a3
```

Listing 16 Vanilla-Converter transformation log TODO to define a correct error code.

Since the correct error code cannot be inferred automatically, the modeler must specify an appropriate value to ensure that error-handling behavior in the transformed Camunda 8 model aligns with the intended semantics of the original process.

Results

Overall, the conversion of the TaxiRide Blueprint process demonstrated that the majority of Camunda 7 modeling constructs can be transformed into Camunda 8 equivalents without requiring manual intervention. The Vanilla-Converter successfully mapped service tasks, gateways, receive tasks, and most event types in a fully automated manner. Some manual TODOs emerged, which stem from stricter execution semantics introduced by Camunda 8 rather than shortcomings of the converter. The transformed models remained structurally valid, with TODO markers transparently indicating where user input is needed to complete the semantic configuration.

3.2 *Case Study 2: Migration of the ELMO Process Landscape*

This case study examines the applicability of the Vanilla-Converter to ELMO, an open-source system designed to coordinate regional social transport services using electric vehicles [16]. ELMO comprises a heterogeneous process landscape spanning three operational domains—Passenger Service, Car Sharing, and Member Management—each reflecting distinct aspects of the system's logistics and customer lifecycle.

Process Landscape

Across all domains, the ELMO process landscape comprises 10 BPMN models, totaling 229 elements. These models feature a broad range of BPMN constructs: 20 start events, 34 end events, 16 service tasks, 26 intermediate catch events, 10 intermediate throw events, five user tasks, 29 send tasks, 15 boundary events, seven call activities, 10 subprocesses, two multi-instance markers, and 28 gateways of various types.

For each model, the Vanilla-Converter was applied to transform the Camunda 7 BPMN definitions into Camunda 8–compatible equivalents. The conversion succeeded for all processes without producing any BPMN validation errors or warnings, confirming that the generated BPMN is structurally valid and executable in Camunda 8.

Conversion Output

An examination of the transformation logs revealed that the majority of BPMN elements were mapped automatically without requiring user intervention. Across all processes in this case study, the converter processed a total of 708 XML elements extracted from the original BPMN models and identified 38 TODOs which are primarily related to missing correlation keys for message events.

Message Correlation in Camunda 7 and Camunda 8

In Camunda 7, message correlation is often performed implicitly using only the message name, allowing the engine to match incoming messages without requiring additional routing information. In contrast, Camunda 8 requires every message to define an explicit correlation key (i.e., an identifier), which is used as a process variable to unambiguously route messages to the correct process instance [8]. Since correlation keys are optional in Camunda 7 but mandatory in Camunda 8, any message event that lacks such a key in the original model must be assigned one during the transformation. Listing 17 shows how a message element is represented in Camunda 7 and Listing 18 how the Vanilla-Converter transforms it into a Camunda 8-compliant element. In the process *car-in-use.bpmn*, the original Camunda 7 model defines a message using only an identifier and a name.

```
<!-- Camunda 7 message definition -->
<bpmn:message id="Message_3utn1jd" name="CarUsageExtended" />
```

Listing 17 Camunda 7 message in the ELMO `car-in-use.bpmn` process.

Since Camunda 8 requires every message to explicitly define a correlation key, the Vanilla-Converter augments the message with a `zeebe:subscription` element that declares such a key.

```
<!-- Transformed Camunda 8 message definition -->
<bpmn:message name="CarUsageExtended" id="Message_3utn1jd">
    <bpmn:extensionElements>
        <zeebe:subscription correlationKey="AddCorrelationKey"/>
    </bpmn:extensionElements>
</bpmn:message>
```

Listing 18 Camunda 8 message in the ELMO `car-in-use.bpmn` process.

Importantly, as shown in Listing 19 the corresponding boundary event that references this message does not require any structural transformation, as the BPMN representation of boundary message events is syntactically compatible between Camunda 7 and Camunda 8.

```
<!-- Boundary event using the message (identical in C7 and C8) --
    >
<bpmn:boundaryEvent xmlns="" attachedToRef="Activity_14376hh"
name="end of usage was extended by driver" id="Event_16qiev5">
<bpmn:outgoing>Flow_1u3kuwg</bpmn:outgoing>
<bpmn:messageEventDefinition messageRef="Message_3utn1jd" id="
    MessageEventDefinition_0j8pw4q"/> </bpmn:boundaryEvent>
```

Listing 19 Boundary event in the ELMO `car-in-use.`bpmn process.

Results

This example highlights the nature of the manual TODOs identified by the converter: the structural mismatch arises not in the event itself but in the message definition it relies on. As Camunda 7 does not enforce explicit correlation semantics, message elements may lack the necessary information for correct execution in Camunda 8. The converter, therefore, flags such cases, ensuring that correlation keys are introduced where needed to preserve unambiguous message routing.

Overall, the ELMO case study demonstrates that the Vanilla-Converter can successfully transform a complex, multi-domain process environment into valid Camunda 8 models with minimal manual effort. The absence of structural errors, combined with the interpretability and relevance of the TODOs, confirms the tool's maturity and practical viability for organizations preparing large-scale migrations of legacy Camunda 7 process landscapes.

4 Discussion

The current implementation of the converter is limited to unidirectional transformations from Camunda 7 to Camunda 8. Supporting reverse transformations (i.e., from Camunda 8 back to Camunda 7) or even enabling interoperability between other BPMN-based workflow engines such as Activiti remains an open challenge. A key obstacle is the fact that different workflow engines often interpret and extend the BPMN standard in proprietary ways, resulting in compatibility issues during model transformation. A promising direction for future research is to conduct a systematic analysis and comparison of BPMN extensions across major process engines. Such an effort could inform the development of a unified extension framework or modeling profile that accommodates engine-specific requirements while preserving core BPMN semantics. This would promote greater interoperability and foster a more engine-agnostic approach to BPMN-based process modeling.

5 Conclusion

In this chapter, we introduced Vanilla-Converter, an open-source command-line tool for automatically converting BPMN models in Camunda 7 format into equivalent Camunda 8 models. The maturity of the tool was evaluated using two case studies that demonstrated the validity of the transformations. The remaining TODOs flagged in the transformation log stem mostly from the fact that Camunda 8 enforces stricter execution semantics than Camunda 7. The tool facilitates the transition to the latest Camunda version by automating the transformation steps and clearly listing TODOs in the transformation log, including both required manual interventions and suggestions for further model improvement. The source code for the Vanilla-Converter and all details on the mapping between the two Camunda versions, as well as the case studies performed, are available at https://github.com/dsunaric/vanilla-converter. A demo video showing how the tool works is available at https://youtu.be/tLOUjrNbE0w.

Acknowledgements It was in 1989 when Barbara and I met the first time, myself being a postdoc fellow in the group of Dennis Tsichritzis at the University of Geneva, Barbara being a visiting professor in Dennis' group. Looking back, it feels somewhat prehistoric—Dennis had built up the very first research group on object-oriented system development in Europe, and both "girls" having a background in office information systems and database modeling, wanted to learn more about this new research branch. There has been a mutual understanding and appreciation from the outset, evident in both hours-long professional discussions and even longer hiking tours in the Alps. Since then, we have followed our different scientific paths, but the rare touchpoints have always felt like "coming home". Barbara, my coauthors and myself, we wish you all the best for the next adventures ahead of you.—Gerti Kappel

References

1. Camunda 7 enterprise end of life (eol) extension announcement. https://camunda.com/blog/2025/02/camunda-7-enterprise-end-of-life-extension/ (n.d.). Accessed 17 May 2025
2. Camunda 8 - bpmn coverage. https://docs.camunda.io/docs/components/modeler/bpmn/bpmn-coverage/ (n.d.). Accessed 17 May 2025
3. Camunda bpm. https://camunda.com/ (n.d.). Accessed 17 May 2025
4. Migrate from camunda 7 - conceptual differences. https://docs.camunda.io/docs/guides/migrating-from-camunda-7/conceptual-differences/ (n.d.). Accessed 17 May 2025
5. Vanillabp. https://www.vanillabp.io/ (n.d.). Accessed 17 May 2025
6. Braun, R., Esswein, W.: Classification of domain-specific bpmn extensions. In: Frank, U., Loucopoulos, P., Pastor, Ó., Petrounias, I. (eds.) The Practice of Enterprise Modeling, pp. 42–57. Springer, Berlin Heidelberg, Berlin, Heidelberg (2014)
7. Camunda Services GmbH: Error events — defining the error (2025). URL https://docs.camunda.io/docs/components/modeler/bpmn/error-events/#defining-the-error. Camunda 8 Documentation. Accessed 15 Dec 2025
8. Camunda Services GmbH: Message events — message correlation (2025). URL https://docs.camunda.io/docs/components/modeler/bpmn/message-events/#message-correlation. Camunda 8 Documentation. Accessed 15 Dec 2025

9. Casati, F., Ceri, S., Pernici, B., Pozzi, G.: Workflow evolution. Data & Knowl. Eng. **24**(3), 211–238 (1998). https://doi.org/10.1016/S0169-023X(97)00033-5. https://www.sciencedirect.com/science/article/pii/S0169023X97000335. ER '96
10. Casati, F., Grazia Fugini, M., Mirbel, I., Pernici, B.: Wires: A methodology for developing workflow applications. Requir. Eng. **7**(2), 73–106 (2002). https://doi.org/10.1007/s007660200006
11. Castano, S., De Antonellis, V., Fugini, M.G., Pernici, B.: Conceptual schema analysis: techniques and applications. ACM Trans. Database Syst. **23**(3), 286–333 (1998). https://doi.org/10.1145/293910.293150
12. Chinosi, M., Trombetta, A.: Bpmn: An introduction to the standard. Comput. Stand. & Inter. **34**(1), 124–134 (2012). https://doi.org/10.1016/j.csi.2011.06.002. https://www.sciencedirect.com/science/article/pii/S0920548911000766
13. David, G., Zmaranda, D.R., Györödi, R.S., Györödi, C.A.: Exploring the impact of workflow engines on business process management in enterprise applications. a case-study: Camunda. In: 2023 17th International Conference on Engineering of Modern Electric Systems (EMES), pp. 1–4 (2023). https://doi.org/10.1109/EMES58375.2023.10171706
14. kurtinaitis: No correct schema for camunda extension bpmn elements. https://github.com/camunda/camunda-modeler/issues/1972 (2020). GitHub issue #1972, camunda/camunda-modeler (closed)
15. Object Management Group: Business process model and notation (bpmn) version 2.0. Tech. Rep. formal/2011-01-03, Object Management Group (OMG) (2011). https://www.omg.org/spec/BPMN/2.0. Accessed 17 May 2025
16. Pelikan, S.: Elmo (2024). https://github.com/stephanpelikan/elmo. Accessed 17 May 2025
17. Pelikan, S.: Taxi ride blueprint for business-processing (micro)services (2024). https://github.com/phactum/taxiride-blueprint. Accessed 17 May 2025
18. Sunaric, D.: Vanilla converter (2025). https://github.com/dsunaric/vanilla-converter
19. Zarour, K., Benmerzoug, D., Guermouche, N., Drira, K.: A systematic literature review on bpmn extensions. Business Proc. Manag. J. **26**(6), 1473–1503 (2020). https://doi.org/10.1108/BPMJ-01-2019-0040

Quality Control Model for the Crowdsourced Task of Vulnerability Discovery

Mortada Al-Banna, Carlos Rodríguez, Boualem Benatallah, and Moshe Chai Barukh

1 Introduction

There is an increasing attention to crowdsourcing vulnerability discovery. For instance, governments are adopting this approach including US Department of Defense[1] and Singapore's Ministry of Defense,[2] large corporations including Google, Facebook and Microsoft.[3] The growing importance of crowdsourced vulnerability discovery[4] indicates that developing quality solutions is a top priority [68, 132].

Research on quality control in crowdsourcing vulnerability discovery has focused on various specific aspects of quality such as incentives for Security Professionals (SecPros) involved in the task [68], or cost-effectiveness of the task [33]. A large body of research reveals that there are several: (i) Quality issues in crowdsourced

[1] https://hackerone.com/deptofdefense.

[2] https://www.hackerone.com/press-release/ministry-defence-singapore-mindef-bolsters-security-second-hackerone-bug-bounty.

[3] https://www.infoworld.com/article/2609040/microsoft-google-and-facebook-team-up-on-new-bug-bounty-program.html.

[4] https://securityboulevard.com/2020/12/bugcrowd-report-shows-marked-increase-in-crowdsourced-security/.

M. Al-Banna
Deloitte, Sydney, Australia
e-mail: mortadaalbanna@gmail.com

C. Rodríguez (✉)
Universidad Católica Nuestra Señora de la Asunción, Asunción, Paraguay
e-mail: carlos.rodriguez@uc.edu.py

B. Benatallah
Dublin City University, Dublin, Ireland
e-mail: boualem.benatallah@dcu.ie

M. C. Barukh
Jellow AI, Sydney, Australia

C. Cappiello et al. (eds.), *Retrospective and Prospective Views on Information Systems Engineering*, https://doi.org/10.1007/978-3-032-19578-4_9

vulnerability discovery tasks [3, 77], (ii) quality assessment methods [129, 130], and (iii) assurance strategies [68, 131]. However, no framework exists to facilitate the understanding of the body of research in this very significant field. Like other research areas, researchers and practitioners can benefit from a framework that brings together fragmented quality problems and solutions in crowdsourced vulnerability discovery. Daniel et al. [26] articulated a framework for analyzing and comparing quality control issues and solutions in crowdsourcing services in general. We believe that due it is significance, work on crowdsourced vulnerability discovery requires similar framework and building blocks in terms of quality control dimensions, attributes, assessment and assurance solutions.

Thus, in this article, inspired by the work done in Daniel et al. [26] on crowdsourcing in general, we propose a holistic framework for understanding, analysing and comparing quality control solutions in vulnerability discovery. More specifically, we make the following contributions:

- A Systematic Literature Review (SLR) on the main issues and solutions in crowdsourced software vulnerability discovery.
- A consolidated framework, as result of our SLR study, for the analysis of crowdsourced vulnerability discovery building blocks in terms of dimensions to identify quality aspects and attributes, assessment and assurance approaches.
- A discussion of shortcomings and limitations of existing solutions along with key challenges and opportunities for future research.
- Recommendations on how to leverage our findings to inform novel and improved techniques for the augmentation of crowdsourcing platforms with capabilities for the effective management of vulnerability discovery processes and services.

This chapter is organized as follows. Section 2 provides background information for this study. Section 3 discusses the methodology adopted in the study. In Sect. 4, we provide the quality model that emerged from the study conducted. Next, in Sect. 5, we illustrate the methods that are used to assess different aspects considered in our quality model such as task performance, quality of reports, expertise of Secpros, among several other aspects. Section 6 illustrates the strategies and actions that are used for quality assurance. While Sect. 7 discusses our findings, identify gaps in research and practice and provide some recommendation. We summarize and conclude this article with finals remarks in Sect. 8.

2 Background

In this section, we provide necessary background and introduce the main concepts and definitions that we use throughout the chapter. We start with an overview of crowdsourcing and its main components, followed by an illustration of the implementation of crowdsourcing for various security tasks and the basic concepts of vulnerability and vulnerability discovery. We then provide an overview of the main approaches for vulnerability discovery along with their main advantages and disadvantages, and close the section with a discussion of the anatomy of a crowdsourced vulnerability discovery task.

2.1 Crowdsourcing

Crowdsourcing is the outsourcing of tasks, typically performed by employees of an organization, to an undefined and large group of people (the crowd) in the form of an open call [46]. Similar to outsourcing, crowdsourcing has two main groups of stakeholders, namely, requesters and workers. The requester is an individual or organization that provides the task to be performed. The worker is a member of the crowd that performs the task. The result obtained by performing the task is called the output. Such output is typically evaluated by the requester, and based of its quality, a reward (monetary or non-monetary) may be issued to the worker. Crowdsourcing has become very popular in the past years due to the facilitated access provided by it to large pool of workers in a cost-effective manner and its appeal as an alternative solution for problems that are out of the reach of state of the art computer-based solutions [127].

Several crowdsourcing platforms exist today (e.g., Amazon Mechanical Turk, Top coder, Innocentive, and Wikipedia). Amazon Mechanical Turk (AMT)[5] is one of the most popular platforms. In AMT, small tasks (also called micro-tasks) are made available in a market place where workers from the crowd can pick and perform the tasks for a monetary reward predefined by the requester. The platform provides the necessary tools for designing tasks, publishing them in the marketplace, recruiting workers, managing rewards, among other activities.

The openness of the call along with the unknown characteristics of workers from the crowd bring a number of challenges when it comes to assuring the overall quality of crowdsourced tasks [4]. For example, the quality of the output depends on the credentials and skills of the worker, which in turn depend on the skills required to perform the task. The overall quality also depends on the clarity of the task description provided by the requester and the rewards offered to workers. Daniel et al. [26] identified a number of quality dimensions and attributes that need to be considered for quality control in this context, which include data quality (e.g., data accuracy), task quality (e.g., task complexity) and people quality (e.g., workers' skills). We will discuss this topic in more details in the following sections.

[5] https://www.mturk.com.

2.2 Crowdsourcing for Security

Crowdsourcing has been also relied on to perform security tasks [104]. One of the security tasks that has adopted crowdsourcing is the evaluation of the security of an application or service (e.g., sharing the perception of an expert in regard to the security of the application or the services) [7, 90]. Cen et al. [21] explored the usage of a crowd-based ranking method for security risk assessment of mobile apps, by leveraging user comments from Google Play store. Similarly, Amini et al. [7] used machine learning along with crowdsourcing to evaluate application behaviour and determine if it is accessing resources that it is not authorised to access. Many services for security and trustworthiness of websites rely on crowdsourcing (e.g., Web of Trust,[6] Avast Browser Security—Web Security Plugin,[7] TrustPilot[8]). Users report their experience on a website and rate its trustworthiness. The community rating of a Website is used to indicate how trustworthy the website is. Crowdsourcing has also been adopted to verify e-mails or websites that aim to steal information (a.k.a. phishing). For example, PhishTank[9] is a community-based platform where users can submit phishing e-mails or websites (e.g., page hijacking), while others evaluate and vote whether they are indeed phishing cases. Moore and Clayton [83] studied the accuracy of a PhishTank and investigated how to leverage crowdsourcing to make security decisions.

Another security task that has adopted crowdsourcing is the sharing of threat information (e.g., malicious actors and their techniques, malicious domains, attack scenarios, etc.). These threat information benefit organization by understanding possible attacks and adjusting their strategy to prevent them from happening [24]. Wagner et al. [119] propose a threat information sharing platform that collects and shares indicators of compromise (IoC) and threat information in the context of financial fraud cases. Sillaber et al. [110] investigated the issues and challenges in data quality when sharing threat information. The authors discovered that the main factors that affect shared threat information is the complexity of the information shared from different sources and how to make sure that integrating and consolidating the information do not affect its usefulness. Tentilucci et al. [113] proposed a tool to crowdsource attacks trees and scenarios (i.e., a characterization of the different types of attacks that can affect a system). The authors highlight that relying on the crowd to provide attack trees and scenarios minimize the possibility that some possible scenarios are overlooked. Various other tools and platforms exists to: share attack information (e.g., ThreatConnect,[10] Open Threat Exchange[11]), gather and distribute

[6] https://www.mywot.com.

[7] https://support.avast.com/en-in/article/18.

[8] https://www.trustpilot.com/.

[9] https://www.phishtank.com.

[10] https://www.threatconnect.com/.

[11] https://www.alienvault.com/open-threat-exchange.

vulnerability-related (e.g., NVD, VulnDB) as well as malware-related (e.g., Virus Total[12]) information.

Securing a device or a system can be a daunting task for novice users [35]. Sharing configurations that would help achieve more security is another security task that has adopted crowdsourcing. Ismail et al. [51] proposed a crowdsourcing approach that leverages people wisdom to assess various security configurations for an application and identify the application's configurations that strike trade-offs between privacy and usability. In the same context, Argwal and Hall [1] relied on crowdsourcing to build a recommendation engine that helps users to decide on the protection settings in iOS applications based on the contribution of protection settings used by other users. Several mobile applications rely on crowdsourcing to acquire permission configurations that would protect users from privacy leakages (e.g., ProtectMyProvacy[13] and XPrivacy[14]). Platforms and communities relied on sharing best practices and templates for hardening security of devices and systems. For instance, StackOverflow contains posts on configuration files to harden the security of systems and devices.[15]

Finally, crowdsourcing has been adopted in vulnerability discovery (a.k.a. bug bounty or vulnerability reward programs). Several organizations like Google, Microsoft and Facebook already adopted this approach and several researchers investigated the crowdsourced task of vulnerability discovery [33, 34, 40, 129]. We discuss in detail the crowdsourced task of vulnerability discovery in following sections.

2.3 Vulnerabilities and Vulnerability Discovery

A vulnerability is a security flaw that arises in the design, implementation or maintenance of hardware (e.g., integrated circuits) and software (e.g., web applications) systems [101]. In this chapter we focus on software vulnerabilities. Vulnerabilities in hardware are equally important and have huge impact on the security of systems (e.g., Spectre and Meltdown[16]). Vulnerabilities are considered highly undesirable because they can be exploited by malicious parties in order to gain unauthorized access to protected resources. One common example of a software vulnerability is SQL injection [17]. A SQL injection occurs when a malicious party constructs a SQL query that is executed through legitimate inputs of the system. By doing so, a malicious party can perform activities such as reading sensitive data from a database, modifying data stored in it, executing administrative operations, among other undesirable activities. The presence of vulnerabilities in a system may pose important risks to organizations because their exploitation may lead to financial loses, reputa-

[12] https://www.virustotal.com/.

[13] https://cydia.saurik.com/package/org.protectmyprivacy.pmp/.

[14] https://github.com/M66B/XPrivacy#xprivacy.

[15] https://security.stackexchange.com/questions/179114/what-are-the-toughest-ssh-daemon-settings-in-terms-of-encryption-handshake-or/179118#179118.

[16] https://techcrunch.com/tag/meltdown-spectre/.

tion damage and private data leakage [79, 99, 117]. Getting exposed to such risks can be avoided altogether by producing software systems that are free of vulnerabilities. But doing so is uncommon, especially in the case of complex software systems [27]. This situation is further exacerbated in scenarios where there is high requirement volatility, which make development teams more likely to produce software that contain vulnerabilities [76]. The task of vulnerability discovery is that of analysing the system in order to find flaws that could be exploited for malicious purposes [71]. There are various ways to discover vulnerabilities in software and we will discuss them next.

2.4 Approaches for Vulnerability Discovery

Several techniques and tools have been proposed in the literature to address the problem of vulnerability discovery [12, 61, 71]. One way of categorizing them is by considering the techniques used, for instance, whether they are expert-based (e.g., code review, black box manual penetration testing), machine-based (e.g., static analysis), or crowd-based (e.g., crowdsourced vulnerability discovery). A vulnerability discovery task may involve one or more of these techniques in the effort of finding vulnerabilities. In this section we briefly explain these approaches.

Expert-Based Vulnerability Discovery

These are techniques that are carried out by experts and rely on their skills and expertise to discover the vulnerability [42]. Some of key techniques are:

Manual code review. This technique consists in inspecting the code of the software to discover vulnerabilities that attackers might exploit [30]. Although manual code review has been highlighted as one of the important techniques to discover vulnerabilities in software [42], it is known for being time-consuming and tedious to perform [45]. This high cost has motivated researchers to investigate code review performance and effectiveness such as the work of Biffl [64]. In a similar context, Munaiah et al. [89] investigated the linguistic features of conversations between developers in a code review, in order to identify factors explaining why developers did not discover a vulnerability during the code review. Since manual code review depends highly on the knowledge and skills of the reviewer, Edmundson et al. [31] investigated the effectiveness of software developers with different backgrounds in performing security code review. The authors discover that if the software developer performing the code review has security knowledge it greatly increases the effectiveness of the code review.

Manual penetration testing. Penetration testing consists in the authorized task of attacking a system (for testing purposes) to gain access to protected resources [37]. Penetration testing involves analyzing a system for detecting vulnerabilities such as flaws in hardware or software, improper configurations, operational weakness in countermeasures, etc. [13]. Relying on manual penetration testing requires the penetration tester to not only have the required skills but also to have creativity to try different approaches [81].

Machine-Based Vulnerability Discovery

These are techniques that rely on automation to discover vulnerabilities. Some of these techniques are presented next:

Static analysis techniques examine the source of a program statically, without attempting to execute it in order to identified vulnerable code snippets [19]. Several researchers proposed static analysis techniques in different environments [55, 72]. Relying on static analysis techniques is prone to having large number of false-positives and affect the adoption of static analysis tools to discover vulnerabilities [9, 54]. Zitser et al. [133] investigated static analysis techniques and test their efficiency and ways to minimize the false-positives. Moser et al. [85] explore the limits of static analysis for the detection of malicious code.

Black box automated vulnerability scanners are a category of techniques that evaluate the security of a software without the need to access the source code. Black box scanners analyse all the input vectors and submit a specially-crafted input values to the application. Scanners would observe the behaviour of the application and give an alert if the input triggers any vulnerability [23]. A challenge of relying on black box vulnerability scanners is the accuracy in identifying vulnerabilities [14, 29]. Doupé et al. [29] investigated eleven black box vulnerability scanners and discovered that they discover different vulnerability types but there is no one tool that was able to discover all types of known vulnerabilities. Similarly, Bau et al. [14] investigated eight black box vulnerability scanners and studied their limitation with respect to the ability to discover vulnerabilities of different types. The authors highlighted the shortcoming of each scanner and the types of vulnerabilities each scanner was discovering efficiently.

Machine learning algorithms has also been used to discover vulnerabilities. Vulnerability prediction models rely on machine learning, data mining and statistical analysis to predict if a software would have vulnerabilities [37]. Shin et al. [109] investigated the usage of software metrics (complexity, code churn, and developer activity metrics) to predict vulnerabilities. Morrison et al. [84] investigated the challenges of relying on vulnerability prediction models specially in term of acquiring practical actionable results, and the accuracy of the models at the binary level. The authors highlighted how impractical the data is for developers to take action and that predictions at the source level are actionable, but the model is inaccurate. Pattern recognition techniques has also been applied to discover vulnerabilities by extracting models and patterns of vulnerable code [37]. Pattern recognition is another machine learning approach that has been investigated by researchers [37, 125]. Pattern recognition for vulnerability discovery rely mainly on gathering a large dataset of vulnerability samples, processing them to extract feature vectors, and build machine learning algorithms to automatically learn a pattern recognition model [37]. Yamaguchi et al. [125] propose vulnerability extrapolations which is a method for assisted discovery of vulnerabilities. The authors use pattern recognition to identify vulnerable code as it shares similar characteristics with known vulnerabilities.

Crowd Based Vulnerability Discovery

In crowd-based vulnerability discovery, organizations submit vulnerability discovery tasks to a community of security professionals (the crowd) who are in charge of discovering vulnerabilities and reporting them to the organization. This approach has recently gained high popularity due to the possibility of accessing a large pool of security professionals with vast and varying security expertise [33, 75, 129]. Crowdsourced vulnerability discovery benefits from the merits of crowdsourcing [46] (i.e., speed, diversity and scale) and hence helps in overcoming some of the shortcomings of other strategies. The next section elaborates in more details the anatomy of the crowdsourced task of vulnerability discovery.

2.5 Anatomy of the Crowdsourced Task of Vulnerability Discovery

Figure 1 illustrate a conceptual model for the crowdsourced task of vulnerability discovery. This model presents the key concepts involved in this approach and shows the relationship among them. We describe bellow the main components of this model.

Task Requester. We refer by this term to the party that owns the software system and is responsible for initiating the crowdsourced task of vulnerability discovery (e.g., companies like Google, public institutions and NGOs) [43]. The task requester can manage and maintain the crowdsourced task by itself or may decide to outsource it to a specialized platform (e.g., Hackerone or Bugcrowd). The task requester is the ultimate responsible of verifying and accepting (or rejecting) the reported vulnerability. If accepted, the requester is also in charge of taking the necessary actions to remediate the vulnerability.

Software. This entity represents the software system that is the subject of the vulnerability discovery task. Possible types of software include web applications, Web services and APIs, desktop applications, mobile applications, among other types.

Vulnerability. This refers a potential flaw that may be present in the software system and that represents the target of the crowdsourced vulnerability discovery task. Common vulnerability types include SQL injection, Cross-Site Scripting (XSS), Cross-Site Request Forgery (CSRF), among other types.

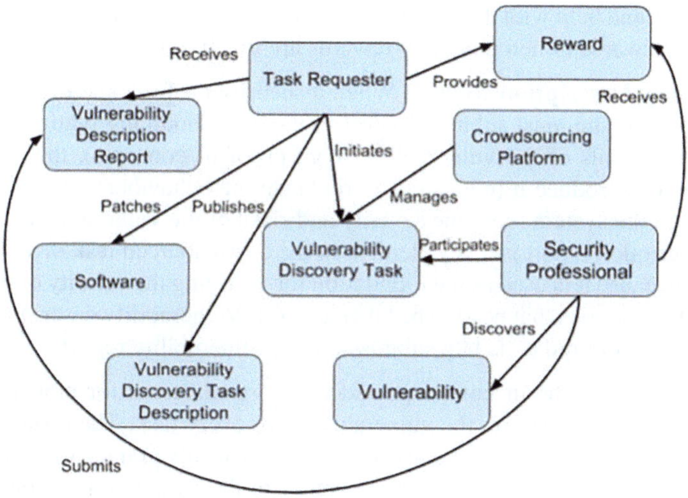

Fig. 1 Crowdsourced vulnerability discovery conceptual model

Vulnerability Discovery Task. Represents the vulnerability discovery task to be performed by the security professions from the crowd. A task can be timeboxed (it runs for a specific time period) or open (it runs indefinitely). Crowdsourced vulnerability discovery tasks are also known as bug bounty programs or vulnerability reward programs.

Vulnerability Discovery Task Description. This is the description of the task as provided by the task requester. It includes the instructions of how to perform the task along with other contextual information (e.g., the types of vulnerabilities targeted by the program and credentials needed to perform the task). These task descriptions are sometimes referred to as the bug bounty brief.[17]

Security Professional. This is a member of the crowd that is in charge of discovering vulnerabilities and submitting the corresponding report to the task requester [2]. Security professionals typically have a diverse background and may include researchers, students, hobbyists and practitioners. Their participation in crowdsourced vulnerability discovery is motivated by different reasons as discussed later in this section.

Crowdsourcing platform. By crowdsourcing platform, we refer to the party that is in charge of managing the crowdsourced vulnerability discovery programs. Two examples of such platforms are Hackerone[18] and Bugcrowd.[19] These crowdsourcing platforms help in offloading some of the management burden of vulnerability discovery tasks from task requesters. In addition, they maintain a pool of security

[17] https://www.bugcrowd.com/resource/anatomy-bug-bounty-brief.

[18] https://www.hackerone.com.

[19] https://www.bugcrowd.com.

professionals and help with the communication, measurement of their reputation and payment of rewards (when monetary rewards are involved).

Vulnerability Description Report. When a security professional discovers a vulnerability, he or she must submit a report to the crowdsourcing platform. A report includes the details of the vulnerability (e.g., proof of concepts), the information about how to reproduce it (e.g., steps to replicate the behaviour), and the impact it may have on the system (e.g., the severity and risks of the vulnerability). A vulnerability description report is a key element in the crowdsourced task of vulnerability discovery because it is used as the foundation for verifying the validity of the vulnerability and the actions that need to be taken to fix it. Vulnerability description reports are sometimes referred to as bug submissions or vulnerability reports.

Reward. These are the incentives provided by organizations for motivating security professionals to perform the vulnerability discovery task. The reward could be monetary or non-monetary. Monetary rewards are typically granted to a security professional depending on the validity and severity of the vulnerability. Non-monetary rewards typically include acknowledgements such as special mentions and messages of gratitude in the organization's website. For example, Facebook maintains a Web page in their website where they thank people that responsibly disclose discovered vulnerabilities to them.[20]

Figure 2 outlines the multiple stages the crowdsourced task of vulnerability discovery typically goes through. The steps (adapted from the work of Tranquillini et al. [116]) decomposes the whole crowdsourced vulnerability discovery task into four stages, namely, task creation, security professional pre-selection, task execution, validation and rewarding. During task creation, the task requester provides a description of the task to be performed by the security professionals, which typically include the scope (e.g., target vulnerabilities), guidelines (e.g., how to report the vulnerability) and access accounts. In the security professional's pre-selection stage, the task

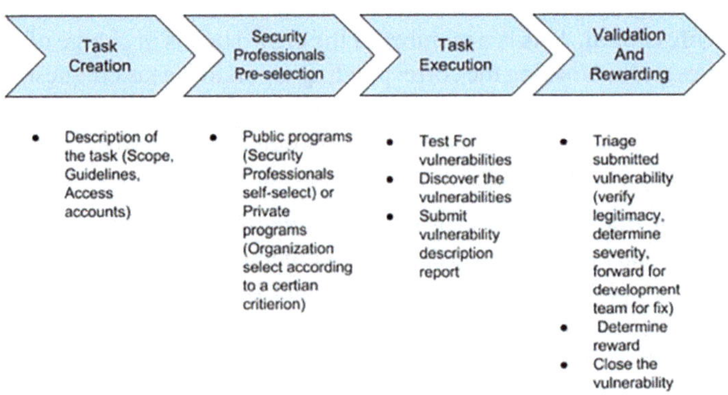

Fig. 2 Steps for crowdsourcing vulnerability discovery

[20] https://www.facebook.com/whitehat/thanks/.

requester decides who is allowed to participate in the execution of the task. In public programs, security professionals self-select tasks based on the target vulnerabilities they are interested in (e.g., based on the offered reward). In private programs, the task requester selects which security professionals can participate based on their profiles and reputation (provided by the crowdsourcing platform). During task execution, security professionals perform the actual task of discovering vulnerabilities. When a vulnerability is discovered, security professionals must create a vulnerability report that provide key information that can help the task requester in validating and fixing the vulnerability. In the final stage, validation and rewarding, the task requester triages the submitted vulnerability to determine its legitimacy and severity, and to decide on the reward that will be assigned to the reporting security professional. After this, the task requester takes all the necessary actions to x the reported vulnerability.

3 Methodology

In order to answer the research questions in this article, we conducted an SLR and platform/tool analysis. For the SRL, we followed the guidelines presented in [91]. Furthermore, in order to form a comprehensive analysis of existing assessment methods and assurance strategies, we also examined existing implementation of platforms used in industry, even though not all of these are the direct result of scientific research.

We reviewed literature by querying Scopus, ACM Digital Library, IEEE XPlore Digital Library and ResearchGate. We applied the following keywords for our queries: ((security AND vulnerability) AND (crowdsourcing OR "vulnerability Market") AND (bounty OR reward) AND (software OR systems)). Since the field of crowdsourcing vulnerability discovery is relatively new, we have limited the literature from 2007–2020. A total of 84 relevant papers were identified after removing from the initial result set references such as posters, duplicates, workshop outlines, etc., and after identifying additional relevant papers through snowballing.

The articles were reviewed in order to identify quality attributes, assessment methods and assurance strategies discussed in literature. Two of the authors actively codified the reviewed articles, while a third author reviewed and revised the resulting coding. In the event of disagreements, the authors engaged in discussions until a consensus was reached.

We relied on the knowledge and expertise of the authors when analyzing existing implementations and platforms for crowdsourcing vulnerability discovery. We included the most popular platforms and crowdsourced tasks that has been running for long periods of time with available public details. We also included tasks that are run by a diverse set of organizations and with different setup strategies (e.g., tasks managed by specialized platform, tasks run directly by the organization, tasks run for open source software, tasks run for closed source software, vulnerability discovery competitions like Pwn2Own[21]). We investigated the blogs, press releases,

[21] https://en.wikipedia.org/wiki/Pwn2Own.

crowdsourced tasks descriptions, rule pages, feature demonstration, public reports and case studies by companies and platform. We relied on the guidelines for online research methods by Wakeford and Cohen [121].

4 Quality Control Model

In this section, we summarize the results according to the analysis of the identified literature and implementations. Based on quality control models from other fields like general crowdsourcing [26], software [120], and services [107], quality models are described as quality dimensions and quality attributes. We followed a similar approach and several quality dimensions and attributes emerged from our analysis. Below, we list these quality dimensions, followed by a discussion of the corresponding attributes.

Task. This is the actual work that needs to be carried out by the SecPros to discover vulnerabilities. The way the task is described and how it is implemented affect the outcome of the task. We discovered the following sub-dimensions:

- *Performance*: This refers to the outcome of the vulnerability discovery task relative to the resources consumed. Different scenarios may yield different outcomes. For example, a task requester may have thousands of SecPros participating in the task, which could generate large volumes of vulnerability submissions that may require a large amount of resources (e.g., time and staff) to verify them. On the contrary, it is also possible for the task requester to go through the whole process of launching a vulnerability discovery task and not get enough useful submissions.
- *Description*. This is the actual description of the vulnerability discovery task to be carried out by SecPros. It includes the instructions on how to perform the task and report the vulnerability along with additional contextual information. The clarity and completeness of the task description as well as it's scope has been shown to impact the seamless disclosure of vulnerabilities to the task requester and minimize the possibility of public disclosure [39].
- *Incentives*. In general, task requesters offer incentives to motivate the SecPros to participate in the task. These incentives could be monetary (e.g., cash rewards and gifts) or non-monetary (e.g., reputation or being mentioned in the hall of fame of the task requester). It has been observed that there is some relation between the incentives and the quality of the output of the task [116] or the overall performance of the task [33].
- *Management*. Tasks can be managed by the requester (e.g., Microsoft vulnerability reward program), or can be fully managed by a specialized platform (e.g., Hackerone managed programs), or the management can be shared by both parties thus becoming a hybrid program (e.g., Hackerone self-managed programs). Depending on how the task is managed, the overall workflow (e.g., including integrations with bug tracking platforms) and time to launch the task (e.g., dur-

ing pre-beta and beta testing of products releases) may vary to help improve its performance [105].

- *Terms and conditions*. Terms and conditions constitute the norms that rule the relationship between task requesters and SecPros. Aspects to be considered in this sub-dimension include the privacy of SecPros and staff/customers of the task requester, information security of the task requester, the protection of intellectual property and legal protection of SecPros (safe haven). Terms and conditions affect how SecPros engage with the task and how the task requester legally deal with participants [57].
- *Complexity and severity*. Tasks differ in their complexity (i.e., the ease of discovering vulnerabilities). The complexity might be because the tasks running for a long time are harder, because all the easy vulnerabilities have been found [130], or the complexity of the system may be different to different audiences [129]. In some cases, platforms and task requesters filter out specific vulnerabilities that are very common and of (typically) low severity.

Outcome. The outcome of the task is the result of discovering a vulnerability in the software and submitting the report describing the details of the vulnerability. Ensuring *high quality reports* is one of the goals of quality control in crowdsourced vulnerability discovery since it would allow the task requester to verify the legitimacy of the submission and remediate the vulnerability [68]. Also, it has been shown that task requesters are more interested in high impact vulnerabilities than low impact ones [130].

People. This dimension refers to the actors involved in the task, including SecPros discovering the vulnerabilities and the task requesters launching the task. We divide this dimension further as follows:

- *SecPros*. These are the security professionals working on the task. They influence the quality of the outcome and the overall quality of the task. Their expertise, satisfaction and trustworthiness are some of the quality attributes that are relevant within this sub-dimension.
- *Task requester*. The task requester is the party that launches the task and receives the vulnerability reports in order to remediate the vulnerability within the software. Impotant quality attributes within this sub-dimension include the fairness, performance and generosity of task requesters, as well as its ability to handle disagreements when conflicts emerge between SecPros and task requesters.
- *Group*. We also consider the quality of the crowd as a whole or as teams working together to accomplish the task. The diversity of the crowd (i.e., a team of SecPros constructed from different backgrounds or areas of expertise) [129], and the level of support for collaboration for SecPros to discover vulnerabilities are examples of interesting topics that have been explored in literature [49].

In the following subsections we describe the quality attributes that characterize the above-mentioned quality dimensions. Table 1 summarize the dimensions, attributes, related literature or resources and their findings.

Table 1 Summary of the quality dimensions, sub-dimensions and attributes

Dimension	Sub-dimension	Attribute	Findings	References
Task	Performance	Cost efficiency	(i) Harvesting vulnerabilities from the white hat community is cost effective and competitive w.r.t. hiring full-time vulnerability researchers. (ii) There are hidden costs for managing the task and verification of submissions to validate legitimate vulnerabilities	[3, 6, 18, 20, 33, 65, 68, 70, 94, 122, 130]
		Effectiveness	(i) Task requesters receive positive number of vulnerabilities monthly. (ii) Running Tasks have beneficial effects on attack diffusion, attack risk, and attack volume. (iii) In some cases, when critical-severity vulnerabilities are considered, external contributions may exceed internal ones	[33, 97, 128]
	Description	Clarity	(i) Clear and explicit procedures facilitate good interactions and allows for vulnerability knowledge to be readily accessible to internal security teams. (ii) Clear descriptions help set guidelines for the program and legal bounds	[28, 65, 77, 124]
		Completeness	(i) Detailed and complete technical specifications describing technical and formal requirements help minimize ambiguities	[65, 124]
		Scope	(i) Specifying the scope of the task (e.g., the types of vulnerabilities eligible for a bounty) helps minimize the false positive submissions. (ii) Tasks vary in their scope (e.g., Website, mobile app, API)	[65, 77, 124, 129]

Table 1 (continued)

Dimension	Sub-dimension	Attribute	Findings	References
	Incentives	Monetary	(i) Setting prices is not easy and the rule of thumb is unclear. (ii) Offering monetary rewards is effective to attract SecPros	[3, 18, 20, 22, 28, 49, 69, 70, 94, 118, 122, 124, 128–130]
		Non-monetary	(i) Acknowledgment and reputation are important motivational elements. (ii) Self-satisfaction (e.g., feeling good to protect the online community) is an important motivation for SecPros. (iii) Popularity of the platform and/or the product attract more SecPros to participate in the task	[20, 22, 28, 47, 65, 118, 122, 124, 128, 129]
	Management	Timeliness	(i) Task requester should not provide the reward to the SecPro before the public is made aware of the vulnerability. (ii) Launching the task in coherence of security events could motivate SecPros to discover vulnerabilities in order to illustrate them in these events. (iii) Launching the task at different product releases (pre-beta testing, beta testing, etc.) can help identify vulnerabilities early	[44, 52, 69, 77, 100, 105, 122]
		Workflow	(i) Integration of the task with the task requester processes and process management technologies could help speed up how the vulnerability is remediated. (ii) Some platforms like Hackerone and Bugcrowd offer integration with the bug tracking platforms like Jira	[18, 44, 65, 124], Hackerone, Bugcrowd

Table 1 (continued)

Dimension	Sub-dimension	Attribute	Findings	References
	Terms and conditions	Information security	(i) There is a risk of disclosing the vulnerability information to a third party or disclosing publicly before the vulnerability is patched. (ii) There is a risk of leakage of information that can be used by malicious parties	[22, 57, 130]
		IP leakage	(i) Agreement for the purchase of the intellectual property of the 0-day vulnerability and all the connected rights. (ii) Copyright infringement (e.g., if the task requester shares software with SecPros to perform testing, SecPros could use the software for personal purposes)	[10, 92]
		Legal protection	(i) Coordinated vulnerability disclosure should allow SecPros to report vulnerabilities withouth fear of legal prosecution	[36, 124]
	Complexity and severity	Complexity	(i) Tasks running for a while usually have the easy-to-find vulnerabilities discovered and only the complex ones remain. (ii) Complex software require special skills in order to the SecPro to be able to discover vulnerabilities. (iii) Products that are perceived as more secure should offer higher reward	[33, 57, 129, 130]
		Severity of vulnerability	(i) Some vulnerabilities are so common (e.g., XSS) and have low severity that they are usually filtered out by platforms or task requesters. (ii) Task requesters aim to receive higher impact and higher severity vulnerabilities because this contributes to making the task more successful	[129, 130]

Table 1 (continued)

Dimension	Sub-dimension	Attribute	Findings	References
Outcome	Quality of report	Duplication	(i) Duplication in submitted reports is a very common issue. (ii) For individuals with larger number of reports in a program (five or more), the highest rediscovery rate is 25% and the mean is 4.25%	[3, 33, 41, 93, 130]
		Clarity	(i) Platforms and task requesters highlight the importance of clarity in submitted reports, because it allows for easier validation	[86], Hackerone, Bugcrowd, Google, Microsoft
		Spamming	(i) Some SecPros submit spam reports in order to promote a service they are offering	[3, 100, 130]
		Completeness	(i) Submissions that come with proofs-of-concept and executables demonstrating consequences are highly valued. (ii) Having the reproduction steps in the submissions affect the reward size	[65, 86, 88]
		Validity	(i) Tasks are riddled with invalid submissions	[3, 68, 130]
People	SecPros	Expertise	(i) The expertise of SecPros is related to how successful they are in performing the task. (ii) SecPros demonstrate their expertise through what is presented in their profile (performance in previous tasks, certification they have, being referred by other SecPros, or the artifacts they contribute)	[2, 40, 49, 100, 118, 129, 130]
		Satisfaction	(i) If the SecPro is satisfied with the rewards, he or she will likely make sure to keep submitting reports and create loyalty to the program	[3, 22]

Table 1 (continued)

Dimension	Sub-dimension	Attribute	Findings	References
		Trustworthiness	(i) There is a risk that vulnerabilities are sold in more than one market. (ii) Some Blackhat hackers participate in crowdsourced task for vulnerability discovery. (iii) Internal engineer from the task requester may collude with a SecPro to introduce vulnerabilities in the software and for the SecPro to submit them for rewards	[3, 10, 65, 70, 96, 100, 102, 103]
	Task requester	Performance	(i) SecPros value the speed of interaction with the task requester. (ii) There is a risk of disclosing vulnerabilities publicly if the task requester shows slow or no response addressing the vulnerability (i.e., it may foster resentment and/or sabotage)	[3, 11, 32, 33, 39, 49, 77, 124]
		Fairness	(i) Task requesters need to assure SecPros that they will indeed pay promised rewards for security bugs. (ii) Task requester may try not to pay for the reward and cheat	[18, 65, 92, 100]
		Generosity	(i) Generous task requesters tend to attract more SecPros to participate in the tasks they are running	[122], Hackerone
		Disagreement	(i) Reasonableness and validity of a bounty amount could be improved through transparency associated to disclosures, thus reducing conflicts between SecPros and task requesters. (ii) A more dangerous situation occurs when the SecPro and the vendor disagree about the disclosure schedule, resulting in the publication of vulnerability details a few days before a patch is made available	[102, 130]

Table 1 (continued)

Dimension	Sub-dimension	Attribute	Findings	References
	Group	Diversity	(i) The whole community of SecPros plays an important role for vulnerability discovery (rather than only a few highly expert SecPros). (ii) Diversity plays a key role in vulnerability discovery, where SecPros with varied backgrounds and expertise may find larger numbers and more varied vulnerabilities	[31, 33, 40, 75, 129, 130]
		Collaboration	(i) Collaboration between SecPros results in a better performance, with higher productivity and diversity in discovered vulnerabilities	[49]

4.1 Task Performance

Two attributes have been studied in the context of task performance: cost efficiency and effectiveness [22, 33, 49, 68, 130]. The overall expected cost of crowdsourced vulnerability discovery tasks is not straightforward to estimate since it depends on the number of vulnerabilities discovered (which is unknown beforehand) and the amount awarded for each vulnerability (which is dependent on the security impact of the vulnerability discovered and unknown beforehand). Finifter et al. [33] compared the cost efficiency of crowdsourcing vulnerability discovery versus hiring an internal security staff to discover vulnerabilities. By analyzing two crowdsourced tasks they concluded that it is more cost efficient to rely on crowdsourcing. Other researchers [20, 22, 68, 130] investigated the cost of managing the task and the verification of the legitimacy of submissions, which is considered a burden on the task requester when dealing with a high number of submissions. The effectiveness of the task could be considered as the number of discovered vulnerabilities that has not been discovered using the traditional methods [33, 49]. Zhao et al. [130] use the term *productivity* and they correlate the number of vulnerabilities discovered with the severity of vulnerabilities. This is used to illustrate the effectiveness of the task in discovering vulnerabilities that would have high impact if it has been discovered by malicious parties [129].

4.2 Task Description

In regard to the quality of task descriptions, clarity and having explicit procedures is considered paramount for a straightforward interaction between task requesters and SecPros [65]. Additionally, the completeness of the task description, where all the technical and formal requirements are provided, will help SecPros in performing the task properly [65]. In order to remove any ambiguities of what SecPros are allowed to test or not, a well-defined scope of the program is very important (e.g., domains for testing, APIs and types of vulnerabilities) [65, 129]. Crowdsourcing platforms for vulnerability discovery (e.g., Bugcrowd, Hackerone and Cobalt) consider the quality of task descriptions as directly impacting the ultimate task performance and having a successful program.[22]

4.3 Task Incentives

Task incentives influence the appeal for SecPros to participate in a particular task. The incentives could be monetary or non-monetary. It has been observed that providing monetary incentives (e.g., cash rewards) would increase the number of participants and hence the number of submissions [33, 49, 130]. Similarly, non-monetary incentives (e.g., being mentioned in the hall of fame, and self-satisfaction) has also been observed to have an effect in motivating SecPros to participate [20, 22, 65, 129].

4.4 Task Management

Crowdsourced task for vulnerability discovery differ in how they are managed by the task requester. One attribute related to task management is the timeliness of the task. Task requesters control when they reward SecPros upon submitting a valid vulnerability report (e.g., Uber reward SecPros as soon as the submission is triaged.[23]). Another aspect of timeliness is the time the task requester launches the task. It has been discovered that SecPros tend to discover more vulnerabilities close to times where a security event is running [52]. Another aspect of task management is the integration of the task with the task requester's processes. Herr et al. [41] highlight that integrating the crowdsourced vulnerability discovery task with the internal processes of the organization helps speed up how vulnerabilities are remediated. Some platforms like Hackerone and Bugcrowd offer integration with bug tracking platforms like Jira.[24]

---

[22] https://www.bugcrowd.com/resource/anatomy-bug-bounty-brief.

[23] https://medium.com/uber-security-privacy/uber-security-bug-bounty-updates-b8256494fd04.

[24] https://docs.hackerone.com/programs/jira-integration.html.

4.5 Terms and Conditions

Tasks for crowdsourced vulnerability discovery typically come with terms and conditions that rule how tasks ought to be performed. Here, information security is one of the most critical aspects and aims to prevent the disclosure of vulnerability information to third parties before the corresponding patch is available [22, 57, 130]. Another key concern is that of IP leakage connected to the IP of 0-day vulnerabilities, as well as the risks of copyright infringements by SecPros when task requesters make their software available (to SecPros) for vulnerability task purposes (e.g., when SecPros use the software for personal and/or commercial purposes outside the scope of the vulnerability discovery task) [10, 92]. Finally, terms and conditions are also there to protect SecPros through so-called coordinated vulnerability disclosure. This allows SecPros to report vulnerabilities without the fear of legal prosecution (safe harbor/haven[25]) [36, 124].

4.6 Complexity and Severity

Crowdsourced tasks for vulnerability discovery differ in their complexity. The complexity can be assessed according to the type of software (e.g., web application, operating system or mobile app) and how easy it is to discover vulnerabilities. It can also be assessed based on the age of the task. Zhao et al. [130] described that the complexity of the task increases after the easy-to-find vulnerabilities are removed and only complex ones remain. It has been observed that once the pool of vulnerabilities is depleted and only the complex vulnerabilities remain the task requesters need to motivate further the SecPros to participate (e.g., adjusting the rewards) in the complex task [27, 33]. Additionally, vulnerabilities that are considered very common and have low severity/impact are often filtered out by task requesters and platforms (e.g., through program policies) so that SecPros can focus on higher severity vulnerabilities [129, 130].

4.7 Quality of Reports

Since vulnerability description reports are the main outcome of tasks, several attributes to assess the quality of such reports are studied. The validity of reports are based on their legitimacy relative to the corresponding task descriptions. One of the challenges with crowdsourced vulnerability discovery tasks is the large number of invalid reports submitted [3, 68]. Munaiah and Meneely [88] investigated the overall quality of reports and their relevance to the rewards offered to SecPros.

[25] https://blog.mozilla.org/security/2018/08/01/safe-harbor-for-security-bug-bounty-participants.

They highlight that the completeness of reports and inclusion of proofs of concept and details for the reproduction of vulnerabilities affect the size of the reward positively. Another challenge under this category are duplicate reports. If two or more SecPros submit reports describing the exact same vulnerability, they are considered duplicates. Duplicates are common in crowdsourced vulnerability discovery tasks [21, 93] and it is not desirable by task requesters [130] because of the additional costs associated to their processing with typically no added-value in return. Finally, spamming is also considered a challenge for the overall quality of reports. Spams are unwanted by task requesters because they typically include irrelevant data or malicious links or code [100, 130]. Platforms for crowdsourcing vulnerability discovery tasks face report spamming regularly. One peculiar type of spamming is what they call *beg bounty*,[26] which is when a report contains irrelevant content plainly asking for reward.

4.8 Expertise of Security Professionals

The expertise of SecPros participating in the crowdsourced task of vulnerability discovery affect the quality of the task [2]. Academic and industrial certifications have been investigated as an indicator of the expertise of SecPros [2]. The performance of the SecPro in discovering vulnerabilities has also been referred to as an indicator of expertise. Zhao et al. [129] considers that the productivity of SecPros discovering large number of vulnerabilities indicates their expertise. Both the effectiveness of the SecPro (i.e., the number of valid submission in comparison to the overall number of submissions) and the impact discovered vulnerabilities has also been studied as a quality attribute indicating the expertise of SecPros [130]. In a previous study reported in [2], the indicators of the expertise of SecPros participating in the task of vulnerability discovery was identified.

4.9 Satisfaction of Security Professionals

The satisfaction SecPros will get from participating in the task refers to how much SecPros are content with what he has received from the task, whether it is of monetary or non-monetary nature [22]. This satisfaction has an impact on SecPros' loyalty to the program and hence the possibility that they will keep searching for vulnerabilities and submitting reports. Platforms like Hackerone and Bugcrowd emphasize the importance of loyalty for a successful program.[27]

[26] https://medium.com/@tareksiddiki/story-of-a-beg-bounty-hunter-e9a1f58ddf9e.

[27] https://blog.bugcrowd.com/four-tips-to-implementing-a-success-bug-bounty-program.

4.10 Trustworthiness of Security Professionals

Since task requesters are delegating the sensitive task of discovering vulnerabilities to a crowd of SecPros, of whom the task requesters typically have limited information about, trustworthiness becomes an important quality attribute [65]. Trustworthiness could be affected by acting maliciously [96], reselling vulnerabilities to the black market [10, 100], leaking information about the vulnerability before it is patched [35], or colluding with internal staff to produce vulnerabilities that the SecPro would discover and submit in exchange of financial gains [92]. Crowdsourcing platforms for vulnerability discovery focus on trustworthiness of SecPros and take measures to monitor and ensure their trustworthiness.[28]

4.11 Task-Requester Reputation

The reputation of the task requester influences how appealing the task is to the SecPro [129]. Several attributes have been studied in regard to the reputation of the task requester. The performance of the task requester in terms of the response time of requesters in answering back to SecPros has been identified as important to SecPros [32, 33], and that the responsiveness of the task requester will minimize the possibility of publicly disclosing vulnerability information before the vulnerability is patched [11, 39, 49]. Also, the timeliness of the reward allocation (i.e., whether to reward the SecPro as soon as the vulnerability is verified or after the patch is release) will make the task more appealing to SecPros since they will be rewarded faster, but it also increases the risk of vulnerability information leakage [105]. Fairness of the task requester when it comes to providing suitable reward for the discovered vulnerability [65, 92, 100]. Generosity of the task requester indicate how well the task requester pays the SecPros in compensation for the time and efforts they invest to perform the task.[29] Finally, disagreement between the task requester and the SecPros on things like the validity of the submission, amount of reward and disclosure timeline can cause undesirable outcomes like the release of vulnerability information before the vulnerability is patched or damages to the reputation of the task requester or the SecPro [35, 130].

4.12 Group Quality

The quality of a group of SecPros, either in terms of the whole crowd participating in the task or smaller teams collaborating to perform the task, has been studied in

[28] https://docs.hackerone.com/hackers/misconduct.html.

[29] https://www.hackerone.com/sites/default/files/2017-05/Bug-Bounty-5-years-in-Uber-Facebook \%20_v2.pdf.

terms of two attributes. The first one is the diversity of the crowd, which refers to the heterogeneity in the type of people, their personality, background, expertise, etc. It has been discovered that the community as a whole play a key role for vulnerability discovery bringing added-value to the task, in contrast with merely having very few expert white hat hackers [129]. For example, SecPros with different views, expertise, and tools tend to discover different kinds of vulnerabilities [27, 33, 55, 130]. The other attribute is the collaboration between SecPros when performing a task, it has been discovered that the collaboration between SecPros to discover vulnerabilities leads to better performance in discovering vulnerabilities [49].

5 Quality Assessment Methods in Crowdsourcing Vulnerability Discovery

Assessing the quality attributes mentioned in the previous section and giving them a concrete measure can be done through manual inspection by individuals (e.g., expert review of submission to determine its legitimacy) or through automated approaches (e.g., content analysis of submissions). In this section we discuss a range of assessment methods that we identified as relevant (see Table 2); we present in two groups according to the technique used and the actors involved.

People-based. Given the manual, human nature of crowdsourced tasks in vulnerability discovery and the qualitative results produced as a result, it is natural to allow people to provide quality assessments for the task. We can split this group further according to the type of actors:

- *Individual*. These are methods that rely on individuals (e.g., SecPros, experts and task requesters) for the verification of the legitimacy of submissions or for providing feedbacks on the satisfaction level of SecPros with respect to their experience in participating in the task [3].
- *Group*. These are methods that require the participation of a group of people to perform the assessment. Voting on the quality of the vulnerability reports or peer review of submissions to determine the vulnerability legitimacy are two examples of group assessment methods. In these examples, even though each single vote and review is casted individually, what matter is the collective action of voting and reviewing and the aggregated results yielded from such action.

Algorithm-based. These are methods that do not require human intervention to perform the assessment (besides the final human judgement required once the assessment metrics and results have been computed by the machine). We can split this group further into:

- *Metric*. These are the values that can be calculated based on the activities within the task such as the number of badges the SecPro acquire and the time the task requester spends to respond to the SecPro [129, 130].

- *Functions*. These are the methods that require an algorithm to perform the assessment such as content analysis of the submission to determine its legitimacy, or entity extraction of some data from the submission to determine its scope.

Table 2 illustrates the assessment methods, the findings, and the tools or literature references that we identified as primarily relevant in this domain.

5.1 Individual Assessment Methods

Security Expert Review

Expert review is a method to rely on individuals that are external to the crowd to perform an assessment. The submissions of the vulnerability discovery tasks are reviewed by experts in order to verify their legitimacy. The experts could be part of the internal staff from the task requester (the case of Facebook, Google, or Microsoft), or the task requester could rely on external parties such as the staff of crowdsourcing platforms like Hackerone or Bugcrowd in their managed programs. Although there is no previous research that investigates the usage of expert review in crowdsourced vulnerability discovery tasks, works like [2, 3, 130] describe the role of expert review in the verification of the legitimacy of submissions.

Rating of the Quality of Vulnerability Report

Rating is the task of assigning a value to an item according to a comparative assessment of its quality. Platforms like Cobalt use ratings provided by task requesters to express the quality of submitted vulnerability reports and SecPros. Similarly, the program run by Mozilla rely on rating to express the quality of submissions.[30] Although, there is no comprehensive research on the usage of rating for quality assessment in crowdsourced vulnerability discovery, Ruohonen et al. [100] discussed the usage of rating in the vulnerability exploit market as a method for quality assessment.

Security Professionals Qualification Test

In the context of crowdsourced vulnerability discovery, a qualification test is a type of examination that is used to measure the skill levels of a SecPros in the context of a given vulnerability discovery task. It typically consists of a set of questions that a SecPro needs to answer correctly in order to be able to participate in the vulnerability discovery task. For example, Giboney et al. [38] developed a tool to discriminate between novice and expert SecPros. They rely on a set of questions to be

---

[30] https://www.mozilla.org/en-US/security/client-bug-bounty.

Table 2 Quality assessment methods

Dimension	Sub-dimension	Assessment method	Findings	References
Algorithmic	SecPros metrics	Number of achievements	(i) The number of vulnerabilities discovered indicates the expertise of the SecPro	[73, 129, 130], Hackerone, Bugcrowd, Cobalt
		Acceptance rate	(i) The ratio of valid versus invalid submissions	Hackerone, Bugcrowd
		Impact	(i)The number of severe vulnerabilities discovered is an indicator of the expertise of the SecPro	[33], Hackerone, Bugcrowd
		Reputation score	(i) Reputation points for the SecPros reflect his/her expertise, providing more chances to get invitations to private tasks and programs	Bugcrowd, Hackerone, Cobalt
	Task metrics	Signal to noise ratio	(i) Measuring the signal to noise ratio can give an indication of the success of the task. (ii) Task requesters desire to have high signal to noise ratio for the program to be more efficient. (iii) Low signal-to-noise ratio is considered an important challenge that needs to be addressed for an effective vulnerability discovery	[22, 41, 130]
		Patching vulnerability Ratio	(i) Vulnerabilities patched by the task requester (the ethics of assuming responsibility and protecting customers) indicate the performance of the task requester	[100]
		Newcomers/ Continuing contribution ratio	(i) Number of SecPros submitting reports for the first time and the number of SecPros being active in a period of time give an indication of the popularity of the task	[129, 130]

Table 2 (continued)

Dimension	Sub-dimension	Assessment method	Findings	References
		Task costs and vulnerability reported ratio	(i) The amount of money paid to SecPros for vulnerabilities indicates the success of the task	[33]
		Average bounty paid	(i) The average of bounties paid to SecPros indicates the generosity of the task requester	Hackerone, Bugcrowd
		Minimum bounty paid	(i) The Minimum amount of reward paid to a SecPro for a valid vulnerability	Hackerone
		Highest bounty range	(i) The range of the highest amount paid to SecPros for valid vulnerabilities	Hackerone
		Response time	(i) The time spent by task requesters to respond to submissions	Hackerone, Bugcrowd
		Number of vulnerabilities discovered	(i) The number of vulnerabilities discovered during the task	[73], Hackerone, Bugcrowd, Cobalt
	Functions	Machine learning	(i) Applying machine learning (collaborative and content filtering) to assess validity of submissions	Cobalt, Hackerone
		Entity extraction	(i) Helps in identifying information that needs to be masked or hidden	Hackerone
People based	Group	Voting	(i) SecPros vote for the quality of the submission	Hackerone
		Consensus	(i) Internal team of the task requester reach decisions about the validity of the submissions	Mozilla
	Individual	Expert review	(i)Internal staff of the task requester validate submissions. (ii) Experts reviewing the submission evaluate the severity of the vulnerability either according to a standard like CVSS or a proprietary scoring system (e.g., Microsoft and Bugcrowd)	[111, 130], Hackerone, Bugcrowd, Google, Microsoft
		Rating	(i) Rating the submission by task requesters indicate the quality of report	[100], Cobalt, Mozilla

Table 2 (continued)

Dimension	Sub-dimension	Assessment method	Findings	References
		Qualification test	(i) Maximizing the generalizability of vulnerability research by checking the legitimacy of SecPros. (ii) Segmentation of SecPros into categories or groups based on their skills	[38], Synack
		Referral	(i) Referral is discovered to be a perceived indicator to the expertise of the SecPro	[2], Zerochopter

answered by the SecPro to measure their level of expertise. Platforms like Synack[31] rely on qualification tests for SecPros to be able to participate in tasks within the platform.

Referral Security Professionals

Referrals imply that someone has recommended someone else for consideration based on their expertise in the field. Referrals and recommendations from other SecPros is a perceived indicator to the expertise of the SecPro [2]. These two mechanisms are acknowledged in the recruitment domain as a means to collect and confirm expertise. For instance, SalesForce stated that referrals are the main recruitment strategy.[32] LinkedIn[33] and ResearchGate[34] allow tagging skills of professionals. Crowdsourcing vulnerability discovery platforms like Zerocopter[35] rely solely on referral and recommendation to invite SecPros on the platform. In [2], referral is highlighted to be one of the indicators to the expertise of SecPros involved in the crowdsourced task of vulnerability discovery.

5.2 Group Assessment Methods

To the best of our knowledge, there is only one work that investigates group assessment methods in the context of crowdsourced vulnerability discovery. Su and Pan

[31] https://www.synack.com.

[32] https://www.salesforce.com/content/blogs/us/en/2015/01/behind-scenes-salesforce-our-1-recruiting-secret.html.

[33] https://www.linkedin.com.

[34] https://www.researchgate.net.

[35] https://www.zerocopter.com.

[111] proposed an approach that relies on collaboration between the task requester's internal staff and the crowd in order to verify the legitimacy of the submitted vulnerability report. Two roles were introduced, script-writers (providing the exploitation script of the vulnerability) and target-providers (building the test environment to run the script). In industry, crowdsourcing platforms for vulnerability discovery rely on group assessment methods to vote on publicly released vulnerability reports to indicate the quality of the report (e.g., Hackerone), relying on consensus between the internal security team of an task requester to decide the legitimacy of a submissions (e.g., Mozilla), aggregating feedback from task requester and peers in order to indicate the quality of the SecPro (see, e.g., Cobalt).

5.3 *Algorithmic Assessment Methods*

Metrics for Security Professionals

The quality of SecPros participating vulnerability discovery tasks can be assessed using various metrics. The number of achievements of the SecPro (e.g., valid submissions, badges, and getting thanks from task requesters) has been highlighted by researchers as a sound method to assess the expertise of SecPros [129, 130]. Finifter et al. [33] highlight that the discovery of high severity vulnerabilities is an indicator of expertise. Platforms like Hackerone, Bugcrowd and Cobalt rely on the reputation score of the SecPro to give indication in regard to his performance within the platform. Some platforms also use fine grained metrics such as the cumulative impact of the vulnerability discovered (see, e.g., Hackerone Impact and Bugcrowd Severity metrics) and the accuracy of the SecPro, which is defined as the ratio between the accepted report to the unaccepted reports submitted by a given SecPro (see, e.g., Hackerone signal and Bugcrowd accuracy metrics).

Metrics for Tasks

There are multiple metrics that are used to assess the quality of vulnerability discovery tasks. The first metric is the signal to noise ratio which is the ratio between the useful vulnerability reports submitted (signal), against the submissions that are invalid or not useful to the requester (noise). Zhao et al. [130] considers that low signal to noise ratio is a key challenge for the effectiveness of the task. Similarly, Laszka et al. [68] coupled the increase of the signal to noise ratio with the success of the program. Platforms (e.g., Bugcrowd, Hackerone) and task requesters (e.g., Facebook, Yelp) have traditionally relied on the signal to noise ratio to indicate the performance of the task and illustrated improvements according to the increase in the signal to noise ratio.

In addition, Ruohonen et al. [100] investigated how the patched vulnerability ratio (i.e., the ratio between the patched vulnerabilities to the unpatched vulnerabilities) may indicate how the task requester is handling the crowdsourced task of vulnerability discovery. Finifter et al. [33] looked at the ratio between the cost of the task and the number of vulnerabilities discovered to associate it to the cost effectiveness of the task. Other researchers explored assessing the popularity of the task by looking at the number of newcomers against the number of continuing contributors ratio [129, 130]. Platforms like Hackerone and Bugcrowd have their own metrics to assess the generosity of the task requester (e.g., average bounty paid, and top bounty paid) and the performance of the task requester responding to the submissions (e.g., average response time).

Functions

Although machine learning models have been used in vulnerability discovery (e.g., vulnerable code pattern recognition, anomaly detection techniques, and vulnerability prediction models) [37], to the best of our knowledge, there is no research work that studies the application of functions for quality assessment specifically oriented to assess quality in crowdsourced vulnerability discovery tasks. However, the use of automated methods to assess the quality of bug reports has been extensively studied in the literature. In this context, researchers such as Behl et al. [15] have investigated the problem of identifying security and non-security bugs using data mining techniques-based term frequency-inverse document frequency (TF-IDF) weights and Naive Bayes. Sun et al. [112] investigated duplicate reports and proposed a tool to detect duplicate reports relying on discriminative models for information retrieval. In addition, Tian et al. [115] focused on the severity of bugs and proposed a tool that rely on information retrieval and similarity functions to predict the severity of the bug report. Platforms like Hackerone use entity extraction functions to assess the quality of submissions[36] or use machine learning functions to recommend actions to process submissions according to their quality like Cobalt.[37]

6 Quality Assurance

Quality assurance is a mechanism where measures are adopted in order to help achieve a desired quality in a product or service [106]. These measures consist of a set of strategies and actions to react to the manifestation of a quality issue (i.e., a reactive measure) or to prevent the manifestation thereof (i.e., a preventive measure) [114]. In this section, we review the strategies and actions that aim to improve the quality of crowdsourced tasks for vulnerability discovery. Many of these strategies require prior quality assessment (e.g., selecting experts require that we first identify and measure expertise), while others do not (e.g., training SecPros could help improve the quality

[36] https://docs.hackerone.com/programs/hackbot.html.

[37] https://cobalt.io/platform.

of submissions). Table 3 illustrate the quality assurance strategies organized into the following categories:

Incentivization. Incentivizing means motivating the SecPros to perform well within the crowdsourced task of vulnerability discovery. There are two sub-strategies within this category:

- *Improvement of monetary incentives*. This strategy consists in actions associated to monetary rewards (e.g., cash rewards, swags, gifts) to motivate the SecPros [129].
- *Improvement of non-monetary incentives*. This strategy leverages actions associated to non-monetary motivations (e.g., gamification, fame and glory).

Controlling vulnerability discovery task execution. These are actions that are to be taken while the task is running and while SecPros are already submitting reports. As an example, if the task requester identifies that they are not receiving an adequate number of submissions they can invite more people to participate in the task [130].

Selection of SecPros. Inviting SecPros according to a set of predefined criteria is another strategy that the task requester can rely on to enhance the quality. The Task requester may select SecPros according to their expertise, past performance and credentials in order to guarantee a pool of suitable candidates for the task [2].

Improvement of crowdsourced vulnerability task design. One of the causes of low quality submissions by SecPros is bad task design (e.g., unclear instructions) [65]. By improving task description, guidelines and design, SecPros will understand better how to effectively discover and submit vulnerabilities (e.g., clarifying the task description will allow SecPros to better understand what they need to do and minimize out of scope submissions) [65].

Improvement of report handling. As submissions can potentially be riddled with noise, this strategy can help in minimizing the burden of dealing with low quality reports and noise (e.g., by filtering out bad reports) [3].

6.1 *Incentivization*

Improvement of Monetary Incentives

One of the most important elements of the of vulnerability discovery tasks is the reward offered to SecPros. By properly choosing the reward, SecPros can be incentivized to participate and put the required efforts to perform a task [68]. Assigning the right amount for the reward has been investigated as a strategy to incentivize and attract SecPros to participate in the task [33, 82, 95, 96]. Some researchers suggested to gradually increase the reward over time to keep the SecPros motivated and to accommodate for the increase of the complexity of the task when the stash of the trivial vulnerabilities (so-called low hanging fruits) is depleted [16, 105, 130]. In addition to the increase in the reward amount, offering bonuses has been discussed

Table 3 Quality assurance strategies

Strategy	Sub-strategy	Action	Findings	References
Incentivization	Improvement of monetary incentives	Adjust reward	(i) Increasing rewards gradually to keep SecPros engaged. (ii) Higher rewards can help prevent SecPros from engaging in black markets or switching to other programs	[3, 16, 77, 94, 95, 105, 118, 130]
		Provide hiring opportunities	(i) Offering hiring opportunities keep SecPros engaged and submitting high quality reports	[22, 33, 129]
		Provide bonus	(i) Offering bonuses to attract newcomers and keep existing SecPros engaged	[33, 130]
		Provide rewards to duplicate reports	(i) Providing rewards for duplicate submissions that increase the quality of the original report. (ii) Incentivize SecPros to submit high quality reports	Microsoft VRP
	Improvement of non-Monetary Incentives	Shorten Vendors response time	(i) Fast response by task requester attracts SecPros to participate in the task. (ii) Fast response by task requesters minimize the possibility of vulnerability information leakage. (iii) Efficient responses is translated to a form of acknowledgement to the SecPros' contributions	[22, 82, 130]
		Gamify the task	(i) Competitions and ranking SecPros keep them engaged in the task. (ii) By comparing SecPros among each other they try to surpass their peers and hence perform better (the gamification effect)	[118], Hackerone, Bugcrowd, Cobalt

Table 3 (continued)

Strategy	Sub-strategy	Action	Findings	References
		Promote Events	(i) Promoting high profile events attract new SecPros and incentivize them to submit high severity vulnerabilities. (ii) Such events can help connect teams from the task requester with SecPros and speedup the discovery of critical vulnerabilities	[28, 33]
		Provide transparency on paid/unpaid bounties	(i) Transparency on paid / unpaid bounties are very importan to build trust between task requesters and Secpros. Blockchain and smart contract technologies can help provide such transparency	[44]
		Acknowledge contribution	(i) Foster the SecPros' altruistic propensity by acknowledging their contribution and the impact on the product or project	[28, 118]
		Provide resources/ hardware	(i) Provide access to resources (such as hardware for IoT) to encourage participation of SecPros, e.g., through hacking events	[28]
Controlling task execution		Run task for longer time	(i) Having a task running for a longer period of time allows SecPros to potentially discover and submit a larger number of vulnerabilities	[130]
		Increase the number of SecPros	(i) Increasing the number of SecPros participating in the task can also increase diversity. (ii) Larger pool of SecPros discover more vulnerabilities of more diverse types	[22, 27, 49, 129, 130]
		Decay in reputation if not submitting for long time	(i) Decreasing the reputation score of a SecPro if not submitting any report for long time keep them engaged to maintain their reputation	Google VRP

Table 3 (continued)

Strategy	Sub-strategy	Action	Findings	References
		Improve communication with SecPros	(i) Use appropriate communication channels that allow task requesters to communicate effectively with Secpros to keep them informed and engaged. (ii) Improved transparency (in processing submissions) and responsiveness will help build trust between vendors and SecPros. (iii) Improve trust, understanding and shared language by consistently keeping contact points with SecPros	[77, 118, 124]
		Timed incentivize Secpros	(i) Payments to SecPros are made only if no *Cobras* (see the *Cobra Effect* [77]) are identified in a given time window	[77]
Selection of SecPros		Filter SecPros	(i) Validating the identity of the SecPros minimizes cheating. (ii) Select SecPros with high level of expertise help improve the quality of submissions. (iii) Using reputation systems to minimize trust issues with SecPros	[3, 15, 48, 77, 100, 130], Hackerone, Bugcrowd
		Select SecPros with high skill diversity	(i) Selecting SecPros with heterogeneous skills can contribute to discovering more varied types of vulnerabilities	[3, 77, 129]
		Recommend tasks	(i) Based on the past performance of the SecPros, recommend tasks where they may excel at	[87], Cobalt
		Reject SecPros	(i) Reject SecPros who perform badly or inappropriately in previous tasks. (ii) Reject SecPros with specific metrics below requirements	Hackerone, Bugcrowd
		Early engagement of SecPros	(i) Pre-qualify skilled SecPros and engage them early to foster a pool of loyal and skilled researchers	[77]

Table 3 (continued)

Strategy	Sub-strategy	Action	Findings	References
Improvement of task design		Clarify terms and conditions	(i) Clarifying the obligations of SecPros regarding the discussion of vulnerabilities without the consent of the task requester minimizes information leakage. (ii) Clear program policies can help reduce exposition of SecPros to legal risks	[3, 28, 65, 80, 82, 124, 128]
		Define reward schemes	(i) Clear reward schemes help minimize controversies when rewards are discussed between task requesters and Secpros	Hackerone
		Clarify submission guidelines	(i) Clear submission guidelines can help minimize out of scope submissions	[3, 77, 124], Hackerone, Bugcrowd
		Enforce security measures in submission platform	(i) Securing the vulnerability submission platforms by measures like strong authentication and encryption of records help minimize information leakage. (ii) Usage of selective revealing to address concerns regarding trustworthiness of SecPros	[3], Hackerone, Bugcrowd, Cobalt
Improve submission handling		Filter submissions	(i) Relying on automation to filter low quality reports minimize the burden on the task requester to (manually) verify the submissions	[3], Cobalt, Hackerone
		Explain reward decisions	(i) Transparency in the reward scheme and decisions minimize possible disagreements with SecPros and trust issues	[77, 82]
		Adopt industry standards for the vulnerability management process	(i) Adopt industry standards to improve governance of coordinated vulnerability disclosure. (ii) Reporting procedures should be made straightforward and guidance must be provided to SecPros to submit reports without the risk of violating the program's policies	[28, 77, 124]

Table 3 (continued)

Strategy	Sub-strategy	Action	Findings	References
		Rate limiting	(i) Prevent SecPros from submitting too many reports in a short time window to help reduce false positives	[77, 124]
		Improve payment fulfillment mechanisms	(i) Employ mechanisms that foster transparency and accountability on the vulnerabilities reported to vendors and enhance assurance regarding compensation to Secpros	[44]
Train SecPros		Teach SecPros	(i) Provide teaching material to help SecPros learn how to perform the task of vulnerability discovery. (ii) Provide online courses and workshops to SecPros to learn how to better write a high-quality vulnerability report	[128], Hackerone, Bugcrowd, Cobalt, Google Bug Bounty Academy
		Provide feedback	(i) Provide feedback to SecPros on their submission to help them improve future submissions. (ii) Allow for public access to vulnerability reports to help SecPros learn from other people mistakes. (iii) Communication with SecPros helps foster shared values and beliefs	[128], Hackerone, Cobalt
		Organize events and workshops	(i) Events and workshops, such as live hacking events, empower Secpros to share resources, help the development of their technical skills and contributes to building meaningful relationships between Secpros	Hackerone, Bugcrowd

Table 3 (continued)

Strategy	Sub-strategy	Action	Findings	References
Improve task requester's capabilities		Educate/train task requester	(i) Training task requesters can help them improve their capabilities, e.g., through workshops, training materials, and experiences reported by other organizations	[3]
		Third party support	(i) Task requesters who do not have the knowledge and expertise to lunch a crowdsourced vulnerability discovery program can rely on third parties to do so	[3]

as a possible strategy to keep the SecPros engaged [33] and incentivize new participants [130]. Finally, providing hiring opportunities has also been studied as a strategy to incentivize SecPros perform better and stay engaged in the task [22, 33, 129]. In [3], reward adjustment has shown to be one of the countermeasures used by task requesters to increase the engagement of SecPros within the task.

Task requesters like Google, Microsoft and Facebook rely on increasing the reward amount to attract SecPros and motivate them to submit high quality submissions (e.g., Google couple the quality of submission with the amount of reward in their Chrome vulnerability reward programs.[38]). Other task requesters like GitHub offer bonuses for clever exploitation of a vulnerability (i.e., chaining multiple low severity vulnerabilities to demonstrate how they can together have high security impact.[39]). Mozilla and Google offer SecPros that perform well permanent jobs within their security team [33]. We also observed other interesting incentive schemes. For instance, Microsoft offered rewards to SecPros even if they submit a duplicate report (i.e., a report that refers to the same vulnerability) as long as it enhances the overall quality of the original submission.

Improvement of Non-monetary Incentives

Non-monetary incentives like reputation increase, being mentioned in the hall of fame and self-satisfaction for securing the cyber space also influence attracting SecPros and keep them engaged. Platforms like Bugcrowd, Hackerone and Cobalt use gamification to make tasks interesting and keep SecPros engaged.[40] Organisations like Facebook, Google, Microsoft and others maintain so-called *Thank you*

[38] https://www.google.com/about/appsecurity/chrome-rewards.

[39] https://www.eweek.com/security/github-bug-bounty-program-offers-bonus-rewards.

[40] https://www.tcs.com/blogs/gamified-hiring-calling-all-hackers.

pages and hall of fame in order to mention SecPros who helped the task requester by discovering vulnerabilities. Promoting high profile events (e.g., competitions like Pwn2Own) has been observed to attract more SecPros and motivate them to submit high severity vulnerabilities [33]. Finally, researchers have observed that there is a relationship between the response time of the task requester and how fast they remediate vulnerabilities, as well as how much SecPros are willing to participate in the task [22, 82, 130].

6.2 Controlling the Execution of the Crowdsourced Vulnerability Discovery Task

Some Actions can be taken at runtime that can have positive effects on the quality of the task. Zhao et al. [130] observed that running the tasks for a longer time helps to discover higher number and more severe vulnerabilities. Another way to increase the quality of tasks is to increase the number of SecPros participating in the task (e.g., when the task requester increases the pool of SecPros in situations where the task originally allowed for invited SecPros only) [22, 49, 92, 129, 130]. Researchers also found a correlation between the number of participants and the diversity in the pool of researchers, which in turn affects the diversity of the vulnerabilities discovered [49, 129]. Other researchers correlated the increase in the number of vulnerabilities to the increase in the number of participating SecPros [22, 92, 130].

There are other actions used by organizations and platforms like notifying SecPros participating in the task of any update or change happening in the task. As an example, Hackerone has a service that would notify SecPros participating in the task of any change or update like adding or removing scope or change in the guidelines of the task.[41] In order to minimize any conflict between SecPros and the task requesters, platforms like Hackerone allow SecPros and task requesters to request the platform to mediate between the two in case of disagreement.[42] This can help in keeping the SecPros engaged in the task and minimizing any friction that may happen between the SecPros and the task requester. Also, in order to keep SecPros engaged in the task, task requesters like Google rely on decreasing the reputation score of the SecPro if he does not submit for a long time, the reason being that this should motivate the SecPros to keep submitting reports so that they do not lose their reputation score.[43]

[41] https://www.hackerone.com/blog/policy-change-notifications.

[42] https://www.hackerone.com/disclosure-guidelines.

[43] https://www.google.com/about/appsecurity/hall-of-fame.

6.3 Selection of SecPros

Selecting SecPros with the required skills and expertise to participate in the task has been observed to influence the quality of the task [48, 129, 130]. Researchers proposed selecting SecPros with a verified identity and credentials to help minimize trust issues and minimize cheating [82, 100]. Foti et al. [15] proposed using the reputation scoring system in platforms to manage the intrinsic untrustworthiness of the task. Zhao et al. [129] proposed to select SecPros with diverse skills as a strategy to increase the number of diverse vulnerability types that SecPros submit. Platforms like Cobalt also rely on the past performance of the SecPro to recommend similar tasks that he can participate in.[44] Also, some platforms (e.g., Hackerone and Bugcrowd) and task requesters (e.g., Google) ban SecPros who behave inappropriately or have had a bad performance in previous tasks.

6.4 Improving the Crowdsourced Vulnerability Discovery Task Design

Researchers investigated the effect of clarifying task descriptions and guidelines on the quality of the task [65, 80, 82]. Kuehn and Mueller [65] suggested that having clear terms and conditions will minimize confusion and help SecPros to perform tasks more efficiently. Mckinney [50] suggested using contracts to prevent information leakage before the reported vulnerability is remediated. Miller [82], instead, suggests that task requesters need to maintain transparency in the reward scheme and when making decisions in regard to the reward amount, the reason being that it will help minimize any possible conflicts between task requesters and SecPros.

Platforms like Hackerone and Bugcrowd emphasize on the importance of the clarity of the task description and the submission guidelines as a way to minimize confusion for SecPros.[45] We have also observed that since existing platforms are the media where SecPros disclose vulnerabilities to task requesters, the security of the platform itself is an important aspect. Platforms rely on security measures like two factor authentication and encryption of the vulnerability repository to make sure there is no unauthorized access to the vulnerabilities.[46] Additionally, existing platforms maintain their own crowdsourced vulnerability discovery tasks (i.e., a vulnerability discovery task for the platform itself) and allow SecPros to discover vulnerabilities in the platform while rewarding them for their submissions, just like any other third-party task hosted by the platform.

---

[44] https://blog.cobalt.io/researcher-vetting-verification-3f3f5ec25f02.

[45] https://www.bugcrowd.com/resources/guides/anatomy-bug-bounty-brief/.

[46] https://cobalt.io/security.

6.5 Improve Report Handling

As the vulnerability discovery tasks is riddled with noise (i.e., invalid submissions) [68], some platforms rely on filtering out the bad submissions to minimize the burden on the task requester when verifying the legitimacy of submissions.[47] Cobalt uses machine learning (e.g., collaborative filtering and content analysis) to recommend to the task requester the likelihood that a given submission will be a valid one.[48] Hackerone on the other hand rely on entity extraction to identify expressions in reports that may deem the submission invalid (e.g., including a domain that is out of scope within the report[49]). Hackerone in their platform offers expert augmented noise reduction service,[50] which relies on expert reviews to help filtering invalid submission.

6.6 Train Security Professionals

Platforms like Hackerone and Bugcrowd, and task requesters like Google, train SecPros to perform better. Hackerone has a free online course to Web security, shares learning materials through blogs and e-books with the community.[51] Google created the Bug Hunter university platform to share learning materials and guidelines[52] with SecPro. Additionally, platforms like Hackerone provide feedback to SecPros on their submissions to help them improve future submissions.[53] Allowing public access to vulnerability reports will also help SecPros learn from other people mistakes and success stories.[54] Platforms like Hackerone offer the ability to make vulnerability reports public.[55] Finally, workshops and other community driven activities also help novice SecPros learn from others and improve how they perform the task of vulnerability discovery.[56]

---

47 https://www.hackerone.com/blog/Double-your-signal-double-your-fun.

48 https://cobalt.io/platform.

49 https://docs.hackerone.com/programs/hackbot.html.

50 https://docs.hackerone.com/programs/human-augmented-signal.html.

51 https://www.hackerone.com/start-hacking.

52 https://sites.google.com/site/bughunteruniversity.

53 https://hackerone.com/reports/297181.

54 https://medium.com/@uranium238/hack-more-learn-more-earn-more-and-get-invited-more-f3fc3c4c67d8.

55 https://docs.hackerone.com/hackers/hacktivity.html.

56 https://www.bsidesau.com.au/2017/bugbounty.html.

7 Discussion

In this section, we examine some of the assessment methods and assurance actions from other domains that employ crowdsourcing—we relate this to our application of crowdsourced for vulnerability discovery tasks. We map the quality attributes we have discovered with the quality assessment methods and assurance actions. This mapping will help researchers to better understand the gap in research and help practitioners achieve better quality for the task. We also provide a discussion of the impact of our work on research and practice and propose potential tools that leverage our findings to improve the quality of crowdsourced tasks in vulnerability discovery.

7.1 Quality Control Techniques Used in General Crowdsourcing

Crowdsourcing vulnerability discovery is relatively new compared to crowdsourcing tasks in other domains. In order to have a better understanding of how to improve quality assessment methods and assurance actions, in this section we analyze and compare methods and actions introduced in other domains and relate their applicability in crowdsourced used for vulnerability discovery. Previous work by Daniel et al. [26] surveyed quality attributes, assessment methods and assurance mechanisms generally in crowdsourcing, albeit this survey does not investigate crowdsourced vulnerability tasks as this requires a domain specific study due to the complexity and sensitivity of the task.

Related Quality Assessment Methods Used in General Crowdsourcing

There are some methods that are yet to be explored for quality assessment as they relate to vulnerability discovery tasks. While trustworthiness is highlighted as a desired quality attribute of SecPros [10, 65] and assessing the expertise of SecPros is investigated by researchers [2, 129], there is currently no study to assess the personality traits of SecPros and the effect of these personality traits in their trustworthiness. For instance, Kazai et al. [58, 59] used the Big Five inventory [53] for assessing personality traits such as agreeableness, extraversion, openness, etc. The authors have identified a positive correlation between openness, consciousness and agreeableness, and the accuracy of the task output; whereas a negative relation has been identified between extraversion and neuroticism w.r.t. the task output accuracy. It would be interesting to investigate the personality traits relevant to SecPros and their effect on trustworthiness (e.g., disclosing vulnerabilities before they are remediated).

Vulnerability discovery task description has been highlighted as a quality dimension that would affect the overall quality of the task [65, 129]. To our knowledge, there is no study or implementation that helps to assess the quality of crowdsourced vulnerability discovery tasks description or design. Khanna et al. [60] relied on user studies to assess the quality of the task description and design. The authors organized controlled study sessions with crowd workers performing image annotation tasks. They discovered that the complexity of instructions and the user interface design of the platform are among the barriers that the crowd workers have faced. On the other hand, Willett et al. [123] have used usability analysis methods to investigate the usability of task user interfaces (understandability and learnability) and identified guidelines to enhance the usability of the task user interface.

Although the usage of algorithms in current implementations to assess the quality of crowdsourced vulnerability discovery tasks has been discussed earlier, there is no deep analysis in literature in regard to the application of algorithmic approaches with respect to crowdsourcing vulnerability discovery. While previous research investigated the identification of duplicates and determining the severity in bug reports [15, 74, 112], to the best of our knowledge the application of these techniques for quality assessment in vulnerability discovery are yet to be investigated. This is specifically important especially since crowdsourced vulnerability discovery tasks tend to attract large number of submissions that have large percentage of submissions being invalid, duplicates, or out of scope [68, 108, 111]. Hence, applying algorithmic techniques like outlier analysis could help minimize these quality issues. Finally, Jung and Lease [56] rely on outliers analysis to find out which workers are considered "noisy" in labeling tasks, while Marcus et al. [78] also leverage outliers analysis for identifying "spammers" in estimation tasks.

Related Quality Assurance Mechanisms Used in General Crowdsourcing

It has been observed that SecPros who collaborate with each other while participating in vulnerability discovery tasks tend to produce higher quality submissions [49]. Although collaboration is generally considered beneficial, we have not observed any platform or task requester that facilitates collaboration to improve quality. We have also observed that SecPros tend to collaborate behind the scenes.[57] Work on crowd collaboration in other areas include Retelny et al. [98], who focused on identifying experts from the crowd and built teams to address complex tasks. Kittur [62] use collaboration between workers for the translation of a poem. Andre et al. [8] investigated creative writing tasks and the effect of providing workers with a shared and collaborative editing space. One of the barriers that may hinder relying on collaborating teams in vulnerability discovery is the possibility of collusiveness between SecPros especially due to the sensitivity of the task. There is also previous research investigating collusion detection like the work of Allahbakhsh et al. [5], where the worker-collusion probability is analyzed based on previous task collaborations between them, and then recommends potentially non-colluding workers for building new teams.

[57] https://twitter.com/zseano/status/864206539241947138?s=03.

There have been actions introduced to improve the design of crowdsourced vulnerability discovery tasks as mentioned in Sect. 5. One of these actions is *task decomposition*, which is applied in other crowdsourcing contexts and could prove interesting to investigate its application to vulnerability discovery. Kittur et al. [63] propose the use of the *map-reduce paradigm* to split tasks into smaller sub-tasks that are solved concurrently to produce intermediate results that are merged together to generate the final output. While Kulkarni et al. [66] use a *price-divide-solve* approach, where the decision to work on a task or to split it further is made by workers, and once the tasks/sub-tasks are solved the corresponding results produced by other workers are merged toghether to produce the final output. Further investigation is needed in regard to splitting the crowdsourced tasks for vulnerability discovery, specifically determining whether allowing SecPros to test modules of the system separately would still help discover all types of vulnerabilities. Determining which vulnerabilities could be discovered in certain modules (e.g., frontend or backend of a web application) and which vulnerabilities can only be discovered with wholesome view of the system (e.g., remote code execution).

7.2 *Mapping Quality Attributes to the Assessment Methods and Assurance Actions*

In order to add more depth to our analysis, we now present a mapping of quality attributes discovered in Sect. 3 with the assessment methods that can be used to measure or assess these attributes. Likewise, we present a similar mapping for the quality attributes with the assurance actions that can help to improve these attributes. While some attributes are mentioned in literature or in current implementation, there is no investigated assessment methods or assurance action related to crowdsourcing vulnerability discovery. In order to provide a more holistic view, we include techniques used in other crowdsourcing contexts or in other research areas.

Mapping Attributes with Assessment Methods

Table 4 shows the mapping between the quality attributes and the corresponding assessment methods. Out of the mapping resulting from Table 4, we make the following observations:

- Assessing the quality amongst crowdsourced vulnerability discovery tasks needs further investigation. Although there are related methods and techniques used in other crowdsourcing contexts or in other research fields, the adoption of these methods and techniques for vulnerability discovery tasks is still lagging behind. Having various assessment methods tested and evaluated would help assessing the quality attributes of the task and determining if an intervention is necessary to improve the quality or prevent a quality issues from happening.

Table 4 Mapping quality attributes with assessment methods

Dimension	Sub-dimension	Attribute	Assessment methods used	Examples
Task	Performance	CosteEfficiency	(i) Metric: Task costs and vulnerability reported ratio. (ii) Metric: Signal to noise ratio	[22, 33, 41, 130]
		Effectiveness	(i) Metric: Newcommers and continuing contribution ratio. (ii) Metric: Task requesters' response time. (iii) Metric: Number of vulnerabilities discovered	[73, 129, 130], Hackerone, Bugcrowd, Cobalt
	Description	Clarity	(i) Functions: Machine learning	[126]
		Completeness	(i) Functions: Machine learning	[126]
		Scope	(i) Functions: Machine learning	[126]
	Incentives	Monetary	(i) Metric: Average bounty paid. (ii) Metric: Minimum bounty paid. (iii) Metric: Highest bounty range	Hackerone, Bugcrowd
		Non-monetary	(i) Metric: Task requesters' response time	Hackerone, Bugcrowd
	Management	Timeliness	(i) Metric: Task requesters' response time	Hackerone, Bugcrowd
		Workflow	(i) Metric: Patching vulnerability ratio	[100]
	Terms and conditions	Information security	(i) Function: Entity extraction	Hackerone
		IP leakage	(i) Function: Entity extraction	Hackerone
		Legal protection	N/A	N/A
	Complexity and severity	Complexity	(i) Metric: Signal to noise ratio. (ii) Number vulnerabilities discovered	[22, 41, 73, 130], Hackerone, Bugcrowd, Cobalt
		Severity of vulnerability	(i) Metric: Patching vulnerability Ratio. (ii) Individual: Expert Review, Rating. (iii) Group: Voting, Consensus	[100, 111, 130], Hackerone, Bugcrowd, Google, Microsoft, Cobalt, Mozilla

Table 4 (continued)

Dimension	Sub-dimension	Attribute	Assessment methods used	Examples
Outcome	Quality of report	Duplication	(i) Individual: Expert Review. (ii) Function: Machine learning	[93, 111, 130], Hackerone, Cobalt, Bugcrowd
		Clarity	(i) Individual: Expert review. (ii) Group: Voting	[111, 130], Hackerone
		Spamming	(i) Individual: Expert review. (ii) Function: Machine learning	[111, 130], Hackerone, Cobalt, Bugcrowd
		Completeness	(i) Individual: Expert review. (ii) Group: Voting	[111, 130], Hackerone
		Validity	(i) Individual: Expert review, Rating (ii) Group: Consensus	[100, 111, 130], Mozilla, Hackerone
People	SecPros	Expertise	(i) Individual: Qualification test, refferral (ii) Metric: Number of achievements, acceptance rate, impact, reputation score	[2, 33, 38, 73, 129, 130], Synack, Cobalt, Hackerone, Bugcrowd, Zerochopter
		Satisfaction	(i) Metric: Newcomers/Continuing contribution ratio	[129, 130]
		Trustworthiness	(i) Individual: Referral	[2], Synack, Cobalt, Zerochopter
	Task requester	Performance	(i) Metric: Response time, patching vulnerability ratio	[100], Hackerone, Bugcrowd
		Fairness	(i) Individual: Expert review, rating	[50, 100, 111, 130]
		Generosity	(i) Individual: Expert review, rating	[50, 100, 111, 130]
		Disagreement	(i) Individual: Expert review, rating	[50, 100, 111, 130]
	Group	Diversity	(i) Individual: Qualification test	[38], Synack
		Collaboration	(i) Metric: Signal to noise ratio, number of vulnerabilities discovered	[22, 41, 73, 130], Hackerone, Bugcrowd, Cobalt

- The industry in crowdsourcing for vulnerability discovery is more active in developing and applying assessment methods in contrast with academia.
- Relying on methods that depend on individuals to assess the quality in crowdsourced vulnerability discovery tasks are the most common approach (e.g., expert review). Methods that rely on groups or automated techniques are not yet explored properly in this domain.
- Although we explored assessment methods from other crowdsourcing contexts to extrapolate methods for assessing some of the quality attributes, for some attributes (e.g. non-monetary incentives, timeliness, workflow, IP leakage, diversity, and collaboration) more research needs to be done to identify methods that can help with their assessment.

Mapping Attributes with Assurance Strategies and Actions

In order to improve the quality of crowdsourced vulnerability discovery tasks, organizations are required to perform actions that would affect related quality attributes. Table 5 illustrates the mapping between quality attributes we have discovered and the corresponding assurance actions. We identify the following:

- The industry in crowdsourcing vulnerability discovery is more active in adopting quality assurance strategies and actions to improve the quality of the crowdsourced vulnerability discovery tasks in contrast to research findings in academia.
- Although there are assurance actions that has been recommended and discussed to have effect on the quality attributes, but there is only limited research on the evaluation of these assurance actions.
- There are assurance actions that affect several quality attributes at the same time. More rigorous research needs to be done to identify these relationships further. Understanding for each assurance action what would be the first order attributes that are affected and what are the ones that are affected as a side effect would help better design of the quality control solution.
- Some actions may have positive effects on some attributes (i.e., improving the quality attributes) and negative effects on others (e.g., increasing the number of SecPros participating in the task may increase the effectiveness of the task through receiving more submissions but at the same time may affect the quality of submissions and cause an increase in the received duplicate reports).

7.3 Study Implications

There is no *one task fits all* solution for crowdsourced vulnerability discovery and, as shown in previous sections, task requester must take into account a number of quality attributes relevant for their programs, the assessment methods they can adopt

Table 5 Mapping assurance strategies and actions with quality attributes

Strategy	Sub-strategy	Action	Related attributes	References
Incentivization	Improvement of monetary incentives	Adjust reward	(i) Effectiveness of the task	[16, 105, 130]
		Provide hiring opportunities	(i) Effectiveness of the task. (ii) Validity of submission	[22, 33, 129]
		Provide bonus	(i) Effectiveness of the task	[33, 130]
		Provide rewards to duplicate reports	(i) Clarity of submission. (ii) Completeness of submission	Microsoft VRP
	Improvement of non-monetary incentives	Shorten vendors response time	(i) Effectiveness of the task. (ii) Information security	[39, 82, 130]
		Gamify the task	(i) Effectiveness of the task. (ii) Cost efficiency of the task. (iii) Clarity of the submissions. (iv) Validity of submissions. (v) Completeness of submissions. (vi) Severity of vulnerabilities	Hackerone, Bugcrowd, Cobalt
		Promote events	(i) Effectiveness of the task. (ii) Severity of vulnerabilities	[33]
		Provide transparency on paid/unpaid bounties	(i) Fairness regarding bounties amount. (ii) Disagreement on bouties amount	[44]
		Acknowledge contribution	(i) Non-monetary incentives. (ii) SecPros' satisfaction. (iii) SecPros' expertise	[28, 118]
		Provide resources/ hardware	(i) Non-monetary incentives. (ii) SecPros' satisfaction. (iii) Task requesters' generosity	[28]
Controlling task execution		Run task for longer time	(i) Effectiveness of the task	[130]
		Increase the number of SecPros	(i) Effectiveness of the task. (ii) Diversity of SecPros	[22, 27, 49, 129, 130]
		Decay in reputation if not submitting for long time	(i) Effectiveness of the task	Google VRP

Table 5 (continued)

Strategy	Sub-strategy	Action	Related attributes	References
		Improve communication with SecPros	(i) SecPros' satisfaction. (ii) Secpros' trusworthiness	[77, 118, 124]
		Timed incentivize Secpros	(i) Task effectiveness. (ii) Non-monetary incentives. (iii) Task timeliness. (iv) SecPros' trustworthiness	[77]
Selection of SecPros		Filter SecPros	(i) Information Security: Trustworthiness. (ii) Clarity of the submissions. (iii) Validity of Submissions. (iv) Completeness of Submissions. (v) Severity of Vulnerabilities	[15, 100, 130], Hackerone, Bugcrowd
		Select SecPros with high skill diversity	(i) Diversity of SecPros	[129]
		Recommend tasks	(i) Validity of submissions	Cobalt
		Reject SecPros	(i) Information security. (ii) Validity of submissions. (iii) Spamming	Hackerone, Bugcrowd
		Early engagement of SecPros	(i) SecPros' expertise. (ii) SecPros' trustworthiness. (iii) Task effectiveness. (iv) Validity of submissions	[77]
Improvement of task design		Clarify terms and conditions	(i) Information Security. (ii) IP leakage. (iii) Legal protection	[65, 80, 82]
		Define reward schemes	(i) SecPros' satisfaction. (ii) Task requesters' fairness. (iii) Disagreements regarding rewards	Hackerone
		Clarify submission guidelines	(i) Task's scope. (ii) Validity of submissions	Hackerone Bugcrowd
		Enforce security measures in submission platform	(i) Information security	Hackerone, Bugcrowd, Cobalt
Improve submission handling		Filter submissions	(i) Task's cost efficiency. (ii) Task requesters' performance in terms of response time	[111], Cobalt, Hackerone
		Explain reward decisions	(i) Disagreement	[82]

Table 5 (continued)

Strategy	Sub-strategy	Action	Related attributes	References
		Adopt industry standards for the vulnerability management process	(i) Task management workflow. (ii) Task requesters' performance	[28, 77, 124]
		Rate limiting	(i) Duplicate submissions. (ii) Spamming. (iii) Validity of submissions	[124]
		Improve payment fulfillment mechanisms	(i) SecPros' satisfaction. (ii) SecPros' trustworthiness. (iii) Task requester's performance. (iv) Task requester's fairness	[44]
Train SecPros		Teach SecPros	(i) Effectiveness of the task. (ii) Clarity of the submissions. (iii) Validity of submissions. (iv) Completeness of submissions. (v) Severity of vulnerabilities	Hackerone, Bugcrowd, Cobalt, Google, Bug Bounty Academy
		Provide feedback	(i) Effectiveness of the task. (ii) Clarity of the submissions. (iii) Validity of submissions. (iv) Completeness of submissions	Hackerone
		Organize events and workshops	(i) Task effectiveness. (ii) Clarity of submissions. (iii) Validity of submissions. (iv) Completeness of submissions. (v) SecPros' expertise. (vi) SecPros' satisfaction. (vii) Secpros' collaboration	Hackerone, Bugcrowd
Improve task requester's capabilities		Educate/train task requester	(i) Task's cost efficiency. (ii) Task's effectiveness. (iii) Clarity, completeness and scope of task description. (iv) Task requesters' performance	[3]
		Third party support	(i) Task's cost efficiency. (ii) Task's effectiveness. (iii) Clarity, completeness and scope of task description. (iv) Task requesters' performance	[3]

and the assurance strategies they need to prioritize and implement. The framework we propose can be used as a roadmap helping them in designing, running and maintaining a crowdsourced task for vulnerability discovery. It has been observed that although crowdsourced vulnerability discovery tasks are gaining an increasing popularity,[58] there are still large numbers of organizations that do not adopt this practice. For instance, as of 2017, the number of Forbes Global 2000 companies using crowdsourcing to discover vulnerabilities were lesser than 6%.[59] We therefore believe our work will help more organizations adopt crowdsourced vulnerability discovery by offering a quality control framework for the crowdsourced vulnerability discovery task. This framework will help design quality control solutions for the task and hence minimize the fears that caused them to be reluctant to use crowdsourcing vulnerability discovery. We have already identified pre-adoption fears that organizations face with regard to adopting crowd-based approach to vulnerability discovery [3]. We believe that the quality control framework would help mitigate these fears.

In the following subsections we discuss potential tools that could leverage our work to support task requesters as well as managers of crowdsourcing vulnerability discovery platforms in reaching their quality goals.

Crowdsourcing Vulnerability Discovery Quality Control Knowledge Graph

We believe it is desirable to provide a repeatable and well-engineered methodology with consolidated concepts and techniques to understand different quality threats and effectively construct quality control mechanisms to address them. This would be feasible through creating a quality-aware knowledge layer to shield developers of vulnerability discovery tasks from the complexity of the underlying quality control mechanisms. By leveraging our findings, it would be possible to create a knowledge base where diverse quality assessment and improvement mechanisms are abstracted and organized.

We propose the development of Crowdsourcing Vulnerability Discovery Quality Control Knowledge Graph (CVQKG). The CVQKG will provide a means to acquire and share relevant knowledge. The type of knowledge captured include entities and constraints representing: (i) Domain concepts describing tasks (e.g., vulnerabilities, vulnerability types, vulnerability disclosure), the actors involved (e.g., SecPros, task requester, experts), the information they need to perform tasks (e.g., task description, scope); (ii) quality control mechanisms (e.g., quality assessment methods, quality assurance actions); and (iii) relationships between entities. The proposed model would feature a vocabulary and constructs for describing elementary entity types (e.g., vulnerability discovery task, SecPro, platform, quality attribute,

[58] https://www.darkreading.com/vulnerabilities---threats/bug-bounty-programs-are-growing-up-fast-and-paying-more/d/d-id/1328428.

[59] https://www.hackerone.com/sites/default/files/2017-06/The%20Hacker-Powered%20Security%20Report.pdf.

quality assessment method, quality assurance action), and relationships among them (e.g., dependencies between artifact-based quality assessment metric and output, between concrete quality indicator and high-level quality properties, and between quality assurance action and high-level quality properties).

Crowdsourcing Vulnerability Discovery Quality Control Knowledge Patterns

In the previous subsection, we propose leveraging our finding to create the CVQKG. Abstracting and unifying disparate quality control concepts and techniques brings several benefits: It separates quality control concerns from the implementation of the functional requirements of a crowd-sourcing application, and it allows development and run-time support to provide assistive and generative functionalities that simplify the automation of crowdsourcing vulnerability discovery quality control. However, specifying what may be a complex quality control solution involving various and interdependent methods of assessment and assurance is a demanding task, especially for novice crowdsourced vulnerability discovery task developers. It is particularly difficult to build effective quality control solutions, because at design time developers must select from among numerous alternative mechanisms to handle quality concerns at various phases of the tasks' lifecycle. We believe that developing a methodology and techniques to provide methodological support and automated decision making to capture, understand, reuse and implement a suitable combination of assessment, and assurance mechanisms is essential.

We propose to encapsulate a quality control solution as first class entities, called: Crowdsourcing Vulnerability Discovery Quality Control Knowledge Patterns (CVQP), which represents a parameterized quality control mechanism template to tackle sample usage and a specific type of quality threat (e.g., high volume of invalid submissions, leakage of information about the vulnerability before it is fixed). A template can be used as both a guideline for developers and input to a tool that automatically generates the quality control code. By making quality control templates reusable and re-configurable, we can radically change how developers design and implement quality-aware crowdsourcing vulnerability discovery tasks, providing incrementally learned patterns that offer developers greater expressive power and mastery of quality control mechanisms. This is similar to codifying common business process behavior as collections of reusable modular reference models built for a specific application domain [25, 67]. In practice, we observe that expert developers of crowdsourcing vulnerability discovery tasks often have valuable knowledge to identify the most appropriate quality control mechanisms. This knowledge is beneficial for reuse and being able to leverage such reuse creates tremendous opportunities to increase the effectiveness of quality control mechanisms. A CVQP would be represented as an entity on the basis of the metadata models proposed in the CVQKG. It has two parts: A recommendation consisting of entities representing quality control components, and a context consisting of conditions under which the recommended components are useful. For instance, a quality component could be an adapter that monitors the number of submissions for a crowdsourced vulnerability discovery task, identifies if there is a decrease in the number of submissions, and increase the rewards offered to attract more submissions. Quality control components will be created, verified, tested, reviewed, and curated by experienced programmers, based on available knowledge or experience, and may be reused in several crowdsourcing vulnerability discovery tasks. Different types of quality control components need to be considered including assessment, improvement, and repair components.

In order to keep the CVQKG up to date and maintain the relevancy of knowledge, we propose to rely on incremental knowledge acquisition techniques. Domain experts would be creating and modifying quality control knowledge, and developers would be attaching code, services, or algorithms that assess or improve the quality of the crowdsourced vulnerability discovery task.

8 Conclusion

According to our analysis, we have observed that literature in this field is significantly lacking and that there are attributes, assessment methods, and assurance actions that are used by industry yet not properly investigated by literature in this field (e.g., clarify of task description as an attribute, algorithmic functions for assessment, the effect of training as an assurance strategy). Researchers can rely on this insight to complement industry implementations with academic research that would greatly help improve and refine these implementations. We also discuss some of the assessment methods and assurance actions used in other crowdsourcing context, but yet to be introduced in crowdsourced vulnerability discovery tasks (e.g., assessing the quality of SecPros according to personality traits, communication skills, improving outcome quality by relying on SecPros collaboration with each other). Leveraging these additional methods and actions from different domains can also greatly help improve the quality of crowdsourced vulnerability discovery tasks.

References

1. Agarwal, Y., Hall, M.: Protectmyprivacy: detecting and mitigating privacy leaks on iOS devices using crowdsourcing. In: Proceeding of the 11th Annual International Conference on Mobile Systems: Applications, and Services, pp. 97–110. Association for Computing Machinery, New York, NY, USA (2013)
2. Al-Banna, M., Benatallah, B., Barukh, M.C.: Software security professionals: expertise indicators. In: 2016 IEEE 2nd International Conference on Collaboration and Internet Computing (CIC), pp. 139–148. IEEE (2016)
3. Al-Banna, M., Benatallah, B., Schlagwein, D., Bertino, E., Barukh, M.C.: Friendly hackers to the rescue: how organizations perceive crowdsourced vulnerability discovery. In: PACIS, p. 230 (2018)

4. Allahbakhsh, M., Benatallah, B., Ignjatovic, A., Motahari-Nezhad, H.R., Bertino, E., Dustdar, S.: Quality control in crowdsourcing systems: issues and directions. IEEE Internet Comput. **17**(2), 76–81 (2013)
5. Allahbakhsh, M., Samimi, S., Motahari-Nezhad, H.R., Benatallah, B.: Harnessing implicit teamwork knowledge to improve quality in crowdsourcing processes. In: 2014 IEEE 7th International Conference on Service-Oriented Computing and Applications, pp. 17–24. IEEE (2014)
6. Allodi, L.: Economic factors of vulnerability trade and exploitation. In: Proceedings of the 2017 ACM SIGSAC Conference on Computer and Communications Security, pp. 1483–1499 (2017)
7. Amini, S., Lin, J., Hong, J.I., Lindqvist, J., Zhang, J.: Mobile application evaluation using automation and crowdsourcing (2013)
8. André, P., Kraut, R.E., Kittur, A.: Effects of simultaneous and sequential work structures on distributed collaborative interdependent tasks. In: Proceedings of the SIGCHI Conference on Human Factors in Computing Systems, pp. 139–148 (2014)
9. Antunes, N., Vieira, M.: Comparing the effectiveness of penetration testing and static code analysis on the detection of SQL injection vulnerabilities in web services. In: 2009 15th IEEE Pacific Rim International Symposium on Dependable Computing, pp. 301–306. IEEE (2009)
10. Armin, J., Foti, P., Cremonini, M.: 0-day vulnerabilities and cybercrime. In: 2015 10th International Conference on Availability, Reliability and Security, pp. 711–718. IEEE (2015)
11. Arora, A., Krishnan, R., Telang, R., Yang, Y.: An empirical analysis of software vendors' patch release behavior: impact of vulnerability disclosure. Inf. Syst. Res. **21**(1), 115–132 (2010)
12. Austin, A., Williams, L.: One technique is not enough: a comparison of vulnerability discovery techniques. In: 2011 International Symposium on Empirical Software Engineering and Measurement, pp. 97–106. IEEE (2011)
13. Bacudio, A.G., Yuan, X., Chu, B.T.B., Jones, M.: An overview of penetration testing. Int. J. Netw. Secur. Its Appl. **3**(6), 19 (2011)
14. Bau, J., Bursztein, E., Gupta, D., Mitchell, J.: State of the art: automated black-box web application vulnerability testing. In: 2010 IEEE Symposium on Security and Privacy, pp. 332–345. IEEE (2010)
15. Behl, D., Handa, S., Arora, A.: A bug mining tool to identify and analyze security bugs using naive bayes and TF-IDF. In: 2014 International Conference on Reliability Optimization and Information Technology (ICROIT), pp. 294–299. IEEE (2014)
16. Böhme, R.: A comparison of market approaches to software vulnerability disclosure. In: International Conference on Emerging Trends in Information and Communication Security, pp. 298–311. Springer, Berlin (2006)
17. Boyd, S.W., Keromytis, A.D.: SQLrand: preventing SQL injection attacks. In: International Conference on Applied Cryptography and Network Security, pp. 292–302. Springer, Berlin (2004)
18. Breidenbach, L., Daian, P., Tramer, F., Juels, A.: The hydra framework for principled, automated bug bounties. IEEE Secur. Priv. **17**(4), 53–61 (2019)
19. Brian, C., Gary, M.: Static analysis for security. IEEE Secur. Priv. **7**(4), 32–36 (2004)
20. Cavusoglu, H., Cavusoglu, H., Raghunathan, S.: Efficiency of vulnerability disclosure mechanisms to disseminate vulnerability knowledge. IEEE Trans. Software Eng. **33**(3), 171–185 (2007)
21. Cen, L., Kong, D., Jin, H., Si, L.: Mobile app security risk assessment: a crowdsourcing ranking approach from user comments. In: Proceedings of the 2015 SIAM International Conference on Data Mining, pp. 658–666. SIAM (2015)
22. Chatfield, A.T., Reddick, C.G.: Cybersecurity innovation in government: a case study of us pentagon's vulnerability reward program. In: Proceedings of the 18th Annual International Conference on Digital Government Research, pp. 64–73 (2017)
23. Chen, J.M., Wu, C.L.: An automated vulnerability scanner for injection attack based on injection point. In: 2010 International Computer Symposium (ICS2010), pp. 113–118. IEEE (2010)

24. Christoforidis, C., Vlachos, V., Androulidakis, I.: A crowdsourcing approach to protect against novel malware threats. In: 2014 22nd Telecommunications Forum Telfor (TELFOR), pp. 1063–1066. IEEE (2014)
25. Cutumisu, M., Onuczko, C., Szafron, D., Schaeffer, J., McNaughton, M., Roy, T., Siegel, J., Carbonaro, M.: Evaluating pattern catalogs: the computer games experience. In: Proceedings of the 28th International Conference on Software Egineering, pp. 132–141 (2006)
26. Daniel, F., Kucherbaev, P., Cappiello, C., Benatallah, B., Allahbakhsh, M.: Quality control in crowdsourcing: a survey of quality attributes, assessment techniques, and assurance actions. ACM Comput. Surv. (CSUR) **51**(1), 1–40 (2018)
27. Dey, P.K., Kinch, J., Ogunlana, S.O.: Managing risk in software development projects: a case study. Ind. Manag. Data Syst. (2007)
28. Ding, A.Y., De Jesus, G.L., Janssen, M.: Ethical hacking for boosting IoT vulnerability management: a first look into bug bounty programs and responsible disclosure. In: Proceedings of the Eighth International Conference on Telecommunications and Remote Sensing, pp. 49–55 (2019)
29. Doupé, A., Cova, M., Vigna, G.: Why Johnny can't pentest: an analysis of black-box web vulnerability scanners. In: International Conference on Detection of Intrusions and Malware, and Vulnerability Assessment, pp. 111–131. Springer, Berlin (2010)
30. Dowd, M., McDonald, J., Schuh, J.: The art of Software Security Assessment: Identifying and Preventing Software Vulnerabilities. Pearson Education (2006)
31. Edmundson, A., Holtkamp, B., Rivera, E., Finifter, M., Mettler, A., Wagner, D.: An empirical study on the effectiveness of security code review. In: International Symposium on Engineering Secure Software and Systems, pp. 197–212. Springer, Berlin (2013)
32. Fang, M., Hafiz, M.: Discovering buffer overflow vulnerabilities in the wild: an empirical study. In: Proceedings of the 8th ACM/IEEE International Symposium on Empirical Software Engineering and Measurement, pp. 1–10 (2014)
33. Finifter, M., Akhawe, D., Wagner, D.: An empirical study of vulnerability rewards programs. In: 22nd {USENIX} Security Symposium ({USENIX} Security 13), pp. 273–288 (2013)
34. Fryer, H., Simperl, E.: Web science challenges in researching bug bounties. In: Proceedings of the 2017 ACM on Web Science Conference, pp. 273–277 (2017)
35. Furnell, S., Tsaganidi, V., Phippen, A.: Security beliefs and barriers for novice internet users. Comput. Secur. **27**(7–8), 235–240 (2008)
36. Gamero-Garrido, A., Savage, S., Levchenko, K., Snoeren, A.C.: Quantifying the pressure of legal risks on third-party vulnerability research. In: Proceedings of the 2017 ACM SIGSAC Conference on Computer and Communications Security, pp. 1501–1513 (2017)
37. Ghaffarian, S.M., Shahriari, H.R.: Software vulnerability analysis and discovery using machine-learning and data-mining techniques: a survey. ACM Comput. Surv. (CSUR) **50**(4), 1–36 (2017)
38. Giboney, J.S., Proudfoot, J.G., Goel, S., Valacich, J.S.: The security expertise assessment measure (seam): developing a scale for hacker expertise. Comput. Secur. **60**, 37–51 (2016)
39. Hafiz, M., Fang, M.: Game of detections: how are security vulnerabilities discovered in the wild? Empir. Softw. Eng. **21**(5), 1920–1959 (2016)
40. Hata, H., Guo, M., Babar, M.A.: Understanding the heterogeneity of contributors in bug bounty programs. In: 2017 ACM/IEEE International Symposium on Empirical Software Engineering and Measurement (ESEM), pp. 223–228. IEEE (2017)
41. Herr, T., Schneier, B., Morris, C.: Taking stock: estimating vulnerability rediscovery. Belfer Cyber Security Project White Paper Series (2017)
42. Herzog, P.: Osstmm 2.2–open source security testing methodology manual. Open source document (2006). www.isecom.org/osstmm
43. Ho, C.J., Vaughan, J.W.: Online task assignment in crowdsourcing markets. In: AAAI, vol. 12, pp. 45–51 (2012)
44. Hoffman, A., Becerril-Blas, E., Moreno, K., Kim, Y.: Decentralized security bounty management on blockchain and IPFS. In: 2020 10th Annual Computing and Communication Workshop and Conference (CCWC), pp. 0241–0247. IEEE (2020)

45. Howard, M.A.: A process for performing security code reviews. IEEE Secur. Priv. **4**(4), 74–79 (2006)
46. Howe, J.: The rise of crowdsourcing. Wired Mag. **14**(6), 1–4 (2006)
47. Huang, C., Liu, J., Fang, Y., Zuo, Z.: A study on web security incidents in China by analyzing vulnerability disclosure platforms. Comput. Secur. **58**, 47–62 (2016)
48. Huang, K., Zhang, J., Tan, W., Feng, Z.: An empirical analysis of contemporary android mobile vulnerability market. In: 2015 IEEE International Conference on Mobile Services, pp. 182–189. IEEE (2015)
49. Huang, K., Zhang, J., Tan, W., Feng, Z.: Shifting to mobile: network-based empirical study of mobile vulnerability market. IEEE Trans. Serv. Comput. (2016)
50. Irani, L.C., Silberman, M.S.: Turkopticon: Interrupting worker invisibility in amazon mechanical Turk. In: Proceedings of the SIGCHI Conference on Human Factors in Computing Systems, pp. 611–620 (2013)
51. Ismail, Q., Ahmed, T., Kapadia, A., Reiter, M.K.: Crowdsourced exploration of security configurations. In: Proceedings of the 33rd Annual ACM Conference on Human Factors in Computing Systems, pp. 467–476 (2015)
52. Joh, H., Malaiya, Y.K.: Seasonal variation in the vulnerability discovery process. In: 2009 International Conference on Software Testing Verification and Validation, pp. 191–200. IEEE (2009)
53. John, O.P., Robins, R.W., Pervin, L.A.: Handbook of Personality: Theory and Research. Guilford Press (2010)
54. Johnson, B., Song, Y., Murphy-Hill, E., Bowdidge, R.: Why don't software developers use static analysis tools to find bugs? In: 2013 35th International Conference on Software Engineering (ICSE), pp. 672–681. IEEE (2013)
55. Jovanovic, N., Kruegel, C., Kirda, E.: Pixy: A static analysis tool for detecting web application vulnerabilities. In: 2006 IEEE Symposium on Security and Privacy (S&P'06), pp. 6–pp. IEEE (2006)
56. Jung, H.J., Lease, M.: Improving consensus accuracy via z-score and weighted voting. In: Workshops at the Twenty-Fifth AAAI Conference on Artificial Intelligence. Citeseer (2011)
57. Kannan, K., Telang, R.: Market for software vulnerabilities? think again. Manage. Sci. **51**(5), 726–740 (2005)
58. Kazai, G., Kamps, J., Milic-Frayling, N.: Worker types and personality traits in crowdsourcing relevance labels. In: Proceedings of the 20th ACM International Conference on Information and Knowledge Management, pp. 1941–1944 (2011)
59. Kazai, G., Kamps, J., Milic-Frayling, N.: The face of quality in crowdsourcing relevance labels: Demographics, personality and labeling accuracy. In: Proceedings of the 21st ACM International Conference on Information and Knowledge Management, pp. 2583–2586 (2012)
60. Khanna, S., Ratan, A., Davis, J., Thies, W.: Evaluating and improving the usability of mechanical Turk for low-income workers in India. In: Proceedings of the first ACM Symposium on Computing for Development, pp. 1–10 (2010)
61. Kim, J., Malaiya, Y.K., Ray, I.: Vulnerability discovery in multi-version software systems. In: 10th IEEE High Assurance Systems Engineering Symposium (HASE'07), pp. 141–148. IEEE (2007)
62. Kittur, A.: Crowdsourcing, collaboration and creativity. XRDS: Crossroads, ACM Mag. Stud. **17**(2), 22–26 (2010)
63. Kittur, A., Smus, B., Khamkar, S., Kraut, R.E.: Crowdforge: crowdsourcing complex work. In: Proceedings of the 24th Annual ACM Symposium on User Interface Software and Technology, pp. 43–52 (2011)
64. Ko, S.T., Lee, J.H.: Aperture coupled metamaterial patch antenna with broad e-plane beamwidth for millimeter wave application. In: 2013 IEEE Antennas and Propagation Society International Symposium (APSURSI), pp. 1796–1797. IEEE (2013)
65. Kuehn, A., Mueller, M.: Shifts in the cybersecurity paradigm: zero-day exploits, discourse, and emerging institutions. In: Proceedings of the 2014 New Security Paradigms Workshop, pp. 63–68 (2014)

66. Kulkarni, A., Can, M., Hartmann, B.: Collaboratively crowdsourcing workflows with Turkomatic. In: Proceedings of the ACM 2012 Conference on Computer Supported Cooperative Work, pp. 1003–1012 (2012)
67. La Rosa, M., Dumas, M., Ter Hofstede, A.H., Mendling, J.: Configurable multi-perspective business process models. Inf. Syst. **36**(2), 313–340 (2011)
68. Laszka, A., Zhao, M., Grossklags, J.: Banishing misaligned incentives for validating reports in bug-bounty platforms. In: European Symposium on Research in Computer Security, pp. 161–178. Springer, Berlin (2016)
69. Li, Z., Liao, Q.: An economic alternative to improve cybersecurity of e-government and smart cities. In: Proceedings of the 17th International Digital Government Research Conference on Digital Government Research, pp. 455–464 (2016)
70. Li, Z., Liao, Q.: Harnessing uncertainty in vulnerability market. In: 2018 27th International Conference on Computer Communication and Networks (ICCCN), pp. 1–9. IEEE (2018)
71. Liu, B., Shi, L., Cai, Z., Li, M.: Software vulnerability discovery techniques: a survey. In: 2012 Fourth International Conference on Multimedia Information Networking and Security, pp. 152–156. IEEE (2012)
72. Livshits, V.B., Lam, M.S.: Finding security vulnerabilities in java applications with static analysis. In: USENIX Security Symposium, vol. 14, pp. 18–18 (2005)
73. Luna, D., Allodi, L., Cremonini, M.: Productivity and patterns of activity in bug bounty programs: analysis of Hackerone and google vulnerability research. In: Proceedings of the 14th International Conference on Availability, Reliability and Security, pp. 1–10 (2019)
74. Maalej, W., Nabil, H.: Bug report, feature request, or simply praise? on automatically classifying app reviews. In: 2015 IEEE 23rd International Requirements Engineering Conference (RE), pp. 116–125. IEEE (2015)
75. Maillart, T., Zhao, M., Grossklags, J., Chuang, J.: Given enough eyeballs, all bugs are shallow? revisiting eric Raymond with bug bounty programs. J. Cybersecur. **3**(2), 81–90 (2017)
76. Malaiya, Y.K., Denton, J.: Requirements volatility and defect density. In: Proceedings 10th International Symposium on Software Reliability Engineering (Cat. No. PR00443), pp. 285–294. IEEE (1999)
77. Malladi, S.S., Subramanian, H.C.: Bug bounty programs for cybersecurity: practices, issues, and recommendations. IEEE Softw. **37**(1), 31–39 (2019)
78. Marcus, A., Karger, D., Madden, S., Miller, R., Oh, S.: Counting with the crowd. Proc. VLDB Endow. **6**(2), 109–120 (2012)
79. McAfee: Economic impact of cybercrime II (2016). http://www.mcafee.com/au/resources/reports/rp-economic-impact-cybercrime2.pdf. Accessed 4 April 2016
80. McKinney, D.: Vulnerability bazaar. IEEE Secur. Priv. **5** (2007)
81. Messier, R.: Penetration Testing Basics. Apress, Berkeley, CA (2016)
82. Miller, C.: The legitimate vulnerability market: the secretive world of 0-day exploit sales. In: WEIS (2007)
83. Moore, T., Clayton, R.: Evaluating the wisdom of crowds in assessing phishing websites. In: International Conference on Financial Cryptography and Data Security, pp. 16–30. Springer, Berlin (2008)
84. Morrison, P., Herzig, K., Murphy, B., Williams, L.: Challenges with applying vulnerability prediction models. In: Proceedings of the 2015 Symposium and Bootcamp on the Science of Security, pp. 1–9 (2015)
85. Moser, A., Kruegel, C., Kirda, E.: Limits of static analysis for malware detection. In: Twenty-Third Annual Computer Security Applications Conference (ACSAC 2007), pp. 421–430. IEEE (2007)
86. Mu, D., Cuevas, A., Yang, L., Hu, H., Xing, X., Mao, B., Wang, G.: Understanding the reproducibility of crowd-reported security vulnerabilities. In: 27th {USENIX} Security Symposium ({USENIX} Security 18), pp. 919–936 (2018)
87. Mumtaz, S., Rodriguez, C., Benatallah, B., Al-Banna, M., Zamanirad, S.: Learning word representation for the cyber security vulnerability domain. In: 2020 International Joint Conference on Neural Networks (IJCNN), pp. 1–8. IEEE (2020)

88. Munaiah, N., Meneely, A.: Vulnerability severity scoring and bounties: why the disconnect? In: Proceedings of the 2nd International Workshop on Software Analytics, pp. 8–14 (2016)
89. Munaiah, N., Meyers, B.S., Alm, C.O., Meneely, A., Murukannaiah, P.K., Prud'hommeaux, E., Wolff, J., Yu, Y.: Natural language insights from code reviews that missed a vulnerability. In: International Symposium on Engineering Secure Software and Systems, pp. 70–86. Springer, Berlin (2017)
90. Nguyen-Dinh, L.V., Blanke, U., Tröster, G.: Towards scalable activity recognition: adapting zero-effort crowdsourced acoustic models. In: Proceedings of the 12th International Conference on Mobile and Ubiquitous Multimedia, pp. 1–10 (2013)
91. Okoli, C., Schabram, K.: A guide to conducting a systematic literature review of information systems research (2010)
92. Ozment, A.: Bug auctions: vulnerability markets reconsidered. In: Third Workshop on the Economics of Information Security, pp. 19–26 (2004)
93. Ozment, A.: The likelihood of vulnerability rediscovery and the social utility of vulnerability hunting. In: WEIS. Citeseer (2005)
94. Parra, C., Subramanian, H.: A bargaining games approach to information security interactions. In: 2019 First International Conference on Digital Data Processing (DDP), pp. 82–87. IEEE (2019)
95. Radianti, J., Gonzalez, J.J.: Understanding hidden information security threats: The vulnerability black market. In: 2007 40th Annual Hawaii International Conference on System Sciences (HICSS'07), pp. 156c–156c. IEEE (2007)
96. Radianti, J., Rich, E., Gonzalez, J.J.: Vulnerability black markets: empirical evidence and scenario simulation. In: 2009 42nd Hawaii International Conference on System Sciences, pp. 1–10. IEEE (2009)
97. Ransbotham, S., Mitra, S., Ramsey, J.: Are markets for vulnerabilities effective? Mis Quarterly, pp. 43–64 (2012)
98. Retelny, D., Robaszkiewicz, S., To, A., Lasecki, W.S., Patel, J., Rahmati, N., Doshi, T., Valentine, M., Bernstein, M.S.: Expert crowdsourcing with flash teams. In: Proceedings of the 27th Annual ACM Symposium on User Interface Software and Technology, pp. 75–85 (2014)
99. Richardson, R.: The latest results from the longest-running project of its kind. CSI Comput. Crime Secur. Surv. (2008)
100. Ruohonen, J., Hyrynsalmi, S., Leppănen, V.: Trading exploits online: a preliminary case study. In: 2016 IEEE Tenth International Conference on Research Challenges in Information Science (RCIS), pp. 1–12. IEEE (2016)
101. Russell, D., Russell, D., Gangemi, G., Gangemi, S., Gangemi Sr, G.: Computer security basics. O'Reilly Media, Inc. (1991)
102. Sabottke, C., Suciu, O., Dumitraş, T.: Vulnerability disclosure in the age of social media: Exploiting twitter for predicting real-world exploits. In: 24th {USENIX} Security Symposium ({USENIX} Security 15), pp. 1041–1056 (2015)
103. Sanagavarapu, L.M., Reddy, Y.R.: Crowdsourcing security-opportunities and challenges. In: 2018 IEEE/ACM 11th International Workshop on Cooperative and Human Aspects of Software Engineering (CHASE), pp. 37–40. IEEE (2018)
104. Sauerwein, C., Gander, M., Felderer, M., Breu, R.: A systematic literature review of crowdsourcing-based research in information security. In: 2016 IEEE Symposium on Service-Oriented System Engineering (SOSE), pp. 364–371. IEEE (2016)
105. Schechter, S.: How to buy better testing using competition to get the most security and robustness for your dollar. In: International Conference on Infrastructure Security, pp. 73–87. Springer, Berlin (2002)
106. Schulmeyer, G.G., McManus, J.I.: Handbook of Software Quality Assurance. Van Nostrand Reinhold Co. (1992)
107. Seth, N., Deshmukh, S., Vrat, P.: Service quality models: a review. Int. J. Qual. Reliab. Manag. (2005)

108. Shafigh, S., Benatallah, B., Rodríguez, C., Al-Banna, M.: Why some bug-bounty vulnerability reports are invalid? study of bug-bounty reports and developing an out-of-scope taxonomy model. In: Proceedings of the 15th ACM/IEEE International Symposium on Empirical Software Engineering and Measurement (ESEM), pp. 1–6 (2021)
109. Shin, Y., Meneely, A., Williams, L., Osborne, J.A.: Evaluating complexity, code churn, and developer activity metrics as indicators of software vulnerabilities. IEEE Trans. Software Eng. **37**(6), 772–787 (2010)
110. Sillaber, C., Sauerwein, C., Mussmann, A., Breu, R.: Data quality challenges and future research directions in threat intelligence sharing practice. In: Proceedings of the 2016 ACM on Workshop on Information Sharing and Collaborative Security, pp. 65–70 (2016)
111. Su, H.J., Pan, J.Y.: Crowdsourcing platform for collaboration management in vulnerability verification. In: 2016 18th Asia-Pacific Network Operations and Management Symposium (APNOMS), pp. 1–4. IEEE (2016)
112. Sun, C., Lo, D., Wang, X., Jiang, J., Khoo, S.C.: A discriminative model approach for accurate duplicate bug report retrieval. In: Proceedings of the 32nd ACM/IEEE International Conference on Software Engineering, vol.1, pp. 45–54 (2010)
113. Tentilucci, M., Roberts, N., Kandari, S., Johnson, D., Stackpole, B., Markowsky, G.: Crowdsourcing computer security attack trees (2015)
114. Tian, J.: Software Quality Engineering: Testing, Quality Assurance, and Quantifiable Improvement. Wiley (2005)
115. Tian, Y., Lo, D., Sun, C.: Information retrieval based nearest neighbor classification for fine-grained bug severity prediction. In: 2012 19th Working Conference on Reverse Engineering, pp. 215–224. IEEE (2012)
116. Tranquillini, S., Daniel, F., Kucherbaev, P., Casati, F.: Modeling, enacting, and integrating custom crowdsourcing processes. ACM Trans. Web (TWEB) **9**(2), 1–43 (2015)
117. Verdon, D., McGraw, G.: Risk analysis in software design. IEEE Secur. Priv. Mag. **2**(4), 79–84 (2004)
118. Votipka, D., Stevens, R., Redmiles, E., Hu, J., Mazurek, M.: Hackers vs. testers: A comparison of software vulnerability discovery processes. In: 2018 IEEE Symposium on Security and Privacy (SP), pp. 374–391. IEEE (2018)
119. Wagner, C., Dulaunoy, A., Wagener, G., Iklody, A.: Misp: The design and implementation of a collaborative threat intelligence sharing platform. In: Proceedings of the 2016 ACM on Workshop on Information Sharing and Collaborative Security, pp. 49–56 (2016)
120. Wagner, S., Goeb, A., Heinemann, L., Kläs, M., Lampasona, C., Lochmann, K., Mayr, A., Plösch, R., Seidl, A., Streit, J., et al.: Operationalised product quality models and assessment: the Quamoco approach. Inf. Softw. Technol. **62**, 101–123 (2015)
121. Wakeford, N., Cohen, K.: Fieldnotes in public: using blogs for research. The SAGE Handbook of Online Research Methods, pp. 307–326 (2008)
122. Walshe, T., Simpson, A.: An empirical study of bug bounty programs. In: 2020 IEEE 2nd International Workshop on Intelligent Bug Fixing (IBF), pp. 35–44. IEEE (2020)
123. Willett, W., Heer, J., Agrawala, M.: Strategies for crowdsourcing social data analysis. In: Proceedings of the SIGCHI Conference on Human Factors in Computing Systems, pp. 227–236 (2012)
124. Woszczynski, A., Green, A., Dodson, K., Easton, P.: Zombies, sirens, and lady gaga-oh my! developing a framework for coordinated vulnerability disclosure for us emergency alert systems. Gov. Inf. Q. **37**(1), 101418 (2020)
125. Yamaguchi, F., Lindner, F., Rieck, K.: Vulnerability extrapolation: assisted discovery of vulnerabilities using machine learning. In: Proceedings of the 5th USENIX conference on Offensive technologies, pp. 13–13 (2011)
126. Yang, J., Redi, J., Demartini, G., Bozzon, A.: Modeling task complexity in crowdsourcing. In: HCOMP, pp. 249–258 (2016)
127. Yuen, M.C., King, I., Leung, K.S.: A survey of crowdsourcing systems. In: 2011 IEEE Third International Conference on Privacy, Security, Risk and Trust and 2011 IEEE Third International Conference on Social Computing, pp. 766–773. IEEE (2011)

128. Zhao, L., Li, Y.: Collaborating with white hat hackers: a study of vulnerability crowdsourcing program from control perspective (2020)
129. Zhao, M., Grossklags, J., Chen, K.: An exploratory study of white hat behaviors in a web vulnerability disclosure program. In: Proceedings of the 2014 ACM Workshop on Security Information Workers, pp. 51–58 (2014)
130. Zhao, M., Grossklags, J., Liu, P.: An empirical study of web vulnerability discovery ecosystems. In: Proceedings of the 22nd ACM SIGSAC Conference on Computer and Communications Security, pp. 1105–1117 (2015)
131. Zhao, M., Laszka, A., Grossklags, J.: Devising effective policies for bug-bounty platforms and security vulnerability discovery. J. Inf. Policy **7**, 372–418 (2017)
132. Zhao, M., Laszka, A., Maillart, T., Grossklags, J.: Crowdsourced security vulnerability discovery: Modeling and organizing bug-bounty programs. In: The HCOMP Workshop on Mathematical Foundations of Human Computation, Austin, TX, USA (2016)
133. Zitser, M., Lippmann, R., Leek, T.: Testing static analysis tools using exploitable buffer overflows from open source code. In: Proceedings of the 12th ACM SIGSOFT Twelfth International Symposium on Foundations of Software Engineering, pp. 97–106 (2004)

Environmental Sustainability in Information Systems Engineering

Xavier Franch

Abstract Environmental sustainability has become a critical concern for information systems engineering (ISE), as digital technologies increasingly shape organizational operations, societal infrastructures, and global energy consumption. While information systems have long been recognized as enablers of efficiency and innovation, their growing environmental footprint–driven by data-intensive applications, cloud infrastructures, and artificial intelligence–raises new challenges for sustainable system design and governance. This chapter, written in honour of Professor Barbara Pernici, one of the pioneering researchers in advancing sustainability within the ISE discipline, examines how environmental sustainability considerations can be systematically incorporated into information systems engineering. It reviews key concepts and approaches delineated by the work of Professor Pernici and her collaborators, and synthesizes the state of the art in the modeling, measurement, assessment, and improvement of environmental sustainability in information systems. The chapter also pays particular attention to AI-enabled systems, highlighting the distinctive challenges introduced by this technology, including increased energy consumption, lifecycle complexity, and the need for sustainability-aware design and governance mechanisms.

1 Introduction

Environmental sustainability is becoming increasingly important in today's world as the impacts of climate change, resource exhaustion, and pollution, grow more visible. With rising global temperatures, declining biodiversity, and scarce natural resources, all societal actors are recognizing the urgent need to adopt practices that protect our environment for future generations. Today, environmental sustainability is no longer optional; it is a key responsibility and a foundation for a healthier, more stable future. In this context, the role of information and communication technologies

X. Franch (✉)
Universitat Politècnica de Catalunya, Vilanova i la Geltrú, Spain
e-mail: xavier.franch@upc.edu

C. Cappiello et al. (eds.), *Retrospective and Prospective Views on Information Systems Engineering*, https://doi.org/10.1007/978-3-032-19578-4_10

(ICT) has been reported as critical. Estimates of the ICT sector footprint vary widely from 1.7 to 4% of global greenhouse gas emissions.[1] Not just this, but also prospects on electricity demand are to triple by 2030.

Given this state of affairs, environmental sustainability has attracted the attention of the ICT research community. In the field of Information System Engineering (ISE), Prof. Barbara Pernici pioneered the efforts on considering this sustainability dimension as far as in 2011, proposing and moderating a panel (which I had the privilege to attend) in the 23rd edition of the CAiSE conference [1, 2]. Participants discussed the two sides of environmental sustainability related to ISE: designing information systems for sustainability (also named *IS for green* in the panel) and designing sustainable information systems (*Green IS*). The panel raised a number of important issues and identified open challenges at that time, many of them still present.

That panel was instrumental to include sustainability in my research priorities, motivating my participation in two literature reviews led by another prominent expert in the field, Prof. Birgit Penzendstadler [3, 4]. In this chapter, I summarize the state of the art in environmental sustainability research in ISE and also reflect on the impact of artificial intelligence (AI) technologies in the field.

2 Background

Sustainable development was originally defined by Bruntland as "meeting the needs of the present without compromising the ability of future generations to meet their own needs" [5]. A rapid review of the literature shows that there are many nuances on this definition, and many categories of this general concept [6]. In this chapter, I consider the five dimensions of sustainability proposed in the Karlskrona Manifesto for Sustainability Design [6] due to its formulation in the context of software systems, therefore close to ISE. Table 1 presents these (interdependent) dimensions and their focus. As one of these five dimensions, environmental sustainability stands up.

In the ISE field, Prof. Barbara Pernici and her group have further investigated the topic of environmental sustainability, at the level of applications (services [7] and cloud systems [8, 9]), data (knowledge graphs [10], data preparation [11]), hardware (data centers [12]) and, of course, IS themselves [13]. In this last work [13], which takes the form of a literature review, Vitali and Pernici identify three main areas for dealing with environmental sustainability in IS, or green IS: measurement, assessment, and improvement (of energy efficiency). In the next section, I analyse the current state of these three areas, preceded by a fourth one, related to modeling, which I find relevant to include.

[1] https://ec.europa.eu/newsroom/dae/redirection/document/116896.

Table 1 Five dimensions of sustainability (from [6])

Dimension	Definition
Environmental	Long-term effects of human activities on natural systems
Social	Societal communities (groups of people, organizations) and the factors that erode trust in society
Economic	Assets, capital and added value
Technical	Longevity of information, systems, and infrastructure and their adequate evolution with changing surrounding conditions
Individual	Well-being of humans as individuals

3 Brief Summary of the State of the Art

3.1 Modeling Environmental Sustainability

In this first subsection, I briefly present three models well-suited for incorporating environmental sustainability aspects: goal models, business process models and enterprise architecture models. As a baseline for all of them, the first subsection examines how knowledge about environmental sustainability can be currently found in the literature.

Representing Knowledge

In absence of established ontologies for environmental sustainability in ISE, we find several metamodels that capture essential environmental sustainability concepts. I highlight Lago et al.'s sustainability metamodel [14] which includes concepts such as sustainability dimensions (with five specializations according to Karlskrona Manifesto [6]), sustainability requirements and evaluation criteria, and also includes environment and stakeholders as first-class elements.

We also find broader sustainability frameworks that coordinate different dimensions. For instance, Duboc et al. introduced SuSAF [15], a question-based sustainability framework proposing a process to elicit and document sustainability requirements. Remarkably, the framework includes a diagram template filled during the elicitation process in order to visualize chains of effects. Condori-Fernández, Lago and colleagues proposed SAF [16, 17], with similar aims as SuSAF but not specifically centered on requirements, instead it produces a software sustainability quality model, and an architectural decision map. Merging the two approaches into a unified framework is undoubtedly a feasible challenge. Furthermore, elaborating ontologies for environmental sustainability, as done by Sales et al. for trust [18], seems a natural objective with respect to knowledge representation.

Goal Models

Goal models have been largely used to specify environmental sustainability concerns. Cabot et al.'s seminal paper [19] modeled sustainability as a softgoal using the *i** language [20]. With *i**, it is possible to identify the contribution of each possible system design decision into sustainability and then systematically search for trade-offs. Since then, other authors have explored the use of goal models, and we can mention the definition of attributes for environmental sustainability in the form of a goal hierarchy [21] and a metamodeling approach in which different layers of sustainability are proposed [22].

As usual in goal models, scalability is a problem, as it can be seen even in Cabot et al.'s paper. The metamodeling approach cited above [21] helps at this respect, because the complexity is distributed at different levels, but still the instantiation in a complex IS may be challenging. A line of research worth pursuing would be the application to model sustainability of structuring mechanisms already explored in goal modeling, such as aspects [23] or modules [24].

Business Process Models

Schoormann et al. [25] synthesised a taxonomy from a literature review showing how BPMN is the preferred notation to express environmental sustainability concerns. In short, they identify two main dimensions related to modeling: *(i)* Representation, which may be textual (the most dominant in the literature), graphical or mathematical; *(ii)* Modeling technique, with a clear dominance of BPMN. The two main research directions in this area are: annotating sustainability information textually in BPMN models [26], and extending BPMN with new modeling elements conveying such sustainability information [27].

Some authors have further explored different aspects related to green process modeling. Remarkably, in a similar vein that done with software quality models (see Sect. 3.2), Hernández González et al. [28] propose adding a Process Greenability characteristic to Kroeger's et al. process quality model [29]. The characteristic is further decomposed into six subcharacteristics (e.g., energy efficiency, resource use) operationalized through a set of indicators.

Enterprise Architecture Models

Enterprise architectures are playing an increasingly important role in providing structure, coherence, and direction to IS design and evolution. Enterprise architectures themselves are commonly described through models, therefore they are also subject of investigation in relation to how these models can incorporate the environmental sustainability dimension.

Vandevenne et al. [30] propose a method to embed environmental sustainability into the core of an organization. It relies on courses of action that incorporate environmental sustainability into the enterprise architecture at different levels, using ArchiMate as modeling language. Example of courses of action are: including planet earth as stakeholder, define key ecological indicators, select efficient machine learning architectures, include energy use in the requirements engineering process, and calculate the CO2 emissions and energy usage of on-premises infrastructure. Putting all these courses of action into practice remains an open challenge.

3.2 Measurement

When we talk about measurement, first challenge is knowing what to measure. At this respect, the classical concept of quality model comes into play. ISO/IEC defines a quality model as "the set of characteristics and the relationships between them which provide the basis for specifying quality requirements and evaluating quality" [31]. However, ISO/IEC quality standards, even the most recent ones, do not include environmental sustainability as part of their definition. Therefore, non-standard quality models are needed.

Calero et al. [32] propose extending the ISO/IEC quality standard (ISO/IEC 25010:2011 at that time [33]) both at the product quality model and the quality in use model by:

- Product Quality: adding a ninth characteristic, Product Greenability, to the eight characteristics proposed by the standard.
- Quality in Use: adding a sixth characteristic, Greenability in Use, to the five characteristics proposed by the standard.

These two characteristics decompose each into several subcharacteristics (see [32] for details), following the ISO/IEC standard structure. Furthermore, new green characteristics and sub-characteristics in both models are linked to the original quality (sub-)characteristics using Bayesian networks.

The same as metamodels can be extended to sustainability frameworks (see section "Representing Knowledge"), quality models and metrics can be embedded into broader measurement frameworks. Guldner et al. propose the Green Software Measurement Model (GSMM) [34]. GSMM puts the focus on the object to be measured. It first derives the sustainability measurement goals, from which metrics, measurements and measurement procedure (including set-up) are derived. The measurements are then executed to produce the measurement data and an analysis report.

3.3 Assessment

Some proposals exist on CMM-based (or at least, CMM-inspired) capability models [35, 36]. One of the most longly reported experiences is the SURF Green

Maturity Model [37], consisting of three generic domains (green ICT in the organization, greening of ICT, and greening of operations with ICT) and one sector-specific domain, each decomposed into several attributes. This maturity model is conceived as a self-assessment tool for organizations. In a subsequent work [38], Hankel et al. report lack of strategic alignment, lack of leadership and misalignment of culture and beliefs in ICT as some of the factors that influence the adoption of green ICT.

Other assessment frameworks have been proposed in the literature. For instance, the Green Software Foundation proposes the Software Carbon Intensity (SCI) specification,[2] aimed at understanding how to improve systems carbon footprint. Remarkably, the proposal includes a precise procedure to calculate and report an SCI score. Other authors have opted by promoting environmental sustainability labels (also called Eco-labels[3]). Deneckère and Rubio propose EcoSoft, an Eco-label for software sustainability [39]. To get the EcoSoft label, a software system must have considered sustainable practices at three different stages: development, usage and retirement. For each of these stages, a number of criteria need to be positively evaluated. A similar type of label has been proposed by Castaño et al. in the context of AI-enabled systems and models [40].

3.4 Improvement

Vitali and Pernici's proposed two dimensions for environmental sustainability improvement: design of green processes and efficient resource management [7]. I add a third dimension: design of green software.

This third dimension addresses sustainability improvement from the software life cycle perspective. Software architecture is the most mentioned life cycle stage with this purpose. For instance, Jagroep et al. address the question of how the software architecture can assist in achieving environmental sustainability goals of an organization [41]. The work relies on several pillars, like coexistence of different viewpoints and adoption of software architecture tactics, such as those defined by Procaccianti et al. for cloud-based systems [42]. At a finer granularity, Noureddine and Le Goaer have recently found that classical Gang of Four design patterns are energy-neutral, paving the way for their safe use in the context of environmental sustainability [43].

4 Impact of AI

While environmental sustainability has been recognized as a concern for ISE since long ago, a disruptive trend has impacted not only this discipline but also related ones such as software engineering [44] and business process management [45]: the

[2] https://sci.greensoftware.foundation/.

[3] https://www.ecolabelindex.com/ecolabels/.

integration of AI in IS. It neets to be mentioned that, oin spite of one of Goodland's hypothesis[4] [46], some researchers question the nature of the problem itself [47]. But in fact, current studies and reports show a growing impact of AI in the energy consumption of socio-technical systems (not to mention today's massive use of large language models at all levels). This growth is mainly due to the availability of high-performance infrastructure (such as data centers and GPUs), which *(i)* makes it possible to address complex computational challenges that were out of reach not many years ago; *(ii)* has made AI available to organizations worldwide. In general, companies tend to prioritize the business value of their solutions over sustainability concerns, and this is particularly true in the case of environmental sustainability, where the return of investment is not obvious at a first glance.

As a reaction to this situation, the research community is creating awareness of the AI's environmental impact by promoting the concept of green AI [48]. Similarly to green IS, green AI aims to balance performance with environmental sustainability, promoting reusable and accessible models and AI-enabled systems.

In the rest of the section, I present a number of lines of action in which the GESSI research group at UPC[5] is working, stemming from the consideration of environmental sustainability in the development and operation of AI-enabled systems.

4.1 Requirements Engineering

In [49], we analyse several aspects related to requirements engineering in the context of AI-enabled systems. Two of them are:

Scope. Several authors remark the existence of requirement scopes that distinguish software, data and AI algorithms [50, 51]. The main consequence is that an environmental sustainability requirement or goal established at the level of the system, may generate other requirements down to the level of data scope. Figure 1 shows such an example of sustainability goal. We remark that some of the emerging requirements (e.g., the one at the data scope) do not seem directly related to sustainability if considered in isolation; still it appeared (in this simplified example) because of the energy efficiency goal).

Roles. Requirements engineers need the support of specialized roles (e.g., data engineer and AI engineer) to analyse the feasibility of requirements and to elaborate them into the scopes mentioned above. Figure 2 illustrates the flow of information and how a sustainability expert needs to be involved in the loop.

[4] Hypothesis 7: "Environmental problems cannot be solved or ameliorated by increases in the rates of consumption of resources."

[5] https://gessi.upc.edu/en.

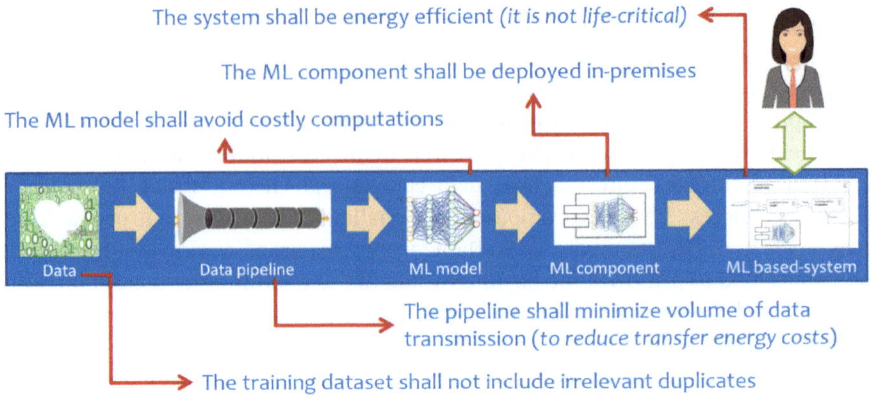

Fig. 1 Requirements scope in the context of AI-enabled systems

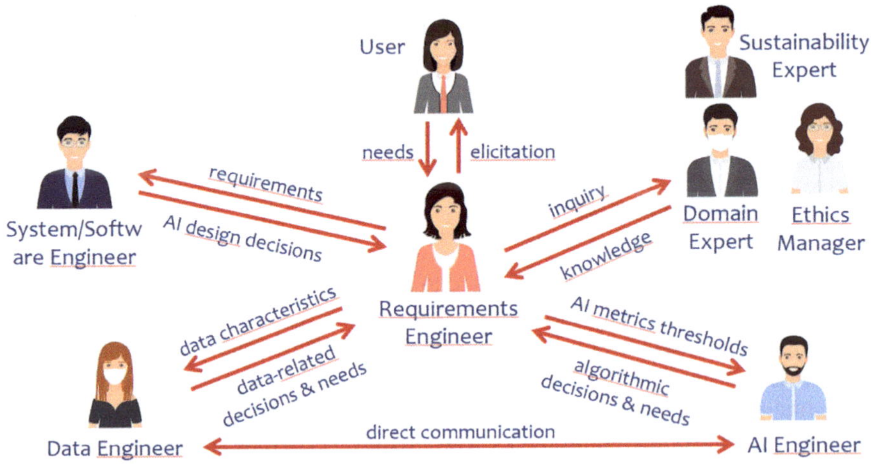

Fig. 2 Requirements engineering roles in the context of AI-enabled systems

4.2 Software Architecture

The structure of the system itself may have a great impact on the energy consumption of the system, therefore any design optimization effort may be worth to implement. Järvenpää et al. [52] present a collection of 30 green architectural tactics classified into six categories: data-centric, algorithm design, model optimization, model training, deployment and management. In a wider perspective, we formulated an architecture-centric approach (GAISSA) [53], integrating a greenability quality model, repositories of green-aware architectural patterns, and a collection of techniques for analysis, decision-making and reporting of architectural decisions.

4.3 Repository Management

AI models and data sets are shared by the community using model repositories. One of them, Hugging Face,[6] has surpassed 2.000.000 entries. It is utterly important to understand the structure of the repository [54], its ecosystem [55, 56] and its evolution dynamics [57]. In relation to environmental sustainability, we have analysed the metadata that model creators include in their entries and found that, as of 2023, the declared CO2 consumption of Hugging Face models decreased in average by a factor of 10 in ca. one year only (until a minimum of 1.24 g in February 2023), although unfortunately the number of models declaring energy consumption was less than 1% [40].

4.4 Deployment

Deploying an AI-enabled system at the right location (edge, fog, or cloud) is critical because it directly affects performance, cost, reliability, security, and feasibility of the system. For instance, deploying in the edge suffers from low latency but improves security and privacy, also supporting adaptability [58]. With techniques as federated learning [59], knowing how to distribute the models and components both in training and inference is of crucial importance. For instance, we have observed that cloud environments are a good option for training complex models or training sporadically, in contrast to local environments, better suited for simpler models [60]. However, every particular context requires a thorough analysis since organizational, system and technical requirements may largely vary.

4.5 The Way Ahead

Green AI is still a young discipline and as such, many research avenues are open. I mention some of them below.

Study aggregation. From the moment the concept appeared, research in green AI is based upon the results of empirical studies (in the form of experiments or mining software repository studies) that explore energy efficiency of AI models or AI-enabled systems in certain conditions, and assess against some kind of performance indicator (accuracy, precision, ...). While valuable by themselves, these studies are difficult to align, because they are conducted in different experimental settings with different research questions, making meta-analysis challenging.

Alternatively, we have explored the use of Structured Synthesis Method (SSM) [61] as a technique to aggregate empirical studies in green AI. SSM aggregates

[6] https://huggingface.co/.

qualitative and quantitative evidence through diagrammatic modeling based on a belief function, which assigns weights to individual studies depending on their robustness. First outcomes on a particular ML model optimization technique (quantization) [62] show promising results. Threats to validity [63] should be integrated into this aggregation process.

Beyond software engineering. So far, green AI research has come mainly from the software engineering community, but of course other disciplines are deeply affected by AI, ISE being among them. We may mention:

- Considering new roles. Besides those mentioned in this section, focused on the requirements engineering stage, others could be identified in direct relation to the problem rather than the solution (e.g., [64])
- Considering new processes. Some new processes emerge around green AI (or even just AI). Just to mention a few: data preparation pipelines; continuous monitoring of model and data set repositories (e.g., Hugging Face); experiments set-up.[7] These processes can be modeled and integrated into the organization main business process models.
- Leveraging technical and modeling patterns into organizational patterns. Architectural [52] and business process [13] patterns and tactics could be leveraged into patterns that organizations could adopt for digital transformation into sustainable businesses.
- Embracing green AI in the enterprise architecture. Following some of the courses of action identified by Vandevenne et al. [30], all the elements above could be integrated into a holistic enterprise architecture covering from the strategy to the technology layers.

Researchers' attitude. While it may be argued that experiments conducted by researchers barely represent a raindrop in the ocean, we may wonder whether the research community should adopt a "greener" attitude when conducting large studies with AI models. Currently, the typical research paper reporting a new model, technique, or method around AI focuses on accuracy, and completely disregards energy consumption. At this respect, two measures could be put in place:

- Include environmental sustainability concerns in the solution design. Energy consumption could be considered in: *(i)* the design of the research; *(ii)* the selection of models and datasets; *(iii)* the deployment of models in training.
- Report the energy consumed (and any other relevant sustainability data) while conducting the research. Particularly, not just raw values, but in reference to well-known activities such as energy required by an overseas flight, a house annual consumption in a particular country, etc.

[7] https://luiscruz.github.io/2021/10/10/scientific-guide.html.

5 Conclusions

In this chapter, and inspired by Prof. Barbara Pernici's pioneering work, I have explored the environmental sustainability dimension in information systems engineering (ISE). While the focus has been in summarizing the current state of the art, I have also delineated some possible avenues of research for the topic.

I would like to conclude with a statement of appreciation for Professor Barbara Pernici. Not only has her outstanding scientific career inspired many, but her personal character and kindness offer a model for us all. Grazie mille, Barbara!

Acknowledgements This work was supported by the project PID2024-156019OB-I00 under funding schema MICIU/AEI/10.13039/501100011033/FEDER, UE.

References

1. Pernici, B.: Panel on green and sustainable IS. In: Proceedings of the 23rd International Conference on Advanced Information Systems Engineering (CAiSE 2011). LNCS 6741, Springer, Berlin (2011)
2. Pernici, B., Aiello, M., vom Brocke, J., Donnellan, B., Gelenbe, E., Kretsis, M.: What IS can do for environmental sustainability: a report from CAiSE'11 panel on green and sustainable IS. Commun. Assoc. Inf. Syst. **30**(18) (2012). https://doi.org/10.17705/1CAIS.03018. https://aisel.aisnet.org/cais/vol30/iss1/18
3. Penzenstadler, B., Bauer, V., Calero, C., Franch, X.: Sustainability in software engineering: a systematic literature review. In: Proceedings of the 16th International Conference on Evaluation & Assessment in Software Engineering (EASE), pp. 32–41 (2012)
4. Penzenstadler, B., Raturi, A., Richardson, D., Calero, C., Femmer, H., Franch, X.: Systematic mapping study on software engineering for sustainability (SE4S). In: Proceedings of the 18th International Conference on Evaluation & Assessment in Software Engineering (EASE), pp. 14:1–14:14 (2014)
5. Brundtland, G.H.: Our Common Future: Report of the World Commission on Environment and Development. United Nations, A/42/427 (1987)
6. Becker, C., Chitchyan, R., Duboc, L., Easterbrook, S., Penzenstadler, B., Seyff, N., Venters, C.C.: Sustainability Design and Software: The Karlskrona Manifesto. In Proceedings of the 37th International Conference on Software Engineering - Volume 2 (ICSE 2015), pp. 467–476. IEEE Press (2015)
7. Pernici, B.: Designing adaptive services: the case of energy efficiency. In: Proceedings of the 7th International Conference on Intelligent Computer Communication and Processing (ICCP). IEEE (2011)
8. Cappiello, C., Datre; S., Fugini; M.G., Melia; P., Pernici; B., Plebani, P.: Monitoring and assessing energy consumption and CO_2 emissions in cloud-based systems. In: Proceedings of 2013 IEEE International Conference on Systems, Man, and Cybernetics (SMC 2013), pp. 127–132 (2013)
9. Vitali, M., Wiesner, P., Kreutz, K., Gandola, R.: Adaptive green cloud applications: balancing emissions, revenue, and user experience through approximate computing. Futur. Gener. Comput. Syst. **176**, 108143 (2026)
10. Ramalli, E., Bono, C.A., Sancricca, C., Cappiello, C., Comuzzi, M., Pernici, B., Vitali, M.: Entity ablation of knowledge graphs: impact on information quality and sustainability. Futur. Gener. Comput. Syst. **175**, 108063 (2026)

11. Pernici, B., Cappiello, C., Ramalli, E., et al.: The future of sustainable data preparation. In: Proceedings of the 32nd Symposium of Advanced Database Systems (SEBD), CEUR Workshop Proceedings, vol. 3741, pp. 486–497 (2024)
12. Kipp, A., Jiang, T., Liu, J., Fugini, M., Vitali, M., Pernici, B., Salomie, I.: Applying green metrics to optimise the energy consumption footprint of IT service centres. Int. J. Space-Based Situated Comput. **2**(3), 158–174 (2012)
13. Vitali, M., Pernici, B.: A survey on energy efficiency in information systems. Int. J. Coop. Inf. Syst. (2014)
14. Lago, P., Akinli Koçak, S., Crnkovic, I., Penzenstadler, B.: Framing sustainability as a property of software quality. Commun. ACM **58**(10), 70–78 (2015)
15. Duboc, L., Penzenstadler, B., Porras, J., et al.: Requirements Engineering for sustainability: an awareness framework for designing software systems for a better tomorrow. Requir. Eng. **25**, 469–492 (2020)
16. Condori-Fernandez, N., Lago, P., Luaces, M.R., Places, á. S.: An action research for improving the sustainability assessment framework instruments. Sustainability **12**(4), 1682 (2020)
17. Lago, P., Condori Fernandez, N., Fatima, I., et al.: The sustainability assessment framework toolkit: a decade of modeling experience. Softw. Syst. Model. **24**, 361–383 (2025)
18. Sales, T.P., Baião, F., Guizzardi, G., Almeida, J.P.A., Guarino, N., Mylopoulos, J.: The common ontology of value and risk. In: Proceedings of the 37th International Conference on Conceptual Modeling (ER), LNCS 11157, Springer, Berlin (2018)
19. Cabot, J., Easterbrook, E., Horkoff, J., Lessard, L., Liaskos, S., Mazon, J.N.: Integrating sustainability in decision-making processes: a modelling strategy. In: Proceedings of the 31st International Conference on Software Engineering - Companion Volume (ICSE): 207-210, IEEE (2009)
20. Yu, E., Yu, E.: Modelling Strategic Relationships for Process Reengineering. Ph.D. Dissertation, University of Toronto (1995)
21. Penzenstadler, B.: GRL for Representing the Sustainability Reference Model. iStar Workshop, pp. 79–84 (2015)
22. Penzenstadler, B., Femmer, H.: A generic model for sustainability with process-and product-specific instances. In: Proceedings of the 2013 Workshop on Green in/by Software Engineering, pp. 3–8 (2013)
23. Mussbacher, G., Amyot, D., Araújo, J., Moreira, A., Weiss, M.: Visualizing aspect-oriented goal models with AoGRL. In: Proceedings of the 2nd International Workshop on Requirements Engineering Visualization (REV), IEEE (2007)
24. Franch, X.: Incorporating modules into the *i** framework. In: Proceedings of the 22nd International Conference on Advanced Information Systems Engineering (CAiSE), LNCS 6051, pp. 439–454. Springer, Berlin (2010)
25. Schoormann, T., Behrens, D., Knackstedt, R.: Sustainability in business process models: a taxonomy-driven approach to synthesize knowledge and structure the field. In: Proceedings of the 38th International Conference on Information Systems (ICIS) (2017)
26. Krogstie, J.: Integrating sustainability awareness analysis and BPMN-modelling. In: Proceedings of the Forum of the 18th IFIP WG 8.1 Working Conference on the Practice of Enterprise Modeling (PoEM), CEUR Proceedings (2025)
27. Recker, J., Rosemann, M., Hjalmarsson, A., Lind, M.: Modeling and analyzing the carbon footprint of business processes. In: Seidel, S., Recker, J., vom Brocke, J. (eds.) Green Business Process Management: Towards the Sustainable Enterprise, pp. 93–109. Springer, Berlin (2012)
28. Hernández González, A., Calero, C., Pérez Parra, D., Mancebo, J.: Approaching green BPM characterisation. J. Softw.: Evol. Process. **31**(2), e2145 (2018)
29. Kroeger, T.A., Davidson, N.J., Cook, S.C.: Understanding the characteristics of quality for software engineering processes: a grounded theory investigation. Inf. Softw. Technol. **56**(2), 252–271 (2014)
30. Vandevenne, N., Van Riel, J., Poels, G.: Green enterprise architecture (GREAN)-leveraging EA for environmentally sustainable digital transformation. Sustainability **15**(19), 1434 (2023)

31. Software Engineering – Product Quality Part 1: Quality Model. Standard, International Organization for Standardization, Geneva, CH (2001)
32. Calero, C., Moraga, M.A., Bertoa, M.F., Duboc, L.: Green Software and Software Quality. Chapter in Calero, C., Piattini, M. (eds.) Green in Software Engineering, pp. 231–260, Springer, Berlin ((2015))
33. Systems and Software Engineering – Systems and Software Quality Requirements and Evaluation (SQuaRE) – Quality-in-use Model. Standard, International Organization for Standardization, Geneva, CH (2011)
34. Guldner, A., Bender, R., Calero, C., et al.: Development and evaluation of a reference measurement model for assessing the resource and energy efficiency of software products and components-green software measurement model (GSMM). Futur. Gener. Comput. Syst. **155**, 402–418 (2024)
35. Standing, C., Jackson, P.: An approach to sustainability for information systems. J. Syst. Inf. Technol. **9**(2), 167–176 (2007)
36. Vásquez, J., Aguirre, S., Puertas, E., et al.: A sustainability maturity model for micro, small and medium-sized enterprises (MSMEs) based on a data analytics evaluation approach. J. Clean. Prod. **311**, 127692 (2021)
37. Hankel, A., Oud, L., Saan, M., Lago, P.A., Oud, L.: A maturity model for green ICT: the case of the SURF green ICT maturity model. In: Proceedings of the 28th International Conference on Informatics for Environmental Protection (EnviroInfo 2014), pp. 33–40 (2014)
38. Hankel, A., Heimeriks, G., Lago, P.: Green ICT adoption using a maturity model. Sustainability **11**(24), 7163 (2019)
39. Deneckère, R., Rubio, G.: EcoSoft: proposition of an eco-label for software sustainability. In: Proceedings of the CAiSE 2020 International Workshops, pp. 121–132, Springer, Berlin (2020)
40. Castaño, J., Martínez-Fernández, S., Franch, X., Bogner, J.: Exploring the carbon footprint of hugging face's ML models: a repository mining study. In: Proceedings of the 17th ACM/IEEE International Symposium on Empirical Software Engineering and Measurement (ESEM) (2023)
41. Jagroep, E., van der Werf, J.M., Brinkkemper, S., et al.: Extending software architecture views with an energy consumption perspective. Computing **99**, 553–573 (2017)
42. Procaccianti, G., Lago. P., Lewis, G.A.: A catalogue of green architectural tactics for the cloud. In: Proceedings of the 8th IEEE International Symposium on the Maintenance and Evolution of Service-oriented and Cloud-based Systems (MESOCA), pp. 29–36 (2014)
43. Noureddine, A., Le Goaer, O.: Investigating the impact of software design patterns on energy consumption. In: Proceedings of the IEEE 22nd International Conference on Software Architecture (ICSA), pp. 153–163 (2025)
44. Cruz, L., Franch, X., Martínez-Fernández, S.: Innovating for tomorrow: the convergence of software engineering and green AI. ACM Trans. Softw. Eng. Methodoloigy **34**(5), 138:1–138:13 (2025)
45. Rosemann, M., Brocke, J.V., Van Looy, A., et al.: Business process management in the age of AI – three essential drifts. ISEB **22**, 415–429 (2024)
46. Goodland, R.: The concept of environmental sustainability. Annu. Rev. Ecol. Syst. **26**, 1–24 (1995)
47. Patterson, D., Gonzalez, J., Hölzle, U., Le, Q., Liang, C., Munguia, L.-M.: The Carbon footprint of machine learning training will plateau, then shrink. Computer **55**(7), 18–28 (2022). IEEE
48. Schwartz, R., Dodge, J., Smith, N.A., Etzioni, O.: Green AI. Commununications ACM **63**(12), 54–63 (2020)
49. Franch, X., Jedlitschka, A., Martínez-Fernández, S.: A requirements engineering perspective to AI-based systems development: a vision paper. In: Proceedings of the 29th International Working Conference on Requirements Engineering: Foundation for Software Quality (REFSQ), LNCS 13975, pp. 223–232, Springer, Berlin (2023)
50. Siebert, J., Joeckel, L., Heidrich, J. et al.: Towards guidelines for assessing qualities of machine learning systems. In: Proceedings of the 13th International Conference on the Quality of Information and Communications Technology (QUATIC), pp. 17–31 (2020)

51. Mohammad Habibullah, K., Gay, G., Horkoff, J.: Non-functional requirements for machine learning: an exploration of system scope and interest. CoRR (2022). arXiv:abs/2203.11063
52. Järvenpää, H., Lago, P., Bogner, J., Lewis, G., Muccini, H., Ozkaya, I.: A synthesis of green architectural tactics for ML-enabled systems. In: Proceedings of the 46th International Conference on Software Engineering: Software Engineering in Society (ICSE-SEIS) (2024)
53. Martínez-Fernández, S., Franch, X., Durán, F.: Towards green AI-based software systems: an architecture-centric approach (GAISSA). In: Proceedings of the 49th Euromicro Conference on Software Engineering and Advanced Applications (SEAA), pp. 432–439 (2023)
54. Ait, A., Izquierdo, J.L.C., Cabot, J.: HFCommunity: a tool to analyze the hugging face hub community. In: Proceedings of the 2023 IEEE International Conference on Software Analysis, Evolution and Reengineering (SANER) (2023)
55. Yang, Z., Shi, J., Devanbu, P., Lo, D.: Ecosystem of Large Language Models for Code (2024). arXiv:2405.16746
56. Laufer, B., Oderinwale, H., Kleinberg, J.: Anatomy of a machine learning ecosystem: 2 million models on hugging face (2025). arXiv:2508.06811
57. Castaño, J., Martínez-Fernández, S., Franch, X., Bogner, J.: Analyzing the evolution and maintenance of ML models on hugging face. In: Proceedings of the 21st International Conference on Mining Software Repositories (MSR), pp. 607–618. ACM Press (2024)
58. Zhu, S., Yu, T., Xu, T., et al.: Intelligent computing: the latest advances, challenges, and future. Intell. Comput. **2**, 0006 (2023)
59. Chen Zhang, Y., Xie, H.B., Bin, Y., Li, W., Yuan Gao, Y.: A survey on federated learning. Knowl.-Based Syst. **216**, 106775 (2021)
60. del Rey, S., Martínez-Fernández, S., Cruz, L., Franch, X.: Do DL models and training environments have an impact on energy consumption? In: Proceedings of the 49th Euromicro Conference on Software Engineering and Advanced Applications (SEAA), pp. 150–158 (2023)
61. Medeiros dos Santos, P.S., Travassos, G.H.: On the representation and aggregation of evidence in software engineering: a theory and belief-based perspective. Electron. Notes Theor. Comput. Sci. **292**, 95–118 (2013)
62. del Rey, S., Medeiros dos Santos, P.S., Travassos, G.H., Franch, X., Martínez-Fernández, S.: Aggregating empirical evidence from data strategies studies: a case on model quantization (2025)
63. Farré, C., Franch, X.: Validity at the forefront: investigating threats in green AI research. In: Intelligent Information Systems. CAiSE 2024. LNBIP 520. Springer, Berlin (2024)
64. Penzenstadler, B., Femmer, H., Richardson, D.: Who is the advocate? stakeholders for sustainability. In: Proceedings of the 2nd International Workshop on Green and Sustainable Software (GREENS), pp. 70–77 (2013)

Beyond GAMES: Energy Efficiency in Information Systems

Alexandre Mello Ferreira, Monica Vitali, and Kyriakos Kritikos

Abstract Computing infrastructures contribute a significant percentage of carbon emissions across the world. Such a percentage is expected to further increase in the context of forthcoming Artificial Intelligence (AI)-dedicated data centres. While initial work focused on the infrastructure layer to reduce energy consumption, it neglected other layers relevant to the adaptive behaviour of the overall information system (IS). The GAMES project attempted to address this gap by proposing a methodology for cross-layer energy-aware IS monitoring and adaptation, leading to Green ISs. The IS group at Politecnico di Milano offered significant contributions to this methodology that paved the way for further research in the context of Green IS. Such research led to novel contributions that can further evolve the Green IS research area. In this respect, the goal of this chapter is to reflect on how the GAMES project catalysed a set of long-lasting research trajectories, spanning goal-oriented frameworks, cross-layer service orchestration, dynamic SLAs, and AI-driven management approaches. We trace the evolution of these ideas across three international research groups and highlight their continued impact on the field.

1 Introduction

The increasing digitalisation of society has led to an unprecedented demand for computing resources, making energy efficiency a central concern in the design and operation of information systems (IS). In the early 2000s, this challenge became

A. M. Ferreira
Recod.ai, State University of Campinas, Campinas, Brazil
e-mail: alexandre.ferreira@unicamp.br

M. Vitali (✉)
Politecnico di Milano, Milan, Italy
e-mail: monica.vitali@polimi.it

K. Kritikos
University of the Aegean, Mytilene, Greece
e-mail: kkritikos@aegean.gr

C. Cappiello et al. (eds.), *Retrospective and Prospective Views on Information Systems Engineering*, https://doi.org/10.1007/978-3-032-19578-4_11

particularly evident with the rapid proliferation of data centres and the emergence of cloud computing, which together contributed significantly to global energy consumption. Traditional research primarily addressed these challenges from an infrastructural perspective, optimising hardware utilisation, cooling systems, and power supply efficiency. However, the role of software and information systems in driving sustainable operations was often overlooked. In this context, the European FP7 **GAMES project** (Green Active Management of Energy in IT Service Centres) emerged as a pioneering effort that redefined energy efficiency as an integral, measurable, and adaptive property of ISs.

GAMES focused on developing a new methodology for modelling, monitoring, and dynamically controlling energy consumption in such environments. The Information Systems (IS) group at Politecnico di Milano (POLIMI) participated in that project and supplied three main contributions: (a) a quality and energy model [12] covering both traditional performance metrics as well as energy and resource efficiency ones; (b) an energy-aware service composition algorithm [9]; (c) the definition of a set of adaptation actions [10, 29] that can facilitate adapting the IS to still satisfy its sustainability goals. In addition, its research in the context of other projects like S-Cube[1] led to basic advancements in Service-Oriented Computing (SOC), which is a significant research area contributing to IS, such as a Service Level Agreement (SLA) template specification language [6] and a rule-based semantic approach for SLA negotiation protocol discovery [7]. It also paved the way for other EU projects like Eco2Cloud,[2] expanding the focus from data centres to cloud computing. All these contributions are considered foundational for Green IS, while paving the way for conducting significant work that can further advance this research area with additional breakthroughs.

For the researchers involved, GAMES represented not only an important scientific collaboration but also a formative experience that inspired several new research trajectories. This chapter aims to highlight these developments and illustrate how the ideas initiated within GAMES have continued to shape and advance the field of Green Information Systems. In particular, we trace the evolution of this research path across three groups distributed worldwide: the RAISE group at Politecnico di Milano in Italy, the IS Labs at FORTH-ICS and the University of the Aegean in Greece, and the Recod.ai Lab at the University of Campinas in Brazil. Their collective work extends the foundations laid by GAMES and includes: (a) goal-oriented frameworks for energy- and data-utility-aware adaptive behaviour in ISs [11, 26, 29]; (b) cross-layer service orchestration algorithms [19, 24]; (c) dynamic SLAs and smart contracts [17, 21]; and (d) learning-based AI methods for Green IS management. Together, these contributions demonstrate how the original vision of GAMES has evolved and expanded, providing a fertile basis for ongoing innovation in IS research.

The rest of this chapter is structured as follows. Section 2 supplies a retrospective of the GAMES project, summarising all of its significant contributions. Section 3

---

[1] https://www.s-cube-network.eu/.

[2] https://www.eco2clouds.polimi.it.

analyses the following research directions that were driven by the GAMES foundational contributions and associates them with further evolutions in Green ISs. Finally, the last section concludes this chapter, supplies the lessons learnt, and outlines extra future work directions.

2 Retrospective: GAMES

In the mid-2000s, the rapid growth of data centres and cloud computing infrastructures raised major concerns about energy consumption, operational costs, and environmental impact. The dominant research at that time focused on hardware optimisation and facility-level efficiency, such as improved cooling and power supply systems. However, these approaches were insufficient to address the systemic nature of energy usage in the multiple layers of IT service centres. The European FP7 **GAMES** project was launched to fill this gap. The main objective of GAMES was to develop a *holistic and active* energy management framework, which covered the range from service design to infrastructure operation. Rather than treating energy as a secondary constraint, the project envisioned energy efficiency as a primary, measurable, and optimizable goal. This vision required new methodologies for modelling, monitoring, and dynamically controlling energy consumption in heterogeneous computing environments (Fig. 1). Within this framework, the project expanded the set of metrics to quantify energy and resource efficiency, bridging the gap between software behaviour, IT resource usage, and power consumption, paving the way for a new paradigm of *energy-aware service management*, where applications, middle-

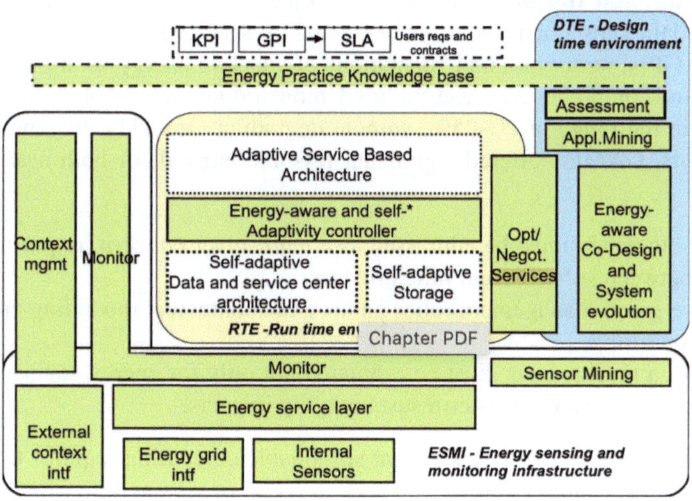

Fig. 1 GAMES architecture overview [1]

ware, and infrastructure collaborate to minimise energy while preserving Quality of Service (QoS). The Information Systems group at Politecnico di Milano, led by Prof. Barbara Pernici, contributed to the modelling and implementation of context-aware and adaptive management techniques that became integral to the GAMES framework. Early work, such as [3, 9], formalised design-time and runtime strategies to integrate energy-awareness into service-based systems. Later studies [10–12] focused on multi-criteria optimisation and intelligent control mechanisms for sustainable data centre operation.

Methodologies and Metrics GAMES proposed a comprehensive methodology to measure, analyse, and optimise energy efficiency. At the metric level, the project adopted and extended existing indicators such as *Power Usage Effectiveness (PUE)* and *Key Performance Indicators (KPIs)*, introducing the notion of *Green Performance Indicators (GPIs)* to capture the energy footprint of services, virtual machines, and workloads at runtime [12]. GPIs enabled cross-layer evaluation, linking business processes, software components, and infrastructure-level parameters within a unified management context. The methodological framework combined **design-time analysis** with **runtime adaptation**. At design time, it provided a way to reason about energy consumption during the composition and deployment of services [9], and to evaluate trade-offs between performance, reliability, and energy efficiency before deployment. At runtime, adaptive management strategies were implemented to respond dynamically to contextual changes in workloads, temperatures, or service priorities. These strategies included *virtual machine migration*, *workload consolidation*, and *dynamic voltage and frequency scaling (DVFS)* policies [10]. The GAMES framework was designed to be applicable in diverse computing environments, ranging from enterprise data centres to early cloud infrastructures, ensuring that its models and metrics could be reused in subsequent research.

Outcomes and Insights The GAMES project delivered several tangible results that shaped the subsequent evolution of Green IT research. These include the formalisation of GPIs, prototype implementations of adaptive energy-aware management systems, and comprehensive case studies demonstrating measurable energy savings, typically in the range of 20–25%, without degrading QoS [11]. Beyond its scientific outputs, GAMES offered significant **lessons learned** for both academia and industry:

- Energy efficiency must be addressed as a *multi-layer concern*, requiring coordination between software and infrastructure;
- Effective green management relies on accurate contextual modelling and continuous monitoring;
- Adaptation mechanisms must be evaluated not only for energy savings, but also for their stability and long-term sustainability impacts.

Ultimately, GAMES demonstrated that sustainable computing requires the integration of energy as a measurable objective in all layers of system design and operation.

3 Beyond GAMES: Research Trajectories Fifteen Years Later

GAMES established the foundation of energy-aware IS, integrating metrics, such as GPIs and KPIs, with service-level objectives (SLA/QoS) to support active monitoring and adaptation of IT infrastructures. This framework introduced the first generation of adaptive and process-aware ISs, capable of adjusting resources and workflows in response to contextual or environmental conditions. Over the following decade, these foundations expanded into more complex, cross-layer architectures, giving rise to Green IS, which coupled business processes, service orchestration, and energy management. Thus, GAMES served as a bridge between the design of energy-efficient IT services and the broader vision of self-adaptive, sustainability-oriented digital ecosystems. Figure 2 summarises the conceptual evolution initiated by the GAMES project. On the right side of the figure, recent developments illustrate the convergence between Green IT and Artificial Intelligence (AI). The emergence of Green AI further extends this trajectory by applying energy-aware principles to the entire AI lifecycle. In essence, GAMES is not an isolated initiative, but the intellectual core of a continuing research lineage that connects sustainability metrics, adaptive software, and data-driven intelligence into a unified vision of environmentally responsible computing.

3.1 A Goal-Driven Approach to Adaptive Information Systems

GAMES provided a significant contribution toward a multi-layered and adaptive approach to Green Information Systems. Two contributions of the project are:

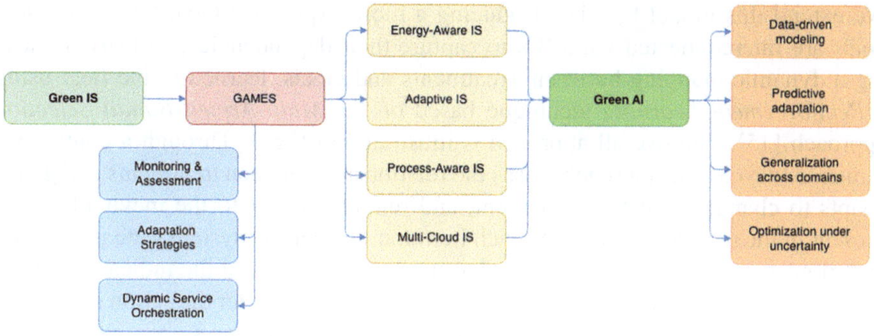

Fig. 2 Evolution from the GAMES project toward adaptive, data-driven, and intelligent Green IS, culminating in the current era of Green AI

- **Monitoring and Assessment**: the definition of a set of metrics capable of evaluating both the quality of service (KPIs), as well as energy efficiency (GPIs);
- **Adaptation Strategies**: the identification and execution of actions that modify system performance or energy consumption, thereby influencing the corresponding indicators.

GAMES suggested to model the dependencies between GPIs/KPIs and adaptation strategies using a goal-driven model. This concept has been further developed in the following research projects in the RAISE group at Politecnico di Milano.

Green Adaptive Information Systems

Following research towards Adaptive Information Systems starts from GAMES and extends its results. The first observation is that *indicators are not independent*: both positive and negative relationships may exist among them. Consequently, actions intended to improve a given indicator may produce unintended side effects on others. To address this issue, in [29] we proposed an approach for automatically learning such relationships and dependencies using a *Bayesian Network* (BN) model. Since indicators are typically continuous variables, constructing the BN required discretising them into three categories: (i) *violated*: the measured value indicates a violation of the user-defined goal; (ii) *satisfied*: the value lies within the desired range; and (iii) *alarm*: the value is close to, but not yet in, violation. Our second observation concerns the need to *identify possible adaptation strategies and understand how they affect the indicators*. However, these effects may vary over time; new strategies may be introduced, and additional system components (applications and/or servers) may become available. Given this environmental dynamism, a static mapping between adaptation strategies and KPIs/GPIs is infeasible.

To address these challenges, we proposed an *adaptive goal-oriented approach* [29]. In a traditional goal-oriented framework [13], *Goals* represent the satisfaction of indicators, while *Treatments* represent adaptive strategies intended to maintain that satisfaction; relationships are expressed through positive or negative contributions. We extend this model by: (i) introducing a more expressive Goal layer, in which goals are interconnected via a BN to capture their dependencies; and (ii) employing a dynamic mapping between Treatments and Goals, learned in the field using a *Reinforcement Learning* technique based on the *Multi-Armed Bandit Selection* approach [15]. The overall approach is illustrated in Fig. 3. Through a continuous refinement cycle, the approach learns the relationship between treatments and goals, adapts to changes in the environment, and remains robust to the inevitable noise present in the monitoring data. At each iteration, the current system state is assessed and, if necessary, an action is selected to improve the status of the indicators, based on its estimated likelihood of producing a positive impact. After the action is enacted, its effect on the indicators is observed through the monitoring system and used to update the model of treatment–indicator impacts.

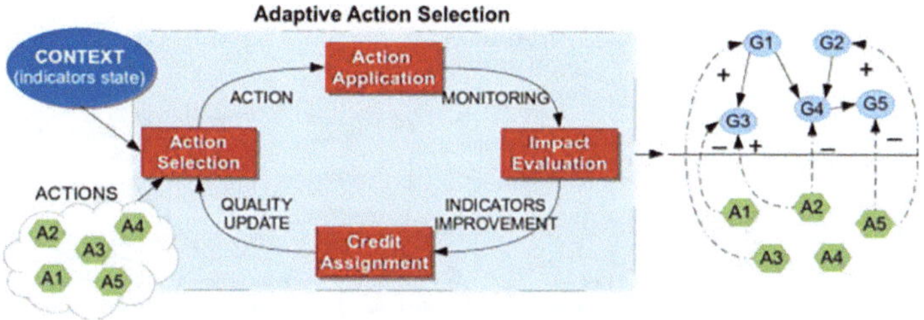

Fig. 3 Adaptive goal-oriented model for energy-efficient information systems management [29]

Goal-Driven Data Sharing in Fog Computing

The same goal-oriented and adaptive principles can be applied beyond energy-efficient information systems. In particular, we extended the approach to a different domain: data sharing in environments involving multiple data providers and consumers, each with heterogeneous requirements on performance, availability, and data management [26]. In this context, the challenge is not only to monitor and maintain QoS levels, but also to decide dynamically where data should be stored or replicated across a diverse set of resources.

For each customer, a goal model captures the negotiated QoS properties of the Data-as-a-Service (DaaS) agreement. A top-level goal (e.g., *High Quality of Service*) is decomposed into subgoals that express the expected reliability, consistency, or performance of the service. AND- and OR-decompositions represent alternative or cumulative ways to satisfy high-level goals, while associated metrics define how satisfaction is assessed at runtime. For instance, a goal such as *Fast data process* may be monitored through the *Response time* metric and considered satisfied when its value remains below a given threshold.

This goal model becomes the basis for continuous monitoring and adaptive decision-making. Potential violations of customer requirements can be detected early, and data movement or replication strategies can be enacted to preserve goal satisfaction. The unified Fog infrastructure, combined with the dynamic and interpretable structure of goals, enables the system to react to changes in demand, resource availability, or data distribution, supporting flexible and scalable data provisioning in multi-provider, multi-consumer environments.

An example of a goal model for the data sharing scenario is shown in Fig. 4. In this setting, goals are no longer represented as a flat structure but organised hierarchically, where high-level objectives are decomposed into combinations of lower-level goals. Only the leaf goals are directly measurable through specific metrics, each associated with a desired value range. This hierarchical organisation enables a more flexible evaluation of requirements, as a high-level goal can be satisfied through multiple alternative patterns of lower-level achievements.

As in the previous scenario, goals are linked to a set of treatments: actions related to data movement or data duplication–each exerting positive or negative influences

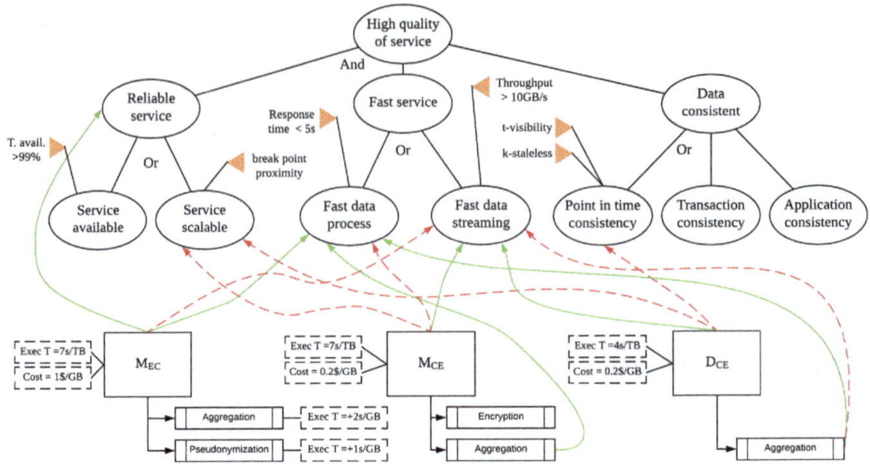

Fig. 4 Example of a diagram for the selection of data movement actions [26]

on the goals they affect. Moreover, a single treatment may be available in different modalities, each characterised by its own execution time or cost, which must be considered during the selection process.

Overall, the goal-oriented framework originally developed in the GAMES project has demonstrated its effectiveness well beyond its initial application domain. By providing a structured and interpretable way to capture dependencies among system objectives, and by supporting dynamic adaptation through learned treatment effects, the model has proved sufficiently general to address challenges in diverse contexts, including complex data-sharing scenarios with multiple stakeholders and heterogeneous infrastructures. This longevity highlights the versatility of goal-based decision models as a foundation for managing evolving requirements in dynamic systems.

3.2 *Towards Adaptive Green Process-Aware Information Systems*

Service-Oriented Computing (SOC), Cloud Computing (CC) and Business Process Management (BPM) are major research areas that paved the way for the development of modern, adaptive process-aware information systems (PAIS). SOC enables to realise PAIS functionalities and supports their adaptation as it can dynamically reconfigure them at runtime by, e.g., replacing services or even whole service compositions implementing business processes (BPs). CC provides the on-demand infrastructure for dynamically provisioning and scaling PAIS based on the current workload. Finally, BPM enables the management and realisation of complete BPs, situated at the very heart of PAIS, allowing to achieve business goals.

As such, we foresee that the evolution of all these research areas can lead to the generation of Green PAIS (GPAIS), i.e., PAIS that are energy-efficient, allowing infrastructures and data centres to reduce their carbon footprint, making them greener. To this end, this subsection's goal is to showcase, starting from initial breakthroughs concerning our work conducted in the IS group, led by Prof. Pernici, how this work has evolved during our participation in the IS lab at FORTH-ICS and the University of the Aegean, and how it can contribute to the generation of Green PAIS.

Work Baseline

Our participation in the IS group at Politecnico di Milano led to the following important results, especially in the context of SOC. One major research result, constituting a significant contribution to GAMES and relating to Green PAIS, was a novel QoS-based and energy-aware service composition algorithm [9]. This algorithm exhibited the following innovative features: (a) it takes into account both GPI and KPI metrics as well as their correlations expressed through dependency functions, enabling to reduce the solution space; (b) it considers that each service has a varied performance and energy consumption as it runs under a dynamic environment; (c) it attempts to satisfy global GPI/KPI constraints across all execution paths in the abstract service execution plan; (e) it can produce a solution even if over-constrained (KPI/GPI) requirements are posed. Another significant result related to the introduction of a rich cross-layer service quality model [4], covering multiple QoS attributes and metrics in different abstraction layers, including the infrastructure and service ones. Such a model was expressed in OWL-Q [20], enabling to have a formal description of quality elements such that they can be uniformly and distinctly referenced in service, thus diminishing any kind of element ambiguity and imprecision. Finally, we proposed two major contributions to support service negotiation. First, in terms of SLA template specification, OWL-Q was extended [6] to express the participants' negotiation strategies, whether QoS metrics can be negotiable, priorities over QoS metrics, plus the requester's budget and the provider's cost function. Second, our semantic rule-based approach [7] allowed the discovery of protocols applicable in the negotiation based on the capabilities of the participants.

Work Evolution

The previous results constituted a baseline, influencing our work's evolution, shortly analysed in the following. First, we have built upon the service composition algorithm to produce more advanced ones that cover multiple abstraction layers. In particular, the service composition algorithm in [24] enables selecting among alternative design decisions for each service task: either select an already available service (from third parties) to realise its functionality or deploy an own service on one of multiple candidate IaaS services. This algorithm was further extended to cover dependencies between the IaaS services' cost and features in [18]. While a green-oriented extension [16] covered the deployment of services near or at the same place where their big data to manage exists to minimise computation costs and communication delays.

The goal-driven approach in [19] specialises in the design of business services (BSs), i.e., BPs implemented via software services and offered to other organisations to fulfil their own goals. Such a design concerns the goal and semantic IO-based composition of BS tasks and the selection of BSs (per BS task) by following an extension of the aforementioned composition algorithm, which exhibits the novelty that it can select both the best among all generated task compositions and the best among all BSs that can implement each task from the selected composition.

The cross-layer service quality model inspired two additional lines of work. On one hand, in the context of BPaaS (i.e., BS offered in the cloud), OWL-Q was extended [22] to model KPIs and link them to business goals where KPIs are specified as conditions on business-level metrics, expressed as compositions of lower-level metrics (e.g., service-based ones). Based on that extension, a specific method to evaluate semantic KPIs for BPaaS was proposed [22], which relies on the semantic lifting of BPaaS measurements and their storage in semantic knowledge bases (KBs), enabling the evaluation of respective KPIs by using SPARQL queries. On the other hand, the CAMEL language, proposed in [22], covers Service-Level Objectives (SLO) and metric specification, utilising similar concepts with OWL-Q, along with other aspects (e.g., provisioning) relevant for cloud-based application management and dynamic provisioning. CAMEL can model various application kinds, including big data [28], micro-service, serverless [23] and polymorphic applications [28], i.e., applications that, along with their components, can change forms at runtime.

Finally, we proposed an SLA-based extension of OWL-Q, called Q-SLA [21], which not only fully models both SLAs and SLA templates but also dynamic service levels (SLs), enabling established SLAs to transit from one SL to another when needed (e.g., in case the current SL cannot be guaranteed by the service provider). Further, OWL-Q was utilised for extending the SLAC language to support the semantic dynamic SLA specification [17]. In fact, SLAC SLAs can be transformed into smart contracts that can be stored and executed on the blockchain.

Green Process-Aware Information Systems

The aforementioned advancements in SOC, CC and BPM can be exploited to realise the GPAIS concept by following the next research directions.

Cross-level energy and quality model: As GAMES proposed a cross-layer service energy model, such a model can be joined with our cross-layer service quality model. The main outcome can then be extended to cover further layers like the BP one as well as additional infrastructural levels, like fog/edge/IoT ones. This rich quality and energy model can then be fully exploited for SLA and adaptation rules specification in order to drive a complete self-adaptive GPAIS behaviour.

Composite and dynamic energy-aware SLAs: GPAIS are intrinsically non-stationary as, e.g., carbon intensity changes frequently, renewable availability is stochastic, edge batteries unexpectedly drain, and workloads are usually dynamically migrated. In this respect, dynamic SLAs, expressed in Q-SLA or SLAC, can come to the rescue, allowing the dynamic SL transitioning when needed. Further, as dynamic SLAs can be transformed into smart contracts, which can support formal SLA verification [27], various GPAIS issues can be solved, like lack of trust in carbon claims, greenwashing and carbon-aware billing. Finally, SLA composition along with smart contracts can enable SLO traceability and precise accountability as well as controlling the overall GPAIS in a distributed, cross-layer manner.

Energy-aware cross-layer adaptive polymorphic service orchestration: The increasing use of cloud-independent technologies to support multi-cloud and mixed-environment service deployment, plus the increasing development of equivalent functionalities in different forms (e.g., micro-services and serverless functions), mapping to different energy profiles, increases service orchestration flexibility and enables to optimise GPAIS adaptive behaviour. In this context, our cross-layer service composition work [24] can be enhanced to support this energy-aware cross-layer polymorphic service orchestration by considering energy-efficiency goals and constraints, dependencies between GPI and GPI metrics, as well as distributed constraint optimisation solving or global-to-local constraint mapping techniques to significantly reduce the vast solution space.

3.3 From GAMES to Artificial Intelligence: A Continuing Vision

The GAMES project represented a pivotal initiative in the evolution of Green IT. Its holistic view of energy efficiency, integrating software design, infrastructure management, and environmental monitoring, challenged the traditional separation between software engineering and operations. By introducing the notion of *active* energy management and defining measurable *Green Performance Indicators*, GAMES provided a rigorous framework to reason about sustainability in information systems.

Concepts such as adaptive control, context modelling, and cross-layer optimisation cultivated an appreciation for systems capable of self-observation and self-improvement. The work developed under Prof. Pernici's supervision, particularly the studies on energy-aware design and adaptive management [3, 9–12], served as a conceptual bridge to **artificial intelligence and machine learning**.

These principles evolved naturally from rule-based adaptation to *data-driven learning*. In the Recod.ai Lab at the University of Campinas, Brazil, the GAMES philosophy of monitoring and adaptation was extended to projects in which systems learn autonomously from complex data. Machine learning offered a new approach to pursuing the same objectives that had motivated GAMES: optimising complex systems under uncertainty, discovering causal relations in dynamic environments, and achieving efficiency without compromising reliability or quality of service. Where GAMES used formal models and context-aware rules, learning-based systems could infer such relations directly from the data, expanding the scope and autonomy of adaptive management.

Machine Learning and Green IT: Recent Developments

Over the last decade, the convergence between machine learning and Green IT has advanced considerably, transforming the management of data centres, cloud infrastructures, and large-scale computing facilities. While GAMES pioneered active and adaptive energy management, recent research has employed modern data-driven techniques to achieve similar goals, leveraging high-frequency monitoring data, large-scale telemetry, and advanced predictive models. Early surveys, such as [8], provided a structured overview of machine-learning techniques applied to specific "green" objectives, such as CPU frequency scaling or dynamic voltage regulation. These studies demonstrated the potential of ML for energy-aware computing, but also revealed a strong fragmentation: each optimisation goal was treated in isolation, without an integrated view of how multiple adaptive strategies interact within complex IT ecosystems. More recently, Kahil et al. [14] published a comprehensive review in Applied Energy, mapping the growing body of research on reinforcement and deep-reinforcement learning (RL/DRL) for data centre energy efficiency, cooling, and virtual-machine scheduling. Their analysis highlights a transition from reactive and heuristic methods to adaptive, model-free control architectures capable of optimising multi-objective energy-performance trade-off in real time. Another important evolution concerns the combination of physical and data-driven modelling. Emerging work on physics-informed machine learning [30] integrates thermal and electrical process models into neural architectures, improving interpretability and reliability–an approach that strongly echoes the model-based rigour pursued in GAMES. Similarly, recent frameworks such as GEECO [25] and the hybrid multi-objective models described by Zhou et al. [31] employ reinforcement learning and predictive scheduling to balance performance, carbon footprint, and energy consumption. These developments also reflect the rise of *Green Artificial Intelligence*, which seeks to make the learning process itself more sustainable. Bolón-Canedo et al. [2] provide a comprehensive review of strategies to reduce the environmental footprint of AI systems through efficient architectures, model compression, pruning, and hardware-aware optimisation. This dual perspective, using AI both *for* energy efficiency and *as* energy-efficient computing, represents the natural continuation of GAMES's vision of sustainability across all system layers.

Despite these advances, many existing works remain specialised, focusing on narrow operational objectives or limited test environments. A comprehensive, holistic, and explainable framework capable of coordinating heterogeneous optimisation actions and understanding their interrelations remains an open challenge. In this sense, the systemic and cross-layer philosophy introduced by the GAMES consortium continues to offer a relevant conceptual foundation for the next generation of intelligent, adaptive, and sustainable computing systems.

Reinterpreting GAMES Through Machine Learning

Modern machine-learning methodologies can be viewed as a natural extension of the GAMES vision. They generalise its concepts and make them scalable across diverse contexts:

- **Data-driven modelling**: statistical learning replaces handcrafted energy models, discovering relations among workload, resource utilisation, and energy consumption directly from data.
- **Predictive adaptation**: probabilistic and reinforcement learning allow systems to anticipate inefficiencies and optimise performance proactively.
- **Generalisation across domains**: transfer and multimodal learning fulfil GAMES's ambition of adaptable frameworks for heterogeneous infrastructures.
- **Optimisation under uncertainty**: Bayesian and causal approaches formalise the trade-offs between energy, reliability, and quality of service, first articulated within GAMES.

Through this perspective, the legacy of GAMES remains profoundly relevant. Machine learning provides the computational means to realise the vision that GAMES anticipated: systems that are not only efficient but also *aware*, capable of learning from their own operation, optimising resource usage, and acting responsibly within their environmental constraints. Following this direction, the principles of GAMES inspire a new generation of intelligent and sustainable computing systems, bridging the past and the future of adaptive and responsible IT.

A key direction lies in the development of self-optimising digital infrastructures, in which intelligent agents continuously monitor, predict, and coordinate energy, thermal, and workload dynamics across data centres. Advances in *causal* [5] and *physics-informed learning* could enable AI systems to reason about the complex relationships between software behaviour, hardware utilisation, and environmental variables, achieving interpretability and stability while preserving adaptability.

At a broader level, the convergence between *Green IT* and *Green AI* creates a dual responsibility. Just as AI can optimise the sustainability of computing infrastructure, those same infrastructures must be optimised to host increasingly large, energy-intensive AI models. Future research must therefore address both sides of this equation by developing energy-aware AI pipelines that are efficient throughout their entire lifecycle.

4 Conclusion

The GAMES project laid the foundations for understanding energy efficiency as a core property of Information Systems, emphasising measurement, adaptation, and integration of sustainability objectives into IS design and operation. Its methodological contributions have provided the conceptual tools that have guided more than a decade of research in Green and Adaptive Information Systems.

Over time, these ideas have evolved in scope and maturity. Energy-aware systems have become integral to broader socio-technical ecosystems, in which performance, quality, and sustainability must be balanced across multiple organisational and technological layers as well as different, heterogeneous environments. Recent advances in data-driven modelling and intelligent automation have extended the GAMES vision, enabling systems to adapt proactively based on observed patterns and contextual data. However, the central challenge remains: designing ISs that reconcile efficiency with reliability, transparency, and environmental responsibility. Emerging technologies, including ML, LLMs, and autonomous agents, create new opportunities to revisit these principles with greater analytical depth and operational reach.

Ultimately, the enduring impact of GAMES lies in its capacity to evolve. What began as a cross-layer framework for energy management has become a blueprint for intelligent, responsible, and adaptive, polymorphic digital ecosystems that learn from their own operations and change forms and behaviours to minimise environmental impact while maximising value for users and society.

Acknowledgements The authors gratefully acknowledge Prof. Barbara Pernici for her exceptional scientific leadership and mentorship. Her guidance fostered rigorous, yet adaptable methodological thinking, shaping research frameworks with enduring relevance across the field of information systems. Her influence continues to inspire the authors' ongoing work toward intelligent, sustainable, and responsible computing.

References

1. Bertoncini, M., Pernici, B., Salomie, I., Wesner, S.: Games: green active management of energy in it service centres. In: International Conference on Advanced Information Systems Engineering, pp. 238–252. Springer, Berlin (2010)
2. Bolón-Canedo, V., Morán-Fernández, L., Cancela, B., Alonso-Betanzos, A.: A review of green artificial intelligence: towards a more sustainable future. Neurocomputing **599**, 128096 (2024)
3. Cappiello, C., Fugini, M., Mello Ferreira, A., Pernici, B., Plebani, P.: Application-driven it service management for energy efficiency. In: Sprouts: Working Papers on Information Systems, vol. 11, issue 165 (2011)
4. Cappiello, C., Kritikos, K., Metzger, A., Parkin, M., Pernici, B., Plebani, P., Treiber, M.: A quality model for service monitoring and adaptation. In: MONA+ Workshop at the ServiceWave Conference. Springer, Berlin (2008)
5. Castro, M., Mendes Júnior, P.R., Soriano-Vargas, A., de Oliveira Werneck, R., Moreira Gonçalves, M., Lusquino Filho, L., Moura, R., Zampieri, M., Linares, O., Ferreira, V., et al.: Time series causal relationships discovery through feature importance and ensemble models. Sci. Rep. **13**(1), 11402 (2023)
6. Comuzzi, M., Kritikos, K., Plebani, P.: Semantic-aware service quality negotiation. In: Mähönen, P., Pohl, K., Priol, T. (eds.) Towards a service-based internet, vol. 5377, pp. 312–323. Springer Berlin Heidelberg, Berlin, Heidelberg (2008). Series Title: LNCS
7. Comuzzi, M., Kritikos, K., Plebani, P.: A semantic based framework for supporting negotiation in service oriented architectures. In: 2009 IEEE Conference on Commerce and Enterprise Computing, pp. 137–145. IEEE, Vienna, Austria (2009)
8. Demirci, M.: A survey of machine learning applications for energy-efficient resource management in cloud computing environments. In: 2015 IEEE 14th International Conference on Machine Learning and Applications (ICMLA), pp. 1185–1190. IEEE (2015)

9. Mello Ferreira, A., Kritikos, K., Pernici, B.: Energy-aware design of service-based applications. In: ServiceWave/ICSOC 2009: ServiceWave Conference, LNCS, vol. 5900, pp. 99–114. Springer, Berlin (2009)
10. Ferreira, A.M., Pernici, B.: Using intelligent agents to discover energy saving opportunities within data centers. In: Proceedings of the Workshops of the 25th International Conference on Advanced Information Systems Engineering (CAiSE 2013), CEUR Workshop Proceedings, vol. 995, pp. 1–12 (2013)
11. Ferreira, A.M., Pernici, B.: Managing the complex data center environment: an integrated energy-aware framework. Computing **98**(7), 709–749 (2016)
12. Ferreira, A.M., Pernici, B., Plebani, P.: Green performance indicators aggregation through composed weighting system. In: ICT as Key Technology Against Global Warming (ICT-GLOW 2012), LNCS, vol. 7453, pp. 79–93. Springer, Berlin (2012)
13. Giorgini, P., Mylopoulos, J., Nicchiarelli, E., Sebastiani, R.: Reasoning with goal models. In: International Conference on Conceptual Modeling, pp. 167–181. Springer, Berlin (2002)
14. Kahil, H., Sharma, S., Välisuo, P., Elmusrati, M.: Reinforcement learning for data center energy efficiency optimization: a systematic literature review and research roadmap. Appl. Energy **389**, 125734 (2025)
15. Koulouriotis, D.E., Xanthopoulos, A.: Reinforcement learning and evolutionary algorithms for non-stationary multi-armed bandit problems. Appl. Math. Comput. **196**(2), 913–922 (2008)
16. Kritikos, K.: Towards dynamic and optimal big data placement. In: 2018 17th IEEE International Conference on Trust, Security and Privacy in Computing and Communications/12th IEEE International Conference on Big Data Science and Engineering (TrustCom/BigDataSE), pp. 1730–1737. IEEE, New York, NY, USA (2018)
17. Kritikos, K., Uriarte, R.B.: Semantic SLA for clouds: combining SLAC and OWL-Q. In: Proceedings of the 7th International Conference on Cloud Computing and Services Science, pp. 432–440. SCITEPRESS - Science and Technology Publications, Porto, Portugal (2017)
18. Kritikos, K., Horn, G.: IaaS service selection revisited. In: Kritikos, K., Plebani, P., De Paoli, F. (eds.) Service-Oriented and Cloud Computing, LNCS, vol. 11116, pp. 170–184. Springer International Publishing, Cham (2018)
19. Kritikos, K., Kubicki, S., Dubois, E.: Goal-based business service composition. SOCA **7**(4), 231–257 (2013)
20. Kritikos, K., Plexousakis, D.: OWL-Q for semantic QoS-based web service description and discovery. In: Noia, T.D., Lara, R., Polleres, A., Toma, I., Kawamura, T., Klusch, M., Bernstein, A., Paolucci, M., Leger, A., Martin, D.L. (eds.) SMR$^{2\$}$2007: Workshop on Service Matchmaking and Resource Retrieval in the Semantic Web, CEUR Workshop Proceedings, vol. 243. CEUR (2007)
21. Kritikos, K., Plexousakis, D., Plebani, P.: Semantic SLAs for services with Q-SLA. Procedia Comput. Sci. **97**, 24–33 (2016)
22. Kritikos, K., Plexousakis, D., Woitch, R.: A flexible semantic KPI measurement system. In: Ferguson, D., Muñoz, V.M., Cardoso, J., Helfert, M., Pahl, C. (eds.) Cloud Computing and Service Science, Communications in Computer and Information Science, vol. 864, pp. 237–261. Springer International Publishing, Cham (2018)
23. Kritikos, K., Skrzypek, P., Moga, A., Matei, O.: Towards the modelling of hybrid cloud applications. In: 2019 IEEE 12th International Conference on Cloud Computing (CLOUD), pp. 291–295. IEEE, Milan, Italy (2019)
24. Kritikos, K., Plexousakis, D.: Towards semantic-based cloud application management. Serv. Trans. Cloud Comput. **3**(3) (2015)
25. Mondal, S., Faruk, F.B., Rajbongshi, D., Efaz, M.M.K., Islam, M.M.: GEECO: green data centers for energy optimization and carbon footprint reduction. Sustainability **15**(21), 15249 (2023)
26. Plebani, P., Salnitri, M., Vitali, M.: Fog computing and data as a service: a goal-based modeling approach to enable effective data movements. In: International Conference on Advanced Information Systems Engineering, pp. 203–219. Springer, Berlin (2018)

27. Uriarte, R.B., Zhou, H., Kritikos, K., Shi, Z., Zhao, Z., De Nicola, R.: Distributed service-level agreement management with smart contracts and blockchain. Concurr. Comput.: Pract. Exp. **33**(14), e5800 (2021)
28. Verginadis, Y., Kritikos, K., Patiniotakis, I.: Data and cloud polymorphic application modelling in multi-clouds and fog environments. In: Advanced Information Systems Engineering, LNCS, vol. 12751, pp. 449–464. Springer International Publishing, Cham (2021)
29. Vitali, M., Pernici, B., O'Reilly, U.-M.: Learning a goal-oriented model for energy efficient adaptive applications in data centers. Inf. Sci. **319**, 152–170 (2015)
30. Wang, R., Cao, Z., Zhang, Q., Tan, R., Wen, Y., Leung, T., Kennedy, S., Teoh, J.: Toward physics-informed machine learning for data center operations: a tropical case study (2025). arXiv:2505.19414
31. Zhou, G., Tian, W., Buyya, R., Xue, R., Song, L.: Deep reinforcement learning-based methods for resource scheduling in cloud computing: a review and future directions. Artif. Intell. Rev. **57**(5), 124 (2024)

Rethinking Personal Sovereignty in the Age of AI-Mediated Ecosystems

Carlo Alberto Bono and Edoardo Ramalli

Abstract The emergence of Artificial Intelligence fundamentally reconfigured the sociotechnical landscape, moving beyond Information Systems as interactive tools to establishing Artificial Intelligence (AI) as an autonomous informational entity. This paradigm shift has generated complex dynamics that risk eroding individual control over the conditions of interaction with such systems. We conceptualize **Personal Sovereignty**, the capacity to define one's domain of agency, set boundaries, and negotiate external impositions, as a critical evaluative metric, and distinguish it from operational autonomy. We propose a framework that models the ecosystem's relationships between formally retain the autonomy Human Agents, AI Agents, Information Systems, and Strategic Actors such as private and public institutional actors. This framework, rooted in structuration theory, operationalizes the assessment of personal sovereignty through measurable properties. The application of this framework to a retrospective case study demonstrates its diagnostic utility in highlighting specific risks, and provides a theoretical basis for designing governance structures that effectively protect individual sovereignty in the age of AI.

1 Introduction

For decades, Information Systems (ISs) have organized, stored, and distributed information, enabling individuals to interact with both data and the world beyond the systems. ISs have revolutionized, for instance, business, education, and research [9], driving organizational changes that transformed technology from a decision support system into a broader strategic tool [15], leveraging and reinforcing data-centric approaches in organizational processes. Similarly, the emergence of AI and Generative Artificial Intelligence (GenAI) represents a structural reorientation of the

C. A. Bono (✉)
Politecnico di Milano, Milan, Italy
e-mail: carlo.bono@polimi.it

E. Ramalli
European Commission-Joint Research Centre, Ispra, Italy
e-mail: edoardo.ramalli@ec.europa.eu

C. Cappiello et al. (eds.), *Retrospective and Prospective Views on Information Systems Engineering*, https://doi.org/10.1007/978-3-032-19578-4_12

sociotechnical landscape. Advancing at an unprecedented pace, AI acted as a disruptive force with uneven and ambivalent effects. What distinguishes it from earlier, disruptive innovations is its transition from a supportive and strategic tool to an active agent participating in decision-making.

As an informational artifact, data has traditionally circulated and gained meaning within the socio-technical space defined by three entities and their interplay: ISs, individual Human Agents (HAs) and Strategic Actors (SAs). The rise of AI and AI agents introduced a distinct and autonomous fourth entity in this ecosystem. AI systems can construct and manipulate abstract representations derived from large-scale data and, crucially, democratize access to this knowledge through natural language interactions. By removing technical barriers and the need for specialized technical skills, and offering on-demand access to domain-specific information, AI increasingly functions as a mediating interface between HAs and ISs. Furthermore, Agentic AI, empowered by GenAI, has made this technology *functionally autonomous*, allowing it to operate as a self-contained entity and construct abstract representations of the available information, while simultaneously raising questions regarding the boundaries of such autonomy [6, 24]. These dynamics are further shaped by upstream data preparation practices, which influence what information becomes available, reusable, and actionable for AI systems, while remaining largely invisible to end users [19]. As a result, information flows acquire meaning not only among individuals, ISs, and SAs, but also through AI entities. This configuration introduces tensions and raises well-known ethical issues and desiderata such as fairness, transparency, privacy, and accountability [12], especially in relation to the *overuse* and *misuse* of AI technologies that may arise from misaligned incentives and adversarial scenarios [7], exacerbating systemic risks such as large-scale manipulation [26] and emergent systemic effects, such as "trained incapacity", where users lose the ability to reflect on or conceive of alternatives to the AI's logic.

Among the other consequences, the advent of AI, as an autonomous informational entity, is reshaping the autonomy of both humans and ISs, aligning with the view that these entities are "constitutively entangled" [18], and shifts in this ecosystem transform roles, responsibilities, and interactions. These transformations are amplified by the growing influence of algorithms in shaping conceptual frameworks and reorganizing social and political structures, a process that can be identified as a form of reontologization [14].

Drawing from Orlikowski's Structuration Theory lens [16, 17], we aim to characterize the bidirectional, recursive dynamics of human-technological interactions. Through this perspective, AI agents are not approached as mere tools, but are framed as active participants that facilitate and constrain human actors through the relations that connect them, that can be interpreted through the "duality of technology": AI shapes human cognition and governance while simultaneously being shaped by them. Among the risks that arise when such interactions become habitual or institutionalized, we specifically focus on the ones related to Personal Sovereignty (PS), the meta-capacity by which individuals delineate and preserve their agency domain as environments progressively become mediated by AI systems, increasingly prestructuring the conditions of action and sense-making. Within this context, we address the following question: *How can personal sovereignty be systematically assessed in AI-mediated sociotechnical environments, considering how the conditions of agency and sense-making are reshaped?*

This chapter offers the following contributions. First, we define the concept of *personal sovereignty* in Sect. 2 as a construct related to autonomy, emphasizing the individual's capacity to define and preserve their own domain of agency in sociotechnical contexts. Then, we introduce a framework that describes the relations, together with their properties, that shape PS in AI-mediated ecosystems, as detailed in Sect. 3. We demonstrate the analytical value of the framework on a relevant use case in Sect. 4. Finally, Sect. 5 presents the discussion, conclusions, and future works.

2 Background

This work adopts the perspective of *Personal Sovereignty* (PS) to characterize the dynamics between humans and technology in AI-mediated ecosystems. We first argue that distinguishing sovereignty and autonomy is crucial for characterizing the impact of AI systems. Traditionally, sovereignty has been viewed as a state-centered concept, i.e., Digital Sovereignty (DS) as a nation's capacity to affirm authority over digital infrastructure and protect citizens and national interests from external interference [20]. Recent studies propose a multi-level perspective, extending sovereignty to the individual level [27]. Moreover, scholars suggest that while sovereignty and autonomy are intertwined, they are independent concepts [23].

As more functions are delegated to AI systems, potential harms may accumulate by excluding human supervision and choice from the interaction loop [7]. We refer to **autonomy** as the capacity to self-govern and decision-making within a given set of options. In contrast, we refer to **personal sovereignty** as the meta-capacity to define the boundaries of one's own domain, to preserve capabilities, e.g., cognitive, epistemic, reflective, and to resist external or indirect imposition.

This distinction is particularly useful in the context of AI systems. In modern digital environments, individual autonomy can be preserved by giving users the ability to choose among options; however, their sovereignty can be eroded since they cannot define or know the conditions of those choices. For instance, the end user of an AI agent retains the *autonomy* to accept a generated recommendation, but often lacks the PS to understand or even interrogate the underlying data, adjust the model's parameters, or define the ethical boundaries of that recommendation. This aspect is especially critical since GenAI has democratized access to information, enabling individuals to generate advanced domain-specific outputs without possessing the prior knowledge necessary to critically evaluate them. Over time, reliance on AI systems ultimately fosters a trust in this technology simply because the individual lacks the expertise to verify the results, leading to unwanted effects such as the AI declination of the Dunning-Kruger effect [8]. This dynamic threatens to erode cognitive and epistemic capabilities, as the user gradually loses the future capacity for independent judgment and critical reflection. Consequently, while users can still choose, they can no longer define, or even properly understand, the *conditions* of their choices.

We choose to frame PS not as an intrinsic property of a user, but rather as a relational characteristic. Coherently within a sociomaterialistic framing [17], we imply that human usage enacts technological structures that, in turn, shape future action, in a recursive loop [16]. When AI systems enter the technological ecosystem, they reconfigure these loops by introducing new forms of dependency, delegation, nudging, surveillance, and "default paths" that can bypass human reflection or awareness. By altering how information is filtered and presented, AI can leave one's *autonomy* intact, the user still acts and chooses, while undermining their *sovereignty*, the user is unaware that their *agency* has been narrowed by the system.

Therefore, PS emphasizes fundamental aspects of one's domain of action and meaning-making capacity, not described by autonomy per se. We study PS over two main components, *agency* and *alignment*, a distinction loosely inspired by Habermas's contrast between structural conditions of action and the individual's interpretive orientation toward them [1], which has parallels in the broader literature [21]. These dimensions capture the fundamental axes through which personal sovereignty is exercised and/or limited:

- **Agency**: the positioning of an individual and their degree of freedom with respect to system-imposed constraints, degree of transparency, or defaults imposed by a system. Agency includes *boundary-drawing*, which is the capacity to demarcate one's domain of action, and *discretionary control*, which is the authority to govern the constraints within the given domain.
- **Alignment**: the degree to which the goals, values, and meaning of the interaction reflect the individual's own intentions rather than those of external actors.

As these two axes are independent, one can retain sovereignty in one axis while losing it in another. AI ecosystems could erode sovereignty not by removing choice per se, but by impacting on the PS axes, e.g., by constricting boundaries, fixing defaults, or imposing interpretive frames, possibly in subtle ways. For example, when using an AI writing assistant, users might maintain high agency, i.e., the ability to edit, override, or reject specific recommendations. However, they may simultaneously lose sovereignty along the alignment axis, as the system imposes subtle stylistic defaults or interpretive frames that reflect the model's training rather than the authors' original intent.

3 Framework

Our primary contribution is a sociotechnical evaluation framework (Fig. 1) for scenario-based PS assessment in AI-mediated ecosystems. This framework deconstructs scenarios by analyzing the relevant actors (Sect. 3.1) and the nature of their interactions (Sect. 3.2), which are characterized by properties (Sect. 3.3) whose impact depends on the scenario. The PS assessment is detailed in Sect. 3.4.

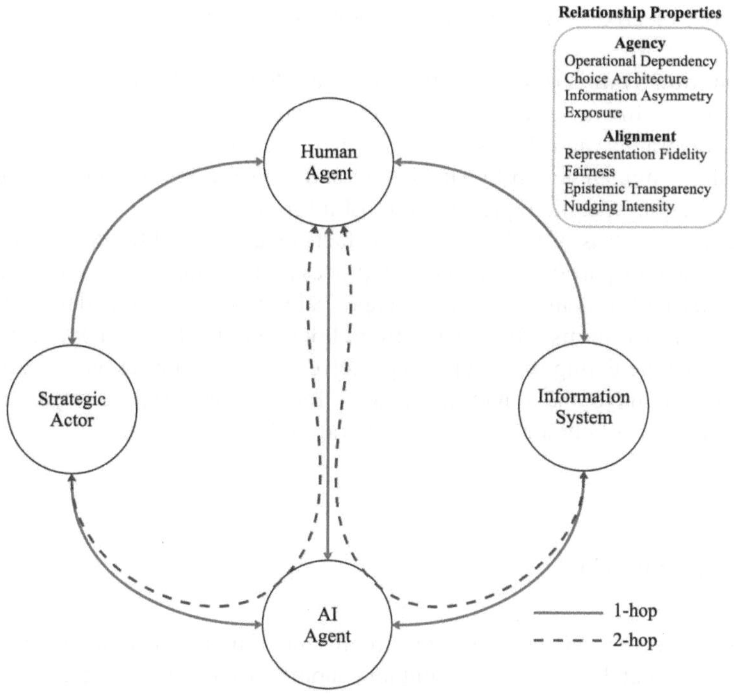

Fig. 1 Overview of the proposed framework

3.1 Actors

The proposed framework accounts for the interplay among four actors, as depicted in Fig. 1. In this setting, we aim to assess PS, especially where AI systems come into play. We recall that PS is a human-centered, relational characteristic. It is worth highlighting, consistently with a sociomaterial perspective, that relations among these actors do not merely represent data flows, but encompass dynamics that emerge with the enactment of the relations [3]:

- **Human Agents (HAs)**: Knowledgeable and reflexive actors whose boundaries emerge through engagement with other actors in the sociotechnical ecosystem. HAs can modify, appropriate, reinterpret, or negotiate structures. In our framework, we assess the *sovereignty* of these agents, specifically their capacity to define the terms of their engagement with the surrounding sociotechnical ecosystem.
- **Strategic Actors (SAs)**: Public, private, and hybrid organizations that shape the sociotechnical environment through norms, rules, incentives, and infrastructural decisions, which all together influence technological behaviors, e.g., by encouraging or sanctioning them [10]. These actors possess strategic agency and may act cooperatively or adversarially toward HAs. Their interventions can either enable,

condition, or erode PS, depending on how they aim to shape the conditions of action.

- **Information Systems (Information Systems (IS))**: Structured technological artifacts that stabilize organizational routines and data flows. ISs embed organizational rules, constraints, and data schemas in their architecture and implementations. They shape human action by supporting and constraining it, and by structuring and privileging specific representations of information.
- **AI Agents**: A class of technological artifacts characterized by interpretive flexibility. AI agents participate in decision processes by generating predictions, classifications, and content. AI agents reshape PS by influencing boundaries, defaults, and interpretive terms. By constructing choice architectures, shaping cognitive frames, and mediating what humans perceive as relevant or actionable, AI agents introduce adaptive and sometimes opaque forms of material agency, modifying the "conditions of choice" which are central to PS.

3.2 Relationships

The arcs connecting the actors in Fig. 1 represent recursive enactments of relationships, that ultimately result in the mutual shaping of the actors; in particular, HAs shape the surrounding technologies through use, and the technologies shape HAs through the repeated application and modification of affordances and constraints [17].

While numerous interactions are enacted within this ecosystem (e.g., SAs regulating AI directly), our analysis of *personal sovereignty* is, by definition, human-centric. We therefore focus on the three primary "front-line" relations where the HA engages with the sociotechnical ecosystem. These relations can be studied as bidirectional flows of *push* (what the system imposes, suggests, or enforces on the human) and *pull* (how the human draws upon, queries, or resists the system). Each arc can be characterized by:

- **Description**: The nature of the relation.
- **Drivers**: The motivations, i.e., why the actors engage and what the relation is optimized to maximize.
- **Impact**: How the relation affects the human's PS, e.g., in terms of degree of freedom in choice, interpretive capacity, resistance, dependence.

We group these front-line relations by 1-hop, which are direct, and 2-hop, which are structural and possibly tied to hidden constraints, since AI introduces indirect effects over PS.

1-Hop

Human Agent (HA) ⇆ Information Systems (IS)

Description HAs interact with ISs to access, store, retrieve, and manipulate data. The IS provides structured information, workflow constraints, and representations of the world; the HA provides inputs, data, corrections, and contextual interpretation. The IS stabilizes routines and embeds organizational logics; HAs appropriate or resist these structures depending on their goals.
Drivers HAs seek efficiency, accuracy, control, and intelligible information. ISs seek consistency, data integrity, and uniform workflows.
Impact on PS This relation enables human agency through access to information and its processing, but also constrains it through workflow rigidity, defaults, and representational choices. PS is then impacted by modifications in terms of friction, dependency, interpretive flexibility, transparency, overrideability, and representational control.

Human Agent (HA) ⇌ Strategic Actor (SA)

Description HAs receive norms, values, expectations, and social pressure from SAs, and in turn influence their agendas and societal discourse. Interactions include cultural narratives, legal and organizational norms, social cues, and knowledge circulation.
Drivers HAs seek legitimacy, belonging, and social recognition; SAs may seek compliance, stability, and norm propagation.
Impact on PS Influences boundaries of action, e.g., via normativity, identity formation, and collective alignment.

Human Agent (HA) ⇌ Artificial Intelligence (AI)

Description AI provides predictions, recommendations, content, and automated judgments directly to humans. This interaction is characterized by a recurring flow of summarized information, decision framing, and suggestions from AI to HAs, and prompts, data traces, and feedback from HAs to AI.
Drivers HAs want convenience, insight, and automation and, by doing so, offload cognitive effort. AI agents seek to optimize predictions in order to satisfy designer/owner objectives and maximize engagement.
Impact on PS AI shapes default paths, dependencies, and cognitive frames that can also bypass conscious human reflection, thereby subtly eroding capacity for independent judgment and critical assessment.

Artificial Intelligence (AI) ⇌ Strategic Actor (SA)

Description SAs train, frame, and validate AI systems via collective knowledge, data traces, norms, and culture; in turn, SAs are shaped by the representations and outputs produced by the AI systems
Drivers SAs wants beneficial effects embedded in AI. AI systems absorb goals, patterns, biases, and norms as a result of their training. This interaction can also be

driven by malicious or non-transparent objectives such as exploitation, surveillance, or deliberate bias injection
Impact on PS Reinforce or reshape behavior at scale, with the risk of amplifying inequalities, including bias propagation, cultural embedding, and harm potential, e.g., misinformation.

Artificial Intelligence (AI) ⇌ Information Systems (IS)

Description AI consumes structured data, metadata, workflows, and constraints from IS; IS receives classifications, predictions, or automations from AI, which may also reconfigure routines.
Drivers IS wants enrichment, automation, quality control. AI wants high-quality data for training and consistent schemas. This interaction can also be influenced by data biases.
Impact on PS IS-AI coupling jointly determines the conditions of action and intelligibility with respect to the technological ecosystem. PS can be influenced because the conditions of choice are determined by IS-level design decisions, which may become opaque once embedded into AI systems, e.g., for example, during training.

2-Hop

The 2-hop relations are composite relationships that HAs enact and experience without directly engaging with the terminal actor. These composite hops possibly represent sovereignty risks, including hidden ones, such as indirect influence and cascading constraints. In these interactions, AI effectively acts as a "man in the middle", mediating the flow of information and shaping outcomes, which necessitates further characterization.

Human Agent (HA) ⇌ Artificial Intelligence (AI) ⇌ Information Systems (IS)

Description AI interprets data originating from ISs and translates it into recommendations, classifications, or automated decisions that HAs receive. HAs do not directly access IS data, but only the mediated AI's interpretation.
Drivers HAs require useful insights; AI strive to obtain accurate predictions; ISs are designed around consistent data structures and workflows.
Impact on PS This chain can obscure provenance and explainability, embed organizational biases and constraints, or impose opaque suggestions onto humans, possibly embedding indirect dependencies. Unlike the direct 1-hop HA ⇌ IS link, here HAs experience only the AI-mediated interpretation of the information and artifacts embedded in one or more ISs, including data, configurations, workflows, and interface outputs. This mediated access can obscure the origin of information, diminish transparency, and introduce hidden constraints that are not recognizable to the HA.

Human Agent (HA) ⇌ Artificial Intelligence (AI) ⇌ Strategic Actor (SA)

Description AI systems serve as the medium through which the norms, values, and objectives of SAs are transmitted to the HA. The HA receives AI-generated output that is inherently influenced by SA goals, often without direct awareness of the underlying representational choices embedded in the model; i.e., AI systems can be trained with specific/multiple goals.

Drivers HAs seek knowledge, personal and cultural understanding, and efficient communication via language-based interaction. AI systems optimize pattern reuse and prediction based on training data. SAs aim to instill specific values, norms, imperatives, and constraints (e.g., regulatory) into the AI models.

Impact on PS Potential reinforcement of stereotypes and biases, as a result of cultural framing and identity influence, or pressure through AI-mediated discourse. In contrast to the 1-hop HA $\rightleftharpoons$ SA interaction, AI mediates the transmission of norms, values, and objectives, subtly shaping the perceptions and decisions of HAs and embedding biases, being them cultural, regulatory, or strategically motivated, in ways that would be more apparent in direct interactions.

3.3 *Properties*

We identify a comprehensive set of properties of the relations; this set characterizes the interactions between actors. While it is designed to be inclusive, allowing a structured assessment of the ecosystem, not every relationship exhibits every property, as some may be irrelevant for PS or inapplicable. Table 1 provides an overview of the properties relevant to each HA-centered relationship. We categorize properties based on which aspect of PS they impact, as introduced in Sect. 2, namely *Agency*, which refers to the capacity to act, and *Alignment*, which refers to the convergence of goals.

Table 1 Mapping relevant properties to framework relationships. Properties are grouped by the PS axis they primarily affect

	Property	HA $\leftrightharpoons$ IS	HA $\leftrightharpoons$ SA	HA $\leftrightharpoons$ AI	HA $\leftrightharpoons$ AI $\leftrightharpoons$ IS	HA $\leftrightharpoons$ AI $\leftrightharpoons$ SA
Agency	Operational dependency	✓	✗	✓	✗	✗
	Choice architecture	✓	✗	✓	✓	✓
	Information asymmetry	✓	✓	✓	✓	✓
	Exposure	✓	✓	✗	✓	✓
Alignment	Representation fidelity	✓	✗	✓	✓	✓
	Fairness	✓	✓	✓	✓	✓
	Epistemic transparency	✓	✓	✓	✓	✓
	Nudging intensity	✓	✗	✓	✓	✓

Properties affecting Agency

- **Operational Dependency**: The degree to which decision-making authority or operational control is transferred from a HA to an external actor. This measures the shift from execution to reliance, quantifying how much of the agency is ceded to the system [22].
- **Choice Architecture** The structural rigidities and workflow limitations embedded in the interaction design that restrict the set of available alternatives. This also includes the "granularity of choice", that is, how coarse or fine the available choices are, and the effort required to deviate from the default path. It assesses the depth of constraints that shape action, possibly without the user's explicit awareness [24].
- **Information Asymmetry** The disparity in knowledge access and interpretative capability between two actors. This property measures whether an actor possesses sufficient context and competence to evaluate the choices presented by the counterparty, or if the distribution of information creates a power imbalance [13].
- **Exposure** The extent to which an actor's internal state, behaviors, or data are visible to external entities. Individual privacy impacts the vulnerability to pressure, traceability, and exposure to behaviour prediction and personalization [29].

Properties affecting Alignment

- **Representation Fidelity** The degree to which the actual intentions, preferences, values, and contextual needs of an actor are reflected, e.g., without distortion, omission, or misinterpretation. This property reflects the extent to which the goals and needs of an actor are accurately represented, which directly affects value alignment and intention alignment [25].
- **Fairness** The extent to which the interaction introduces or amplifies distortions, inequities, or prejudices, whether strictly algorithmic or emerging from governance logic. This property measures if the system acts neutrally or whether it systematically disadvantages some HAs relative to their legitimate intentions, rights, and scope of action [2].
- **Epistemic Transparency** The degree to which a system's outputs, the logic that produced them, and the underlying data provenance are understandable to a HA, ensuring the rationale behind automated decisions is clear [4].
- **Nudging Intensity** The degree to which an interaction design shapes, steers, or biases the decisions of a human agent in ways that reflect system-predefined objectives rather than the agent's own intentions, especially when such influence happens without explicit awareness [28].

3.4 Personal Sovereignty Assessment

The objective of the framework is to provide a structured assessment of PS, through the properties of the relationships qualitatively discussed in Sect. 3.2, which measure

Table 2 Framework template. Rows are populated according to Table 1, scores are filled according to the evaluation criteria

Relationship		Property	Score
...	Agency	Operational dependency	[1–5]
		Choice architecture	[1–5]
		Information asymmetry	[1–5]
		Exposure	[1–5]
	Alignment	Representation fidelity	[1–5]
		Fairness	[1–5]
		Epistemic transparency	[1–5]
		Nudging intensity	[1–5]
...		...	...

the reported impact on PS from the perspective of HAs. The framework is structured as an evaluative matrix, whose template is provided in Table 2. While, in principle, any scoring mechanism could be employed, the framework utilizes a Likert scale from a minimum value of 1 (lowest impact) to a maximum of 5 (highest impact). The framework consists of two elements:

Relations The assessment is performed for each of the relations defined in Sect. 3.2. Depending on the specific scenario requirements, a subset of one-hop and two-hop relationships that are applicable could be identified.

Analytical properties The relationships are assessed against the relevant analytical properties defined in Sect. 3.3 according to Table 1. Therefore, each score measures the impact of a property of a precise relationship with respect to PS.

The matrix is intended to be completed by multiple experts with different backgrounds, roles, and responsibilities, including both external observers and actors directly involved in the scenario under analysis.

This allows for the identification of trade-offs, side effects, and imbalances at different granularity levels, e.g., global, relationship, and property of the relationship. For instance, a relationship-level assessment can be obtained by aggregating individual scores reported by different experts. As an alternative, scores can be aggregated across relationships, providing a global property-centered overview. Both aggregations could be further grouped by expert roles, possibly highlighting differences among them and contributing insights to the overall evaluation.

4 Use Cases

This section illustrates the outcome of a possible application of the framework introduced in Sect. 3 through a real-world scenario drawn from the gig economy [5]. The use case regards the PS of riders in platform-mediated food delivery companies, con-

Table 3 Personal Sovereignty assessment for the food delivery scenario, considering relations that involve HA and AI

Relationship		Property	Score
HA $\leftrightharpoons$ AI	Agency	Operational dependency	2.5
		Choice architecture	4.5
		Information asymmetry	4.0
		~~Exposure~~	–
	Alignment	Representation fidelity	3.0
		Fairness	4.5
		Epistemic transparency	3.5
		Nudging intensity	2.5
HA $\leftrightharpoons$ AI $\leftrightharpoons$ IS	Agency	~~Operational dependency~~	–
		Choice architecture	1.0
		Information asymmetry	3.0
		Exposure	4.0
	Alignment	Representation fidelity	3.0
		Fairness	4.5
		Epistemic transparency	3.0
		Nudging intensity	1.5
HA $\leftrightharpoons$ AI $\leftrightharpoons$ SA	Agency	~~Operational dependency~~	
		Choice architecture	5.0
		Information asymmetry	3.0
		Exposure	4.5
	Alignment	Representation fidelity	4.0
		Fairness	3.0
		Epistemic transparency	3.0
		Nudging intensity	4.0

sidering them as HAs, the delivery platform's algorithmic management system as the AI agent, and the management of the delivery company as the SA. The analysis is centered on relationships involving AI; an analogous reasoning can be applied to other relationships.

According to the proposed methodology, the framework has been applied by collecting inputs from multiple experts. Table 3 presents a possible aggregated assessment derived from multiple interviews. We recall, as anticipated in Sect. 3.3, that not all properties apply to all relationships.

The relationship between HA and the AI exhibits high scores for Choice Architecture (4.5) and Information Asymmetry (4.0). These values reflect the rigid structuring of action space imposed by the platform and the opacity of the algorithmic decision-making process. It is worth noticing that, once an AI model is trained and deployed, its operational logic is difficult for riders to influence. In contrast, Operational Dependency is perceived as less impactful, as the scenario defaults already set stringent

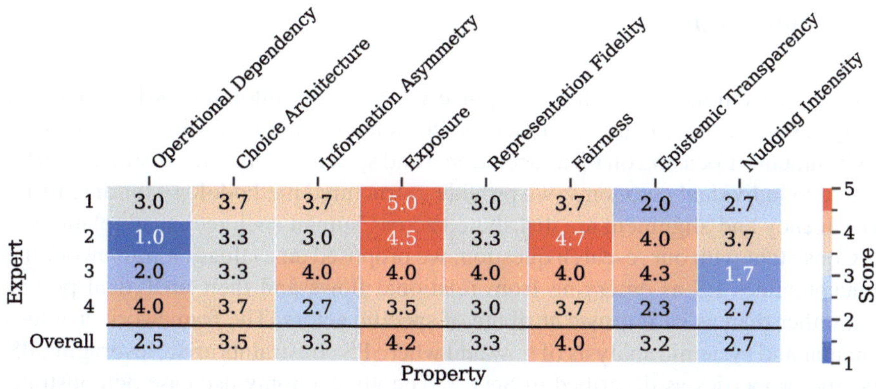

Fig. 2 Expert-level assessment heatmap for the food delivery scenario, averaged over relationships

expectations for HAs. Moreover, the Fairness (4.5) score is high, since the model is trained on large-scale datasets that may embed historical or structural biases, further exacerbating knowledge disparities.

When the IS is also considered, Exposure (4.0) emerges as a salient concern. This reflects riders' perceived vulnerability arising from extensive data collection on performance, behavior, and availability, which could enable continuous monitoring and evaluation, and contributes to a sense of persistent surveillance. Analogous considerations apply to Fairness (4.5), in line with the previous paragraph.

Finally, in the relationship involving the HA, the AI, and the SA, Choice Architecture reaches its maximum value (5.0), highlighting the control exerted by the company over the structure of work and subsequent choice possibilities. High reported values for Exposure (4.5) and Nudging Intensity (4.0) further indicate that organizational influence and data-driven governance operate at a systemic level, shaping AI, for example, through incentives, rankings, and performance feedback loops.

Overall, in this scenario, while HAs formally retain the autonomy to accept or reject individual tasks, they lack sovereignty over critical aspects of their labor, such as task allocation logic, or the ability to understand opaque decisions, which are determined unilaterally also through the AI. As a result, agency is exercised only within a tightly constrained procedural space, while strategic control remains fundamentally external to the HA. This configuration produces high procedural confinement and contributes to the erosion of the capacity for self-definition [11], with authority effectively delegated to an algorithm shaped primarily by company interests.

Figure 2 presents another possible analysis enabled by our framework. For each expert involved, the property scores are aggregated across relationships, highlighting expertise-centric judgements. In addition, an overall PS score is also provided, highlighting critical aspects and potential intervention points from a global perspective.

5 Conclusions

This work examined how the emergence of AI as an autonomous informational entity reshapes the conditions under which humans interact in digitally mediated environments. Focusing on PS as a relational and systemic construct, distinct from but related to individual autonomy, we provide a structured methodology for diagnosing how agency and alignment are distributed across human-sociotechnical relations.

Consistent with our research question, we proposed an evaluation framework that conceptualizes PS as emerging from relational flows and their analytical properties, rather than as an intrinsic attribute of specific actors. The framework enables a granular and systemic analysis of how and where PS constraints arise, leveraging PS-specific properties as described in Sect. 2. The gig economy use case demonstrates how this approach reveals layered and compounding tensions that would otherwise remain obscured, enabling the systematic identification of critical intervention points.

Several directions for future work can be pursued. First, the framework can be extended and validated across diverse empirical contexts. Second, further work is needed to refine the interpretation and aggregation of expert assessments, especially in light of their different expertise areas or roles. Third, the framework opens to the translation of diagnostic insights into design and governance implications, supporting the development of organizational and regulatory mechanisms that are explicitly aimed at preserving PS in AI-mediated ecosystems.

Overall, this work positions PS as a fundamental evaluative perspective for characterizing AI agents as participants in dynamic relational configurations that shape how individuals can define, negotiate, and preserve their autonomy.

References

1. Anderson, J.: Autonomy, Agency and the Self, pp. 91–112. Acumen Publishing, Key Concepts (2011)
2. Barocas, S., Hardt, M., Narayanan, A.: Fairness and Machine Learning: Limitations and Opportunities. MIT Press (2023)
3. Baygi, R.M., Introna, L.D., Hultin, L.: Everything flows: studying continuous socio-technological transformation in a fluid and dynamic digital world1. Manag. Inf. Syst. Q. **45**(1), 423–452 (2021)
4. Burrell, J.: How the machine 'thinks': Understanding opacity in machine learning algorithms. Big Data & Soc. **3**(1), 2053951715622512 (2016)
5. Christiaens, T.: Digital Working Lives: Worker Autonomy and the Gig Economy. Rowman & Littlefield (2022)
6. Enqvist, L.: 'Human oversight' in the EU artificial intelligence act: what, when and by whom? Law Innov. Technol. **15**(2), 508–535 (2023)
7. Floridi, L., Cowls, J., Beltrametti, M., Chatila, R., Chazerand, P., Dignum, V., Luetge, C., Madelin, R., Pagallo, U., Rossi, F., Schafer, B., Valcke, P., Vayena, E.: AI4People - An ethical framework for a good AI society: opportunities, risks, principles, and recommendations. Mind. Mach. **28**(4), 689–707 (2018)
8. Guan, J., He, X., Su, Y., Zhang, X.: The Dunning–Kruger effect and artificial intelligence: knowledge, self-efficacy and acceptance. Manag. Dec. (2025)

9. Hirschheim, R., Klein, H.K.: A glorious and not-so-short history of the information systems field. J. Assoc. Inf. Syst. **13**(4), 5 (2012)
10. Jobin, A., Ienca, M., Vayena, E.: The global landscape of ai ethics guidelines. Nat. Mach. Intell. **1**(9), 389–399 (2019)
11. Koutsimpogiorgos, N., Van Slageren, J., Herrmann, A.M., Frenken, K.: Conceptualizing the gig economy and its regulatory problems. Policy & Internet **12**(4), 525–545 (2020)
12. Kowald, D., Scher, S., Pammer-Schindler, V., Müllner, P., Waxnegger, K., Demelius, L., Fessl, A., Toller, M., Estrada, I.G.M., Šimić, I., Sabol, V., Trügler, A., Veas, E., Kern, R., Nad, T., Kopeinik, S.: Establishing and evaluating trustworthy ai: overview and research challenges. Front. Big Data **7** 2024 (2024)
13. Maas, J.: Machine learning and power relations. AI & Soc. **38**(4), 1493–1500 (2023)
14. Mittelstadt, B.D., Allo, P., Taddeo, M., Wachter, S., Floridi, L.: The ethics of algorithms: mapping the debate. Big Data & Soc. **3**(2), 2053951716679679 (2016)
15. Mukherji, A.: The evolution of information systems: their impact on organizations and structures. Manag. Decis. **40**(5), 497–507 (2002)
16. Orlikowski, W.J.: The duality of technology: rethinking the concept of technology in organizations. Organ. Sci. **3**(3), 398–427 (1992)
17. Orlikowski, W.J.: Sociomaterial practices: exploring technology at work. Organ. Stud. **28**(9), 1435–1448 (2007)
18. Orlikowski, W.J., Scott, S.V.: Sociomateriality: challenging the separation of technology, work and organization. Acad. Manag. Ann. **2**(1), 433–474 (2008)
19. Pernici, B., Cappiello, C., Bono, C.A., Sancricca, C., Catarci, T., Angelini, M., Filosa, M., Palmonari, M., De Paoli, F., Bergamaschi, S., Simonini, G., Mozzillo, A., Zecchini, L.: Sustainable quality in data preparation. J. Data Inf. Qual. **17**(4) (2025)
20. Pohle, J., Thiel, T.: Digital sovereignty. Internet Pol. Rev. **9**(4), 1–19 (2020)
21. Prunkl, C.: Human autonomy at risk? an analysis of the challenges from AI. Mind. Mach. **34**(3), 26 (2024)
22. ...Rahwan, I., Cebrian, M., Obradovich, N., Bongard, J., Bonnefon, J.-F., Breazeal, C., Crandall, J.W., Christakis, N.A., Couzin, I.D., Jackson, M.O., Jennings, N.R., Kamar, E., Kloumann, I.M., Larochelle, H., Lazer, D., McElreath, R., Mislove, A., Parkes, D.C., Pentland, A.S., Roberts, M.E., Shariff, A., Tenenbaum, J.B., Wellman, M.: Machine behaviour. Nature **568**(7753), 477–486 (2019)
23. Robles-Carrillo, M.: Sovereignty vs. digital sovereignty. J. Dig. Technol. Law **1**(3) (2023)
24. Shneiderman, B.: Human-centered artificial intelligence: reliable, safe & trustworthy. Int. J. Human-Comput. Int. **36**(6), 495–504 (2020)
25. Suresh, H., Guttag, J.: A framework for understanding sources of harm throughout the machine learning life cycle. In: Proceedings of the 1st ACM Conference on Equity and Access in Algorithms, Mechanisms, and Optimization, EAAMO '21, New York, NY, USA (2021). Association for Computing Machinery
26. Susser, D., Roessler, B., Nissenbaum, H.: Technology, autonomy, and manipulation. Internet Pol. Rev. **8**(2) (2019)
27. K.L. Tan, C.-H. Chi, K.-Y. Lam, Survey on digital sovereignty and identity: from digitization to digitalization. ACM Comput. Surv. **56**(3), 1–36 (2023)
28. R.H. Thaler, C.R. Sunstein, Nudge: Improving Decisions About Health, Wealth, and Happiness. Penguin Publishing Group (2009)
29. Zuboff, S.: The Age of Surveillance Capitalism: The Fight for a Human Future at the New Frontier of Power, 1st edn. (2018)

MIX
Papier aus verantwortungsvollen Quellen
Paper from responsible sources
FSC® C105338

If you have any concerns about our products,
you can contact us on
ProductSafety@springernature.com

In case Publisher is established outside the EU,
the EU authorized representative is:
Springer Nature Customer Service Center GmbH
Europaplatz 3, 69115 Heidelberg, Germany

Printed by Libri Plureos GmbH
in Hamburg, Germany